MznLnx

Missing Links Exam Preps

Exam Prep for

Calculus

Larson, Hostetler, Edwards, 7th Edition

The MznLnx Exam Prep is your link from the texbook and lecture to your exams.
The MznLnx Exam Preps are unauthorized and comprehensive reviews of your textbooks.

All material provided by MznLnx and Rico Publications (c) 2010
Textbook publishers and textbook authors do not particpate in or contribute to these reviews.

MznLnx

Rico
Publications

Exam Prep for Calculus
7th Edition
Larson, Hostetler, Edwards

Publisher: Raymond Houge
Assistant Editor: Michael Rouger
Text and Cover Designer: Lisa Buckner
Marketing Manager: Sara Swagger
Project Manager, Editorial Production: Jerry Emerson
Art Director: Vernon Lowerui

Product Manager: Dave Mason
Editorial Assitant: Rachel Guzmanji
Pedagogy: Debra Long
Cover Image: Jim Reed/Getty Images
Text and Cover Printer: City Printing, Inc.
Compositor: Media Mix, Inc.

(c) 2010 Rico Publications
ALL RIGHTS RESERVED. No part of this work covered by the copyright may be reproduced or used in any form or by an means--graphic, electronic, or mechanical, including photocopying, recording, taping, Web distribution, information storage, and retrieval systems, or in any other manner--without the written permission of the publisher.

For more information about our products, contact us at:
Dave.Mason@RicoPublications.com

For permission to use material from this text or product, submit a request online to:
Dave.Mason@RicoPublications.com

Printed in the United States
ISBN:

Contents

CHAPTER 1
Swimming Speed: Taking It to the Limit — 1

CHAPTER 2
Section Project: Graphs and Limits of Trigonometric Functions — 28

CHAPTER 3
Applications of Differentiation — 42

CHAPTER 4
The Wankel Rotary Engine and Area — 55

CHAPTER 5
Plastics and Cooling — 67

CHAPTER 6
Constructing an Arch Dam — 93

CHAPTER 7
Integration Techniques, L'Hopital' — 104

CHAPTER 8
The Koch Snowflake: Infinite Perimeter? — 116

CHAPTER 9
Conics, Parametric Equations, and Polar Coordinates — 140

CHAPTER 10
Suspension Bridges — 156

CHAPTER 11
Race Car Cornering — 175

CHAPTER 12
Satellite Receiving Dish — 187

CHAPTER 13
Hyperthermia Treatments for Tumors — 207

CHAPTER 14
Vector Analysis — 219

CHAPTER 15
Functions — 230

ANSWER KEY — 238

TO THE STUDENT

COMPREHENSIVE

The *MznLnx* Exam Prep series is designed to help you pass your exams. Editors at MznLnx review your textbooks and then prepare these practice exams to help you master the textbook material. Unlike study guides, workbooks, and practice tests provided by the texbook publisher and textbook authors, *MznLnx* gives you **all** of the material in each chapter in exam form, not just samples, so you can be sure to nail your exam.

MECHANICAL

The MznLnx Exam Prep series creates exams that will help you learn the subject matter as well as test you on your understanding. Each question is designed to help you master the concept. Just working through the exams, you gain an understanding of the subject--its a simple mechanical process that produces success.

INTEGRATED STUDY GUIDE AND REVIEW

MznLnx is not just a set of exams designed to test you, its also a comprehensive review of the subject content. Each exam question is also a review of the concept, making sure that you will get the answer correct without having to go to other sources of material. You learn as you go! Its the easiest way to pass an exam.

HUMOR

Studying can be tedious and dry. MznLnx's instructional design includes moderate humor within the exam questions on occassion, to break the tedium and revitalize the brain

Chapter 1. Swimming Speed: Taking It to the Limit 1

1. In mathematics, the _____ of a non-negative integer n, denoted by n!, is the product of all positive integers less than or equal to n. For example,

$$5! = 1 \times 2 \times 3 \times 4 \times 5 = 120$$

and

$$6! = 1 \times 2 \times 3 \times 4 \times 5 \times 6 = 720.$$

The notation n! was introduced by Christian Kramp in 1808.

The _____ function is formally defined by

$$n! = \prod_{k=1}^{n} k \qquad \forall n \in \mathbb{N}$$

or recursively defined by

$$n! = \begin{cases} n \leq 1 & 1 \\ n > 1 & n(n-1)! \end{cases} \qquad \forall n \in \mathbb{N}.$$

Both of the above definitions incorporate the instance

$$0! = 1$$

as an instance of the fact that the product of no numbers at all is 1.

a. Constraint counting
b. Factorial
c. BDDC
d. 15 theorem

2. In mathematics, the _____ is a conic section, the intersection of a right circular conical surface and a plane parallel to a generating straight line of that surface. Given a point (the focus) and a line (the directrix) that lie in a plane, the locus of points in that plane that are equidistant to them is a _____.

A particular case arises when the plane is tangent to the conical surface of a circle.

a. BIBO stability
b. BDDC
c. 15 theorem
d. Parabola

3. A _____ is an algebraic equation in which each term is either a constant or the product of a constant and (the first power of) a single variable. Linear equations can have one, two, three or more variables. Linear equations occur with great regularity in applied mathematics.

Chapter 1. Swimming Speed: Taking It to the Limit

a. Cubic function
b. Linear equation
c. Quartic function
d. Quadratic formula

4. In calculus, a branch of mathematics, the _____ is a measurement of how a function changes when its input changes. Loosely speaking, a _____ can be thought of as how much a quantity is changing at some given point. For example, the _____ of the position (or distance) of a vehicle with respect to time is the instantaneous velocity (respectively, instantaneous speed) at which the vehicle is traveling.

The process of finding a _____ is called differentiation. The fundamental theorem of calculus states that differentiation is the reverse process to integration.

a. Bounded function
b. Stationary phase approximation
c. Semi-differentiability
d. Derivative

5. _____ (including exponential decay) occurs when the growth rate of a mathematical function is proportional to the function's current value. In the case of a discrete domain of definition with equal intervals it is also called geometric growth or geometric decay (the function values form a geometric progression.)

_____ is said to follow an exponential law; the simple-_____ model is known as the Malthusian growth model.

a. Isomonodromic deformation
b. Oscillating
c. Inseparable differential equation
d. Exponential growth

6. _____ is used to describe the steepness, incline, gradient, or grade of a straight line. A higher _____ value indicates a steeper incline. The _____ is defined as the ratio of the 'rise' divided by the 'run' between two points on a line, or in other words, the ratio of the altitude change to the horizontal distance between any two points on the line.

a. Sequence
b. Y-intercept
c. 15 theorem
d. Slope

7. In coordinate geometry, the _____ is the y-value of the point where the graph of a function or relation intercepts the y-axis of the coordinate system.

In other words, the _____ of a function is the y-value of the point at which it intersects the line x=0 (the y-axis.) Thus, if the function is specified in form y = f(x), the _____ is easy to find by calculating f.

a. Y-intercept
b. 15 theorem
c. Sequence
d. Slope

8. _____ generally conveys two primary meanings. The first is an imprecise sense of harmonious or aesthetically-pleasing proportionality and balance; such that it reflects beauty or perfection. The second meaning is a precise and well-defined concept of balance or 'patterned self-similarity' that can be demonstrated or proved according to the rules of a formal system: by geometry, through physics or otherwise.

a. BDDC
b. 15 theorem
c. BIBO stability
d. Symmetry

9. A _____ is a type of map characterized by large-scale detail and quantitative representation of relief, usually using contour lines in modern mapping, but historically using a variety of methods. Traditional definitions require a _____ to show both natural and man-made features.

The Canadian Centre for Topographic Information provides this definition of a _____:

Other authors define topographic maps by contrasting them with another type of map; they are distinguished from smaller-scale 'chorographic maps' that cover large regions, 'planimetric maps' that do not show elevations, and 'thematic maps' that focus on specific topics.

a. BDDC
b. BIBO stability
c. Topographic map
d. 15 theorem

10. _____ is the tendency of a force to rotate an object about an axis (or fulcrum or pivot.) Just as a force is a push or a pull, a _____ can be thought of as a twist. The symbol for _____ is τ, the Greek letter tau.

a. 15 theorem
b. BIBO stability
c. BDDC
d. Torque

11. In geometry, a _____ (pl. tori) is a surface of revolution generated by revolving a circle in three dimensional space about an axis coplanar with the circle, which does not touch the circle. Examples of tori include the surfaces of doughnuts and inner tubes.

a. Hyperbolic paraboloid
b. Paraboloid
c. Prolate
d. Torus

12. In mathematics and its applications, a _____ system is a system for assigning an n-tuple of numbers or scalars to each point in an n-dimensional space. This concept is part of the theory of manifolds. 'Scalars' in many cases means real numbers, but, depending on context, can mean complex numbers or elements of some other commutative ring.

a. Spherical coordinate system
b. 15 theorem
c. Coordinate
d. Cylindrical coordinate system

13. The function $\log_b(x)$ depends on both b and x, but the term _____ in standard usage refers to a function of the form $\log_b(x)$ in which the base b is fixed and so the only argument is x. Thus there is one _____ for each value of the base b (which must be positive and must differ from 1.) Viewed in this way, the base-b _____ is the inverse function of the exponential function b^x.

a. BIBO stability
b. Logarithm function
c. 15 theorem
d. BDDC

14. In computer science and information science, _____ could also be a method or an algorithm. Again, an example will illustrate: There are systems of counting, as with Roman numerals, and various systems for filing papers, or catalogues, and various library systems, of which the Dewey Decimal _____ is an example. This still fits with the definition of components which are connected together (in this case in order to facilitate the flow of information.)

a. 15 theorem
b. System
c. BIBO stability
d. BDDC

15. The _____ is a function in mathematics. The application of this function to a value x is written as exp(x). Equivalently, this can be written in the form e^x, where e is a mathematical constant, the base of the natural logarithm, which equals approximately 2.718281828, and is also known as Euler's number.

   a. Exponential function
   b. Area hyperbolic functions
   c. ACTRAN
   d. Integral part

16. In statistics, _____ is a form of regression analysis in which the relationship between one or more independent variables and another variable, called dependent variable, is modeled by a least squares function, called _____ equation. This function is a linear combination of one or more model parameters, called regression coefficients. A _____ equation with one independent variable represents a straight line.

   a. Correlation
   b. Standard deviation
   c. Linear regression
   d. Probability

17. In calculus, the _____ determines whether a given critical point of a function is a maximum, a minimum, or neither.

Suppose that f is a function and we want to determine if f has a maximum or minimum at x. If f is increasing to the left of x and decreasing to the right of x, then x is a local maximum of f.

   a. Test for Divergence
   b. Continuous function
   c. Partial sum
   d. First Derivative Test

18. The largest and the smallest element of a set are called extreme values, absolute extrema, or extreme records.

For a differentiable function f, if $f(x_0)$ is an _____ for the set of all values f(x), and if x_0 is in the interior of the domain of f, then x_0 is a critical point, by Fermat's theorem.

In the case of a general partial order one should not confuse a least element (smaller than all other) and a minimal element (nothing is smaller.)

   a. Extreme Value
   b. Integration by substitution
   c. Extreme Value Theorem
   d. Infinitesimal

19. In calculus, the _____ states that if a real-valued function f is continuous in the closed and bounded interval [a,b], then f must attain its maximum and minimum value, each at least once. That is, there exist numbers c and d in [a,b] such that:

$$f(c) \geq f(x) \geq f(d) \quad \text{for all } x \in [a, b].$$

A related theorem is the boundedness theorem which states that a continuous function f in the closed interval [a,b] is bounded on that interval. That is, there exist real numbers m and M such that:

$$m \leq f(x) \leq M \quad \text{for all } x \in [a, b].$$

The _____ enriches the boundedness theorem by saying that not only is the function bounded, but it also attains its least upper bound as its maximum and its greatest lower bound as its minimum.

- a. Uniform convergence
- b. Integral of secant cubed
- c. Extreme Value Theorem
- d. Infinitesimal

20. In mathematics, given a subset S of a partially ordered set T, the _____ (sup) of S, if it exists, is the least element of T that is greater than or equal to each element of S. Consequently, the _____ is also referred to as the least upper bound, lub or LUB. If the _____ exists, it may or may not belong to S.
- a. BDDC
- b. 15 theorem
- c. BIBO stability
- d. Supremum

21. In mathematics, a _____ is an ordered list of objects (or events). Like a set, it contains members (also called elements or terms), and the number of terms (possibly infinite) is called the length of the _____. Unlike a set, order matters, and the exact same elements can appear multiple times at different positions in the _____.
- a. 15 theorem
- b. Y-intercept
- c. Sequence
- d. Slope

22. In mathematics, especially in order theory, an _____ of a subset S of some partially ordered set (P, >≤) is an element of P which is greater than or equal to every element of S. The term lower bound is defined dually as an element of P which is lesser than or equal to every element of S. A set with an _____ is said to be bounded from above by that bound, a set with a lower bound is said to be bounded from below by that bound.

A subset S of a partially ordered set P may fail to have any bounds or may have many different upper and lower bounds. By transitivity, any element greater than or equal to an _____ of S is again an _____ of S, and any element lesser than or equal to any lower bound of S is again a lower bound of S. This leads to the consideration of least upper bounds: (or suprema) and greatest lower bounds (or infima.)

- a. AUSM
- b. ALGOR
- c. ACTRAN
- d. Upper bound

23. In mathematics, a _____ is a curve in a Euclidian plane (cf. space curve.) The most frequently studied cases are smooth plane curves (including piecewise smooth plane curves), and algebraic plane curves.
- a. Vector area
- b. Lipschitz domain
- c. Plane curve
- d. Gyroid

24. A _____ is an expression which compares quantities relative to each other. The most common examples involve two quantities, but in theory any number of quantities can be compared. In mathematical terms, they are represented by separating each quantity with a colon, for example the _____ 2:3, which is read as the _____ 'two to three'.
- a. 15 theorem
- b. Ratio
- c. Sequence
- d. Y-intercept

25. In mathematics, a (topological) _____ is defined as follows: let I be an interval of real numbers (i.e. a non-empty connected subset of $\mathbb{R}$); then a _____ γ is a continuous mapping $\gamma : I \to X$, where X is a topological space. The _____ γ is said to be simple if it is injective, i.e. if for all x, y in I, we have $\gamma(x) = \gamma(y) \implies x = y$. If I is a closed bounded interval $[a, b]$, we also allow the possibility $\gamma(a) = \gamma(b)$ (this convention makes it possible to talk about closed simple _____.)

a. Curve
b. Prolate cycloid
c. Tractrix
d. Closed curve

26. If a function has an integral, it is said to be integrable. The function for which the integral is calculated is called the _____. The region over which a function is being integrated is called the domain of integration.

a. Integration by parts
b. Order of integration
c. Integral test for convergence
d. Integrand

27. In mathematics, an _____ on a real vector space is a choice of which ordered bases are 'positively' oriented and which are 'negatively' oriented. In the three-dimensional Euclidean space, the two possible basis orientations are called right-handed and left-handed (or right-chiral and left-chiral), respectively. However, the choice of _____ is independent of the handedness or chirality of the bases (although right-handed bases are typically declared to be positively oriented, they may also be assigned a negative _____.)

a. ALGOR
b. Unit vector
c. ACTRAN
d. Orientation

28. A _____ officer is an officer of high military rank. The term or equivalent is used by nearly every country in the world. _____ can be used as a generic term for all grades of _____ officer, or it can specifically refer to a single rank that is just called _____.

a. BDDC
b. BIBO stability
c. General
d. 15 theorem

29. In mathematics, the _____ of a function y = f(x) is a function that, in some fashion, 'undoes' the effect of f The _____ of f is denoted f $^{-1}$. The statements y=f(x) and x=f $^{-1}$(y) are equivalent.

a. ALGOR
b. Inverse
c. ACTRAN
d. AUSM

30. The method of _____ or ordinary _____ is used to solve overdetermined systems. _____ is often applied in statistical contexts, particularly regression analysis.

_____ can be interpreted as a method of fitting data. The best fit in the _____ sense is that instance of the model for which the sum of squared residuals has its least value, a residual being the difference between an observed value and the value given by the model.

a. BDDC
b. BIBO stability
c. 15 theorem
d. Least squares

31. Let f be a differentiable function, and let f'(x) be its derivative. The derivative of f'(x) (if it has one) is written f''(x) and is called the _____ of f. Similarly, the derivative of a _____, if it exists, is written f'''(x) and is called the third derivative of f.

a. Second Derivative
b. Vertical asymptote
c. Slant asymptote
d. Stationary phase approximation

32. In calculus, a branch of mathematics, the _____ is a criterion often useful for determining whether a given stationary point of a function is a local maximum or a local minimum.

The test states: If the function f is twice differentiable at a stationary point x, meaning that $f'(x) = 0$, then:

- If $f''(x) < 0$ then f has a local maximum at x.
- If $f''(x) > 0$ then f has a local minimum at x.
- If $f''(x) = 0$, the _____ says nothing about the point x, has a possible inflection point.

In the last case, the function may have a local maximum or minimum there, but the function is sufficiently 'flat' that this is undetected by the second derivative. In this case one has to examine the third derivative. Such an example is f(x) = x^4.

a. Symmetric derivative
b. Stationary point
c. Second Derivative Test
d. Linearity of differentiation

33. In a totally ordered set all elements are mutually comparable, so such a set can have at most one minimal element and at most one maximal element. Then, due to mutual comparability, the minimal element will also be the least element and the maximal element will also be the greatest element. Thus in a totally ordered set we can simply use the terms minimum and _____.

a. Leibniz rule
b. Racetrack principle
c. Maximum
d. Nth term

34. The _____ of an angle is the ratio of the length of the opposite side to the length of the hypotenuse. In our case

$$\sin A = \frac{\text{opposite}}{\text{hypotenuse}} = \frac{a}{h}.$$

Note that this ratio does not depend on size of the particular right triangle chosen, as long as it contains the angle A, since all such triangles are similar.

The cosine of an angle is the ratio of the length of the adjacent side to the length of the hypotenuse.

a. Trigonometric
b. Sine integral
c. Trigonometric functions
d. Sine

35. The terms '_____' and 'independent variable' are used in similar but subtly different ways in mathematics and statistics as part of the standard terminology in those subjects. They are used to distinguish between two types of quantities being considered, separating them into those available at the start of a process and those being created by it, where the latter (dependent variables) are dependent on the former (independent variables.)

In traditional calculus, a function is defined as a relation between two terms called variables because their values vary.

a. BIBO stability
b. BDDC
c. 15 theorem
d. Dependent variable

36. The terms 'dependent variable' and '_____' are used in similar but subtly different ways in mathematics and statistics as part of the standard terminology in those subjects. They are used to distinguish between two types of quantities being considered, separating them into those available at the start of a process and those being created by it, where the latter (dependent variables) are dependent on the former (independent variables.)

In traditional calculus, a function is defined as a relation between two terms called variables because their values vary.

a. AUSM
b. ACTRAN
c. Independent variable
d. ALGOR

37. In mathematics, the _____ (or replacement set) of a given function is the set of 'input' values for which the function is defined. For instance, the _____ of cosine would be all real numbers, while the _____ of the square root would be only numbers greater than or equal to 0 (ignoring complex numbers in both cases.) In a representation of a function in a xy Cartesian coordinate system, the _____ is represented on the x axis (or abscissa.)

a. 15 theorem
b. BIBO stability
c. BDDC
d. Domain

38. In mathematics, the _____ of a function is the set of all 'output' values produced by that function. Sometimes it is called the image, or more precisely, the image of the domain of the function. If a function is a surjection then its _____ is equal to its codomain.

a. Piecewise-defined function
b. Range
c. Surjective
d. Constant function

39. An injective function is called an injection, and is also said to be a _____ function (not to be confused with _____ correspondence, i.e. a bijective function.)

A function f that is not injective is sometimes called many-to-one. (However, this terminology is also sometimes used to mean 'single-valued', i.e. each argument is mapped to at most one value.)

a. Injective function
b. Onto
c. One-to-one
d. One-to-one function

40. An injective function is called an injection, and is also said to be a _____ (not to be confused with one-to-one correspondence, i.e. a bijective function.)

A function f that is not injective is sometimes called many-to-one. (However, this terminology is also sometimes used to mean 'single-valued', i.e. each argument is mapped to at most one value.)

a. One-to-one
b. Onto
c. Injective function
d. One-to-one function

41. In mathematics, a function f is said to be surjective or _____, if its values span its whole codomain; that is, for every y in the codomain, there is at least one x in the domain such that f(x) = y .

Said another way, a function f: X → Y is surjective if and only if its range f(X) is equal to its codomain Y. A surjective function is called a surjection.

- For any set X, the identity function id_X on X is surjective.
- The function f: R → R defined by f(x) = 2x + 1 is surjective (and even bijective), because for every real number y we have an x such that f(x) = y: an appropriate x is (y - 1)/2.
- The natural logarithm function ln: (0,+∞) → R is surjective.
- The function f: Z → {0,1,2,3} defined by f(x) = x mod 4 is surjective.
- The function g: R → R defined by g(x) = x^2 is not surjective, because (for example) there is no real number x such that x^2 = −1. However, the function g: R → [0,+∞) defined by g(x) = x^2 (with restricted codomain) is surjective.

Every function with a right inverse is a surjection. The converse is equivalent to the axiom of choice.

a. One-to-one
b. Onto
c. Injective function
d. One-to-one function

42. In mathematics, a function f is said to be _____ or onto, if its values span its whole codomain; that is, for every y in the codomain, there is at least one x in the domain such that f(x) = y .

Said another way, a function f: X → Y is _____ if and only if its range f(X) is equal to its codomain Y. A _____ function is called a surjection.

- For any set X, the identity function id_X on X is _____.
- The function f: R → R defined by f(x) = 2x + 1 is _____, because for every real number y we have an x such that f(x) = y: an appropriate x is (y - 1)/2.
- The natural logarithm function ln: (0,+∞) → R is _____.
- The function f: Z → {0,1,2,3} defined by f(x) = x mod 4 is _____.
- The function g: R → R defined by g(x) = x^2 is not _____, because (for example) there is no real number x such that x^2 = −1. However, the function g: R → [0,+∞) defined by g(x) = x^2 (with restricted codomain) is _____.

Every function with a right inverse is a surjection. The converse is equivalent to the axiom of choice.

a. Constant function
b. Range
c. Piecewise-defined function
d. Surjective

43. In mathematics, the _____ (or modulus) of a real number is its numerical value without regard to its sign. So, for example, 3 is the _____ of both 3 and −3.

The _____ of a number a is denoted by $|a|$.

a. Area hyperbolic functions
b. Absolute value
c. ACTRAN
d. Exponential function

44. In mathematics, an _____ is a function that always returns the same value that was used as its argument. In terms of equations, the function is given by f = x.

Formally, if M is a set, the _____ f on M is defined to be that function with domain and codomain M which satisfies

f = x for all elements x in M.

a. Onto
b. One-to-one function
c. One-to-one
d. Identity function

45. The principal _____ $f(x) = \sqrt{x}$ (usually just referred to as the '_____') is a function which maps the set of non-negative real numbers $R^+ \cup \{0\}$ onto itself, and, like all functions, always returns a unique value. The _____ also maps rational numbers into algebraic numbers (a superset of the rational numbers); $\sqrt{x}$ is rational if and only if x is a rational number which can be represented as a ratio of two perfect squares. In geometrical terms, the _____ maps the area of a square to its side length.

a. Hyperbolic tangent
b. Multiplicative inverse
c. Hyperbolic cosine
d. Square root function

46. The _____ is a test to determine if a relation or its graph is a function or not. For a relation or graph to be a function, it can have at most a single y-value for each x-value. Thus, a vertical line drawn at any x-position on the graph of a function will intersect the graph at most once.

a. BIBO stability
b. BDDC
c. 15 theorem
d. Vertical line test

47. In mathematics, a _____ is a constant multiplicative factor of a certain object. For example, in the expression $9x^2$, the _____ of x^2 is 9.

The object can be such things as a variable, a vector, a function, etc.

a. Degree of the polynomial
b. Resultant
c. Coefficient
d. Binomial type

48. _____ is a type of motion in which the velocity of an object changes equal amounts in equal time periods. An example of an object having _____ would be a ball rolling down a ramp. The object picks up velocity as it goes down the ramp with equal changes in time.

a. ACTRAN
b. ALGOR
c. AUSM
d. Uniform Acceleration

49. In mathematics, a _____ is a function whose values do not vary and thus are constant. For example, if we have the function f(x) = 4, then f is constant since f maps any value to 4. More formally, a function f : A → B is a _____ if f(x) = f(y) for all x and y in A.
   a. Constant function
   b. Range
   c. Surjective
   d. Piecewise-defined function

50. In mathematics, the _____ of a polynomial is the term of degree 0. For example, in the polynomial

    X³ + 2X + 3

over the variable X, the _____ is 3. Here, the _____ is given by a numeral, but it may also be specified by a letter that is a parameter rather than a variable, as in the polynomial

    ax² + bx + c,

in the variable x, where a, b, and c are parameters so that c is the _____.

   a. Discriminant
   b. Constant term
   c. Symmetric function
   d. Resultant

51. In mathematics, a _____ is a function of the form

$$f(x) = ax^3 + bx^2 + cx + d,$$

where a is nonzero; or in other words, a polynomial of degree three. The derivative of a _____ is a quadratic function. The integral of a _____ is a quartic function.

   a. Cubic function
   b. Quartic function
   c. Quadratic formula
   d. Linear equation

52. When a polynomial is expressed as a sum or difference of terms (e.g., in standard or canonical form), the exponent of the term with the highest exponent is the _____. The degree of a term is the sum of the powers of each variable in the term. The words degree and order are used interchangeably.
   a. Degree of the polynomial
   b. Symmetric function
   c. Binomial type
   d. Quadratic polynomial

53. In mathematics, an _____ is a function built from a finite number of exponentials, logarithms, constants, one variable, and nth roots through composition and combinations using the four elementary operations (+ - × ÷.) The trigonometric functions and their inverses are assumed to be included in the elementary functions by using complex variables and the relations between the trigonometric functions and the exponential and logarithm functions.

Elementary functions are considered a subset of special functions.

a. Elementary function
b. ACTRAN
c. AUSM
d. ALGOR

54. For the largest k where $a_k \neq 0$, a_k is called the _____ of P because most often, polynomials are written starting from the left with the largest power of x. So for example the _____ of the polynomial

$$4x^5 + x^3 + 2x^2$$

is 4.

The coefficients of polynomial also may be in the other order:

$$Q(x) = a_0 x^k + a_1 x^{k-1} + \cdots + a_{k-1} x^1 + a_k$$

and must be $a_0 \neq 0$ and a_0 is the _____ of Q.

a. Discriminant
b. Leading coefficient
c. Resultant
d. Symmetric function

55. A _____, in mathematics, is a polynomial function of the form $f(x) = ax^2 + bx + c$, where $a \neq 0$. The graph of a _____ is a parabola whose major axis is parallel to the y-axis.

The expression $ax^2 + bx + c$ in the definition of a _____ is a polynomial of degree 2 or a 2nd degree polynomial, because the highest exponent of x is 2.

a. Leading coefficient
b. Quadratic function
c. Resultant
d. Discriminant

56. In mathematics, an _____ is informally a function which satisfies a polynomial equation whose coefficients are themselves polynomials. For example, an _____ in one variable x is a solution y for an equation

$$a_n(x) y^n + a_{n-1}(x) y^{n-1} + \cdots + a_0(x) = 0$$

where the coefficients $a_i(x)$ are polynomial functions of x. A function which is not algebraic is called a transcendental function.

a. ACTRAN
b. ALGOR
c. Algebraic function
d. AUSM

57. In mathematics, a _____ represents the application of one function to the results of another. For instance, the functions f: X → Y and g: Y → Z can be composed by first computing f(x) and then applying a function g to the output of f(x.)

Thus one obtains a function g ∘ f: X → Z defined by (g ∘ f)(x) = g(f(x)) for all x in X. The notation g ∘ f is read as 'g circle f', or 'g composed with f', 'g after f', 'g following f', or just 'g of f'.

a. Composite function
b. Constant function
c. Piecewise-defined function
d. Surjective

58. In mathematics, a _____ is any function which can be written as the ratio of two polynomial functions.

$$y = \frac{x^2 - 3x - 2}{x^2 - 4}$$

In the case of one variable, x, a _____ is a function of the form

$$f(x) = \frac{P(x)}{Q(x)}$$

where P and Q are polynomial function in x and Q is not the zero polynomial. The domain of f is the set of all points x for which the denominator Q(x) is not zero.

a. BDDC
b. BIBO stability
c. 15 theorem
d. Rational function

59. A _____ is a function that does not satisfy a polynomial equation whose coefficients are themselves polynomials, in contrast to an algebraic function, which does satisfy such an equation. In other words a _____ is a function which 'transcends' algebra in the sense that it cannot be expressed in terms of a finite sequence of the algebraic operations of addition, multiplication, and root extraction.

Examples of transcendental functions include the exponential function, the logarithm, and the trigonometric functions.

a. BIBO stability
b. 15 theorem
c. Transcendental function
d. BDDC

60. In vector calculus, there are two ways of multiplying three vectors together, to make a _____ of vectors. Three vectors defining a parallelepiped

The scalar _____ is defined as the dot product of one of the vectors with the cross product of the other two.

Geometrically, the scalar _____

$$\mathbf{a} \cdot (\mathbf{b} \times \mathbf{c})$$

is the (signed) volume of the parallelepiped defined by the three vectors given.

a. Green's theorem
b. Divergence
c. Gradient theorem
d. Triple product

61. In elementary mathematics, physics, and engineering, a _____ is a geometric object that has both a magnitude (or length), direction and sense, (i.e., orientation along the given direction.) A _____ is frequently represented by a line segment with a definite direction, or graphically as an arrow, connecting an initial point A with a terminal point B, and denoted by

The magnitude of the _____ is the length of the segment and the direction characterizes the displacement of B relative to A: how much one should move the point A to 'carry' it to the point B.

Many algebraic operations on real numbers have close analogues for vectors.

a. BDDC
b. 15 theorem
c. Linear partial differential operator
d. Vector

62. In mathematics, even functions and odd functions are functions which satisfy particular symmetry relations, with respect to taking additive inverses. They are important in many areas of mathematical analysis, especially the theory of power series and Fourier series. They are named for the parity of the powers of the power functions which satisfy each condition: the function $f(x) = x^n$ is an _____ if n is an even integer, and it is an odd function if n is an odd integer.

a. Integral of secant cubed
b. Infinite series
c. Operational calculus
d. Even function

63. In mathematics, even functions and odd functions are functions which satisfy particular symmetry relations, with respect to taking additive inverses. They are important in many areas of mathematical analysis, especially the theory of power series and Fourier series. They are named for the parity of the powers of the power functions which satisfy each condition: the function $f(x) = x^n$ is an even function if n is an even integer, and it is an _____ if n is an odd integer.

a. Even function
b. Integration by substitution
c. Integral of secant cubed
d. Odd function

64. The _____, H, also called the unit step function, is a discontinuous function whose value is zero for negative argument and one for positive argument. It seldom matters what value is used for H, since H is mostly used as a distribution. The function is used in the mathematics of control theory and signal processing to represent a signal that switches on at a specified time and stays switched on indefinitely.

a. Hyperbolic functions
b. Hyperbolic sine
c. Square root function
d. Heaviside step function

Chapter 1. Swimming Speed: Taking It to the Limit 15

65. In geometry, the _____ (or simply the tangent) to a curve at a given point is the straight line that 'just touches' the curve at that point (in the sense explained more precisely below.) As it passes through the point of tangency, the _____ is 'going in the same direction' as the curve, and in this sense it is the best straight-line approximation to the curve at that point. The same definition applies to space curves and curves in n-dimensional Euclidean space.

a. Lie derivative
b. Tangent line
c. North pole
d. Minimal surface

66. A _____ of a curve is a line that (locally) intersects two points on the curve. The word secant comes from the Latin secare, for to cut.

It can be used to approximate the tangent to a curve, at some point P. If the secant to a curve is defined by two points, P and Q, with P fixed and Q variable, as Q approaches P along the curve, the direction of the secant approaches that of the tangent at P, assuming there is just one.

a. Witch of Agnesi
b. Curve
c. Secant line
d. Kappa curve

67. In mathematics, the concept of a '_____' is used to describe the behavior of a function as its argument or input either 'gets close' to some point, or as the argument becomes arbitrarily large; or the behavior of a sequence's elements as their index increases indefinitely. Limits are used in calculus and other branches of mathematical analysis to define derivatives and continuity.

In formulas, _____ is usually abbreviated as lim

a. BDDC
b. BIBO stability
c. 15 theorem
d. Limit

68. The _____ is the derived unit of energy in the International System of Units. It is defined as:

$$1\,\text{J} = 1\,\text{kg} \cdot \text{m}^2 \cdot \text{s}^{-2}$$

One _____ is the amount of energy required to perform the following physical actions:

- The work done by a force of one newton travelling through a distance of one metre;
- The work required to move an electric charge of one coulomb through an electrical potential difference of one volt; or one coulomb volt, with the symbol CÂ·V;
- The work done to produce the power of one watt continuously for one second; or one watt second (compare kilowatt hour), with the symbol WÂ·s. Thus a kilowatt hour is 3,600,000 joules or 3.6 megajoules;

1 _____ is equal to:

- 1×10^7 ergs (exactly)
- 1.6022×10^{19} eV (electronvolts)
- 0.2390 cal (gram calories or small calories)
- 2.3901×10^{-4} kcal (kilocalories, kilogram calories, large calories or food calories)
- 9.4782×10^{-4} BTU (British thermal unit)
- 0.7376 ft·lbf (foot-pound force)
- 23.7 ft·pdl (foot-poundals)
- 2.7778×10^{-7} kilowatt-hour
- 2.7778×10^{-4} watt-hour
- 9.8692×10^{-3} litre-atmosphere
- 1×10^{-44} Foe (exactly)

Units defined in terms of the _____ include:

- 1 thermochemical calorie = 4.184 J
- 1 International Table calorie = 4.1868 J
- 1 watt hour = 3600 J
- 1 kilowatt hour = 3.6×10^6 J (or 3.6 MJ)
- 1 ton TNT exploding = 4.184 GJ

Useful to remember:

- 1 _____ = 1 newton × 1 meter = 1 watt × 1 second

One _____ in everyday life is approximately:

- the energy required to lift a small apple one metre straight up.
- the energy released when that same apple falls one meter to the ground.
- the energy released as heat by a quiet person, every hundredth of a second.
- the energy required to heat one gram of dry, cool air by 1 degree Celsius.
- one hundredth of the energy a person can receive by drinking a drop of beer.
- the kinetic energy of an adult human moving a distance of about a handspan every second.

- Conversion of units
- Orders of magnitude (energy)
- Fluence

a. BIBO stability
c. BDDC
b. 15 theorem
d. Joule

69. A _____ is a statement of the meaning of a word or phrase. The term to be defined is known as the definiendum . The words which define it are known as the definiens .
   a. 15 theorem
   b. BDDC
   c. BIBO stability
   d. Definition

70. Integration is an important concept in mathematics, specifically in the field of calculus and, more broadly, mathematical analysis. Given a function f of a real variable x and an interval [a, b] of the real line, the _____

$$\int_a^b f(x)\,dx,$$

is defined informally to be the net signed area of the region in the xy-plane bounded by the graph of f, the x-axis, and the vertical lines x = a and x = b.

The term '_____' may also refer to the notion of antiderivative, a function F whose derivative is the given function f.

   a. Integral
   b. Integral test for convergence
   c. Indefinite integral
   d. Integrand

71. In mathematics, the _____ for convergence is a method used to test infinite series of non-negative terms for convergence. An early form of the test of convergence was developed in India by Madhava in the 14th century, and by his followers at the Kerala School. In Europe, it was later developed by Maclaurin and Cauchy and is sometimes known as the Maclaurin-Cauchy test.
   a. ALGOR
   b. AUSM
   c. ACTRAN
   d. Integral Test

72. In vector calculus, the _____ is shorthand for either the _____ matrix or its determinant, the _____ determinant.

In algebraic geometry the _____ of a curve means the _____ variety: a group variety associated to the curve, in which the curve can be embedded.

These concepts are all named after the mathematician Carl Gustav Jacob Jacobi.

   a. Saddle surface
   b. Vector Laplacian
   c. Critical point
   d. Jacobian

73. The _____ states that the total amount of energy in an isolated system remains constant. A consequence of this law is that energy cannot be created or destroyed. The only thing that can happen with energy in an isolated system is that it can change form, that is to say for instance kinetic energy can become thermal energy.

Chapter 1. Swimming Speed: Taking It to the Limit

a. 15 theorem
b. BDDC
c. Potential energy
d. Law of Conservation of Energy

74. In complex analysis, a mathematical discipline, a _____ of a meromorphic function is a certain type of singularity that behaves like the singularity of $\frac{1}{z^n}$ at z = 0. This means that, in particular, a _____ of the function f(z) is a point z = a such that f(z) approaches infinity uniformly as z approaches a.

Formally, suppose U is an open subset of the complex plane C, a is an element of U and f : U {a} → C is a function which is holomorphic over its domain.

a. Lacunary function
b. Pole
c. Complex logarithm
d. Bieberbach conjecture

75. Trigonometry is a branch of mathematics that deals with triangles, particularly those plane triangles in which one angle has 90 degrees (right triangles.) Trigonometry deals with relationships between the sides and the angles of triangles and with the _____ functions, which describe those relationships.

Trigonometry has applications in both pure mathematics and in applied mathematics, where it is essential in many branches of science and technology.

a. Trigonometric
b. Trigonometric integrals
c. Trigonometric functions
d. Sine

76. In mathematics, the _____ are functions of an angle. They are important in the study of triangles and modeling periodic phenomena, among many other applications. _____ are commonly defined as ratios of two sides of a right triangle containing the angle, and can equivalently be defined as the lengths of various line segments from a unit circle.

a. Trigonometric integrals
b. Sine integral
c. Trigonometric functions
d. Trigonometric

77. In differential geometry there are a number of second-order, linear, elliptic differential operators bearing the name _____

The connection _____ is a differential operator acting on the various tensor bundles of a manifold, defined in terms of a Riemmanian- or pseudo-Riemannian metric.

a. Laplacian
b. Dirac operator
c. Semi-elliptic operator
d. Peetre theorem

78. In calculus and other branches of mathematical analysis, an _____ is an algebraic expression obtained in the context of limits. Limits involving algebraic operations are often performed by replacing subexpressions by their limits; if the expression obtained after this substitution does not give enough information to determine the original limit, it is known as an _____. The indeterminate forms include 0^0, $0/0$, 1^∞, $\infty - \infty$, ∞/∞, $0 \times \infty$, and ∞^0.

a. ALGOR
b. ACTRAN
c. AUSM
d. Indeterminate form

79. The _____ is the chord parallel to the directrix and passing through the focus (or one of the two foci.)

The semi-_____ (l) is half the _____.

The focal parameter (p) is the distance from the focus (or one of the two foci) to the directrix.

a. BDDC
b. 15 theorem
c. Foci
d. Latus rectum

80. In calculus, the _____ is a theorem regarding the limit of a function.

The _____ is a technical result which is very important in proofs in calculus and mathematical analysis. It is typically used to confirm the limit of a function via comparison with two other functions whose limits are known or easily computed.

a. Table of limits
b. Limit of a sequence
c. 15 theorem
d. Squeeze Theorem

81. In physics, _____ is defined as the rate of change of position. it is vector physical quantity; both speed and direction are required to define it. In the SI (metric) system, it is measured in meters per second: (m/s) or ms^{-1}.

a. BIBO stability
b. BDDC
c. 15 theorem
d. Velocity

82. In geometry, a disk (also spelled disc) is the region in a plane bounded by a circle.

A disk is said to be closed or open according to whether or not it contains the circle that constitutes its boundary. In Cartesian coordinates, the open disk of center (a,b) and radius R is given by the formula

$$D = \{(x, y) \in \mathbb{R}^2 : (x-a)^2 + (y-b)^2 < R^2\}$$

while the _____ of the same center and radius is given by

$$\overline{D} = \{(x, y) \in \mathbb{R}^2 : (x-a)^2 + (y-b)^2 \leq R^2\}.$$

The area of a closed or open disk of radius R is πR^2

a. 15 theorem
b. BIBO stability
c. BDDC
d. Closed disk

83. In mathematics, the _____, sometimes called the direct _____ is a criterion for convergence or divergence of a series whose terms are real or complex numbers. The test determines convergence by comparing the terms of the series in question with those of a series whose convergence properties are known.

The _____ states that if the series

$$\sum_{n=1}^{\infty} b_n$$

is an absolutely convergent series and

$$|a_n| \leq |b_n|$$

for sufficiently large n, then the series

$$\sum_{n=1}^{\infty} a_n$$

converges absolutely.

a. Telescoping series
c. Comparison Test
b. Conditionally convergent
d. Ratio test

84. The _____ is a type of definite integral extended to functions of more than one real variable, for example, f(x, y) or f (x, y, z.)

Introduction

Just as the definite integral of a positive function of one variable represents the area of the region between the graph of the function and the x-axis, the double integral of a positive function of two variables represents the volume of the region between the surface defined by the function (on the three dimensional Cartesian plane where z = f(x,y)) and the plane which contains its domain. (Note that the same volume can be obtained via the triple integral -- the integral of a function in three variables -- of the constant function f(x, y, z) = 1 over the above-mentioned region between the surface and the plane.)

a. Quadratic integral
c. Risch algorithm
b. Multiple integral
d. Surface of revolution

85. In metric topology and related fields of mathematics, a set U is called _____ if, intuitively speaking, starting from any point x in U one can move by a small amount in any direction and still be in the set U. In other words, the distance between any point x in U and the edge of U is always greater than zero.

As an example, consider the _____ interval (0, 1) consisting of all real numbers x with 0 < x < 1. Here, the topology is the usual topology on the real line. We can look at this in two ways.

a. AUSM
b. ALGOR
c. ACTRAN
d. Open

86. In algebra, a _____ is a function depending on n that associates a scalar, det(A), to an n×n square matrix A. The fundamental geometric meaning of a _____ is a scale factor for measure when A is regarded as a linear transformation. Determinants are important both in calculus, where they enter the substitution rule for several variables, and in multilinear algebra.

For a fixed nonnegative integer n, there is a unique _____ function for the n×n matrices over any commutative ring R. In particular, this function exists when R is the field of real or complex numbers.

a. BDDC
b. 15 theorem
c. BIBO stability
d. Determinant

87. Continuous functions are of utmost importance in mathematics and applications. However, not all functions are continuous. If a function is not continuous at a point in its domain, one says that it has a _____ there. The set of all points of _____ of a function may be a discrete set, a dense set, or even the entire domain of the function.

a. Vector
b. 15 theorem
c. Discontinuity
d. BDDC

88. In mathematics, the _____ is a binary operation on two vectors in a three-dimensional Euclidean space that results in another vector which is perpendicular to the plane containing the two input vectors. The algebra defined by the _____ is neither commutative nor associative. It contrasts with the dot product which produces a scalar result.

a. 15 theorem
b. Permutation
c. Fundamental theorem of algebra
d. Cross product

89. In mathematics and computer science, the floor and ceiling functions map a real number to the next smallest or next largest integer. More precisely, floor(x) is the largest integer not greater than x and ceiling(x) is the smallest integer not less than x.

The _____ is also called the greatest integer or entier function, and the floor of a nonnegative x may be called the integral part or integral value of x. Computer languages (other than APL) commonly use ENTIER(x) (Algol), floor(x), or int(x) (C and C++).

a. Hyperbolic functions
b. Hyperbolic tangent
c. Multiplicative inverse
d. Floor function

90. In mathematical optimization, the method of Lagrange multipliers provides a strategy for finding the maximum/minimum of a function subject to constraints.

For example, consider the optimization problem

$$\text{maximize } f(x, y)$$
$$\text{subject to } g(x, y) = c.$$

We introduce a new variable (λ) called a _____, and study the Lagrange function defined by

$$\Lambda(x, y, \lambda) = f(x, y) - \lambda\big(g(x, y) - c\big).$$

If (x,y)≈ is a maximum for the original constrained problem, then there exists a λ such that (x,y,λ)≈ is a stationary point for the Lagrange function (stationary points are those points where the partial derivatives of Λ are zero.) However, not all stationary points yield a solution of the original problem.

a. BDDC
c. BIBO stability
b. 15 theorem
d. Lagrange multiplier

91. In calculus, a _____ is either of the two limits of a function f(x) of a real variable x as x approaches a specified point either from below or from above. One should write either:

$$\lim_{x \to a^+} f(x) \text{ or } \lim_{x \downarrow a} f(x)$$

for the limit as x decreases in value approaching a (x approaches a 'from above' or 'from the right'), and similarly

$$\lim_{x \to a^-} f(x) \text{ or } \lim_{x \uparrow a} f(x)$$

for the limit as x increases in value approaching a (x approaches a 'from below' or 'from the left'.)

The two one-sided limits exist and are equal if and only if the limit of f(x) as x approaches a exists.

a. ACTRAN
c. AUSM
b. ALGOR
d. One-sided limit

92. In mathematics, a function on the real numbers is called a _____ (or staircase function) if it can be written as a finite linear combination of indicator functions of intervals. Informally speaking, a _____ is a piecewise constant function having only finitely many pieces.
a. Hyperbolic sine
c. Square root function
b. Multiplicative inverse
d. Step function

93. Let S be a set with a binary operation *. If e is an identity element of (S, *) and a * b = e, then a is called a _____ of b and b is called a right inverse of a. If an element x is both a _____ and a right inverse of y, then x is called a two-sided inverse, or simply an inverse, of y.

a. Completing the square
b. Hurwitz quaternion order
c. Left Inverse
d. Closed-form expression

94. A curve γ is said to be closed or a loop if $I = [a, b]$ and if $\gamma(a) = \gamma(b)$. A _____ is thus a continuous mapping of the circle S^1; a simple _____ is also called a Jordan curve or a Jordan arc. The Jordan curve theorem states that such curves divide the plane into an 'interior' and an 'exterior'.

a. Bullet-nose curve
b. Curve
c. Kappa curve
d. Closed curve

95. A _____ is one of the most curvilinear basic geometric shapes:It has two faces, zero vertices, and zero edges. The surface formed by the points at a fixed distance from a given straight line, the axis of the _____. The solid enclosed by this surface and by two planes perpendicular to the axis is also called a _____.

a. 15 theorem
b. Cylinder
c. Right circular cylinder
d. BDDC

96. In economics, the _____ functional form of production functions is widely used to represent the relationship of an output to inputs. It was proposed by Knut Wicksell (1851-1926), and tested against statistical evidence by Charles Cobb and Paul Douglas in 1900-1928.

For production, the function is

$Y = AL^\alpha K^\beta$,

where:

- Y = total production (the monetary value of all goods produced in a year)
- L = labor input
- K = capital input
- A = total factor productivity
- α and β are the output elasticities of labor and capital, respectively. These values are constants determined by available technology.

Output elasticity measures the responsiveness of output to a change in levels of either labor or capital used in production, ceteris paribus. For example if α = 0.15, a 1% increase in labor would lead to approximately a 0.15% increase in output.

a. BIBO stability
b. BDDC
c. 15 theorem
d. Cobb-Douglas

97. The _____ of an angle is the ratio of the length of the adjacent side to the length of the hypotenuse. In our case

$$\cos A = \frac{\text{adjacent}}{\text{hypotenuse}} = \frac{b}{h}.$$

The tangent of an angle is the ratio of the length of the opposite side to the length of the adjacent side. In our case

$$\tan A = \frac{\text{opposite}}{\text{adjacent}} = \frac{a}{b}.$$

The remaining three functions are best defined using the above three functions.

a. Trigonometric
c. Sine integral

b. Trigonometric functions
d. Cosine

98. In mathematics, a _____ is a function which preserves the given order. This concept first arose in calculus, and was later generalized to the more abstract setting of order theory.

In calculus, a function f defined on a subset of the real numbers with real values is called monotonic (also monotonically increasing or non-decreasing), if for all x and y such that x >≤ y one has f(x) >≤ f(y), so f preserves the order.

a. Monotonic function
c. 15 theorem

b. Pettis integral
d. Pseudo-differential operator

99. In mathematics, an _____ is a theorem with a statement beginning 'there exist(s) ..' y, ... there exist(s) ...'. That is, in more formal terms of symbolic logic, it is a theorem with a statement involving the existential quantifier.

a. AUSM
c. Existence theorem

b. ALGOR
d. ACTRAN

100. In mathematical analysis, the _____ states that for each value between the least upper bound and greatest lower bound of the image of a continuous function there is a corresponding value in its domain mapping to the original. _____

- Version I. The _____ states the following: If the function y = f(x) is continuous on the interval [a, b], and u is a number between f(a) and f(b), then there is a c ∈ [a, b] such that f(c) = u.

- Version II. Suppose that I is an interval [a, b] in the real numbers R and that f : I → R is a continuous function. Then the image set f(I) is also an interval, and either it contains [f(a), f(b)], or it contains [f(b), f(a)]; that is,

    f(I) ⊇ [f(a), f(b)], or f(I) ⊇ [f(b), f(a)].

It is frequently stated in the following equivalent form: Suppose that f : [a, b] → R is continuous and that u is a real number satisfying f(a) < u < f(b) or f(a) > u > f(b).) Then for some c ∈ [a, b], f(c) = u.

This captures an intuitive property of continuous functions: given f continuous on [1, 2], if f(1) = 3 and f(2) = 5 then f must take the value 4 somewhere between 1 and 2.

a. AUSM
c. ALGOR
b. ACTRAN
d. Intermediate Value Theorem

101. In geometry, _____ is the division of something into two equal or congruent parts, usually by a line, which is then called a bisector. The most often considered types of bisectors are segment bisectors and angle bisectors. _____ of a line segment using a compass and ruler _____ of an angle using a compass and ruler Line DE bisects line AB at D, line EF is a perpendicular bisector of segment AD at C and the interior bisector of right angle AED

A line segment bisector passes through the midpoint of the segment.

a. BIBO stability
c. Bisection
b. BDDC
d. 15 theorem

102. In mathematics, the _____ is a root-finding algorithm which repeatedly divides an interval in half and then selects the subinterval in which a root exists. It is a very simple and robust method, but it is also rather slow.

Suppose we want to solve the equation

$$f(x) = 0,$$

where f is a continuous function.

a. BDDC
c. 15 theorem
b. BIBO stability
d. Bisection method

103. In mathematics, the sign function is an odd mathematical function that extracts the sign of a real number. To avoid confusion with the sine function, this function is often called the _____ .

In mathematical expressions the sign function is often represented as sgn.

a. Hyperbolic tangent
c. Hyperbolic functions
b. Heaviside step function
d. Signum function

104. Cantor defined two kinds of _____ numbers, the ordinal numbers and the cardinal numbers. Ordinal numbers may be identified with well-ordered sets, or counting carried on to any stopping point, including points after an _____ number have already been counted. Generalizing finite and the ordinary _____ sequences which are maps from the positive integers leads to mappings from ordinal numbers, and transfinite sequences.

a. ALGOR
c. ACTRAN
b. AUSM
d. Infinite

105. An _____ of a real-valued function y = f(x) is a curve which describes the behavior of f as either x or y tends to infinity.

In other words, as one moves along the graph of f(x) in some direction, the distance between it and the _____ eventually becomes smaller than any distance that one may specify.

a. AUSM

b. ALGOR

c. Asymptote

d. ACTRAN

106. The line x = a is a _____ of a curve y=f(x) if at least one of the following statements is true:

1. $\lim_{x \to a} f(x) = \pm\infty$
2. $\lim_{x \to a^-} f(x) = \pm\infty$
3. $\lim_{x \to a^+} f(x) = \pm\infty$

Intuitively, if x = a is an asymptote of f, then, if we imagine x approaching a from one side, the value of f(x) grows without bound; i.e., f(x) becomes large (positively or negatively), and, in fact, becomes larger than any finite value.

Note that f(x) may or may not be defined at a: what the function is doing precisely at x = a does not affect the asymptote. For example, consider the function

$$f(x) = \begin{cases} \frac{1}{x} & \text{if } x > 0, \\ 5 & \text{if } x \leq 0 \end{cases}$$

As $\lim_{x \to 0^+} f(x) = \infty$, f(x) has a _____ at 0, even though f(0) = 5.

Another example is $f(x) = 1/(x-1)$ which has a _____ of x=1 as shown by the limit

$$\lim_{x \to 1^+} \frac{1}{x - 1} = \infty$$

In the graph of $f(x) = x + \frac{1}{x}$, the y-axis (x = 0) and the line y = x are both asymptotes.

When a linear asymptote is not parallel to the x- or y-axis, it is called either an oblique asymptote or equivalently a slant asymptote.

a. Third derivative

b. Vertical asymptote

c. Ramp function

d. Monodromy

107. The _____ is a doubly ruled surface shaped like a saddle. In a suitable coordinate system, it can be represented by the equation

$$z = \frac{x^2}{a^2} - \frac{y^2}{b^2}.$$

This is a _____ that opens up along the x-axis and down along the y-axis.

Paraboloid of revolution

With a = b an elliptic paraboloid is a paraboloid of revolution: a surface obtained by revolving a parabola around its axis.

a. Parametric surface
c. Paraboloid
b. Hyperbolic paraboloid
d. Torus

108. In mathematics, a _____ is a quadric surface of special kind. There are two kinds of paraboloids: elliptic and hyperbolic. The elliptic _____ is shaped like an oval cup and can have a maximum or minimum point.

a. Torus
c. PDE surfaces
b. Hyperbolic paraboloid
d. Paraboloid

Chapter 2. Section Project: Graphs and Limits of Trigonometric Functions

1. The function difference divided by the point difference is known as the _____, it is also known as Newton's quotient):

$$\frac{\Delta F(P)}{\Delta P} = \frac{F(P + \Delta P) - F(P)}{\Delta P} = \frac{\nabla F(P + \Delta P)}{\Delta P}.$$

If ΔP is infinitesimal, then the _____ is a derivative, otherwise it is a divided difference:

$$\text{If } |\Delta P| = iota: \quad \frac{\Delta F(P)}{\Delta P} = \frac{dF(P)}{dP} = F'(P) = G(P);$$

$$\text{If } |\Delta P| > iota: \quad \frac{\Delta F(P)}{\Delta P} = \frac{DF(P)}{DP} = F[P, P + \Delta P].$$

Regardless if ΔP is infinitesimal or finite, there is (at least--in the case of the derivative--theoretically) a point range, where the boundaries are P ± (.5)ΔP (depending on the orientation--ΔF(P), δF(P) or ∇F(P)):

    LB = Lower Boundary; UB = Upper Boundary;

Anyone familiar with derivatives knows that they can be regarded as functions themselves, harboring their own derivatives. Thus each function is home to sequential degrees ('higher orders') of derivation, or differentiation. This property can be generalized to all difference quotients. As this sequencing requires a corresponding boundary splintering, it is practical to break up the point range into smaller, equi-sized sections, with each section being marked by an intermediary point ('P_i''), where LB = P_0 and UB = P_{A_n}, the nth point, equaling the degree/order:

LB = P_0 = P_0 + 0Δ_1P = P_{A_n} - (Åf-0)Δ_1P; P_1 = P_0 + 1Δ_1P = P_{A_n} - (Åf-1)Δ_1P; P_2 = P_0 + 2Δ_1P = P_{A_n} - (Åf-2)Δ_1P; P_3 = P_0 + 3Δ_1P = P_{A_n} - (Åf-3)Δ_1P; ↓↓↓↓ P_{A_n-3} = P_0 + (Åf-3)Δ_1P = P_{A_n} - 3Δ_1P; P_{A_n-2} = P_0 + (Åf-2)Δ_1P = P_{A_n} - 2Δ_1P; P_{A_n-1} = P_0 + (Åf-1)Δ_1P = P_{A_n} - 1Δ_1P; UB = P_{A_n-0} = P_0 + (Åf-0)Δ_1P = P_{A_n} - 0Δ_1P = P_{A_n};

ΔP = Δ_1P = P_1 - P_0 = P_2 - P_1 = P_3 - P_2 = ...

    a. Notation for differentiation   b. Directional derivative
    c. Continuously differentiable   d. Difference quotient

2. A _____ of a curve is a line that (locally) intersects two points on the curve. The word secant comes from the Latin secare, for to cut.

It can be used to approximate the tangent to a curve, at some point P. If the secant to a curve is defined by two points, P and Q, with P fixed and Q variable, as Q approaches P along the curve, the direction of the secant approaches that of the tangent at P, assuming there is just one.

a. Kappa curve
c. Curve

b. Secant line
d. Witch of Agnesi

3. _____ is used to describe the steepness, incline, gradient, or grade of a straight line. A higher _____ value indicates a steeper incline. The _____ is defined as the ratio of the 'rise' divided by the 'run' between two points on a line, or in other words, the ratio of the altitude change to the horizontal distance between any two points on the line.

a. Slope
c. 15 theorem

b. Y-intercept
d. Sequence

4. A _____ is a cubic curve generated by increasing or diminishing the radius vector of a variable point P on a straight line by the distance PA of the point from the foot of the perpendicular drawn from the origin to the fixed line.

The polar equation is

$$r = a \, \cos 2\theta \sec \theta.$$

The Cartesian equation is

$$y^2 = x^2 \, l,$$

where a is the distance of the line from the origin.

a. Macbeath surface
c. Dolbeault operator

b. Kampyle of Eudoxus
d. Strophoid

5. In geometry, the _____ (or simply the tangent) to a curve at a given point is the straight line that 'just touches' the curve at that point (in the sense explained more precisely below.) As it passes through the point of tangency, the _____ is 'going in the same direction' as the curve, and in this sense it is the best straight-line approximation to the curve at that point. The same definition applies to space curves and curves in n-dimensional Euclidean space.

a. Minimal surface
c. Lie derivative

b. North pole
d. Tangent line

6. In mathematics, the _____, sometimes called the direct _____ is a criterion for convergence or divergence of a series whose terms are real or complex numbers. The test determines convergence by comparing the terms of the series in question with those of a series whose convergence properties are known.

The _____ states that if the series

$$\sum_{n=1}^{\infty} b_n$$

is an absolutely convergent series and

$$|a_n| \leq |b_n|$$

for sufficiently large n , then the series

$$\sum_{n=1}^{\infty} a_n$$

converges absolutely.

a. Ratio test
c. Comparison Test
b. Conditionally convergent
d. Telescoping series

7. In calculus, a branch of mathematics, the _____ is a measurement of how a function changes when its input changes. Loosely speaking, a _____ can be thought of as how much a quantity is changing at some given point. For example, the _____ of the position (or distance) of a vehicle with respect to time is the instantaneous velocity (respectively, instantaneous speed) at which the vehicle is traveling.

The process of finding a _____ is called differentiation. The fundamental theorem of calculus states that differentiation is the reverse process to integration.

a. Bounded function
c. Stationary phase approximation
b. Semi-differentiability
d. Derivative

8. In infinitesimal calculus, a _____ is traditionally an infinitesimally small change in a variable. For example, if x is a variable, then a change in the value of x is often denoted Δx (or δx when this change is considered to be small.) The _____ dx represents such a change, but is infinitely small.

a. Local maximum
c. Dirichlet integral
b. The Method of Mechanical Theorems
d. Differential

9. A _____ is a mathematical equation for an unknown function of one or several variables that relates the values of the function itself and of its derivatives of various orders. they play a prominent role in engineering, physics, economics and other disciplines.

A simplified real world example of a _____ is modeling the acceleration of a ball falling through the air (considering only gravity and air resistance.)

a. Phase line
c. Differential equation
b. Structural stability
d. Caloric polynomial

Chapter 2. Section Project: Graphs and Limits of Trigonometric Functions

10. In metric topology and related fields of mathematics, a set U is called _____ if, intuitively speaking, starting from any point x in U one can move by a small amount in any direction and still be in the set U. In other words, the distance between any point x in U and the edge of U is always greater than zero.

As an example, consider the _____ interval (0, 1) consisting of all real numbers x with 0 < x < 1. Here, the topology is the usual topology on the real line. We can look at this in two ways.

a. ALGOR
b. ACTRAN
c. AUSM
d. Open

11. In complex analysis, a mathematical discipline, a _____ of a meromorphic function is a certain type of singularity that behaves like the singularity of $\frac{1}{z^n}$ at z = 0. This means that, in particular, a _____ of the function f(z) is a point z = a such that f(z) approaches infinity uniformly as z approaches a.

Formally, suppose U is an open subset of the complex plane C, a is an element of U and f : U {a} → C is a function which is holomorphic over its domain.

a. Pole
b. Bieberbach conjecture
c. Complex logarithm
d. Lacunary function

12. f'(x) is twice the absolute value function, and it does not have a derivative at zero. Similar examples show that a function can have k derivatives for any non-negative integer k but no (k + 1)-order derivative. A function that has k successive derivatives is called _____.

a. Differential coefficient
b. Differential calculus
c. Power series
d. K times differentiable

13. In mathematics, a _____ that describes a line D is any vector

$$\vec{AB}$$

where A and B are two distinct points on the line D. If v is a _____ for D, so is kv for any nonzero scalar k; and these are in fact all of the direction vectors for the line D. Under some definitions, the _____ is required to be a unit vector, in which case each line has exactly two direction vectors, which are negatives of each other (equal in magnitude, opposite in direction.)

Any line in two-dimensional Euclidean space can be described as the set of solutions to an equation of the form

ax + by + c = 0

where a, b, c are real numbers. Then one _____ of (D) is (− b,a).

a. Direction cosines
b. Dot product
c. Direction vector
d. Vector-valued function

14. In elementary mathematics, physics, and engineering, a _____ is a geometric object that has both a magnitude (or length), direction and sense, (i.e., orientation along the given direction.) A _____ is frequently represented by a line segment with a definite direction, or graphically as an arrow, connecting an initial point A with a terminal point B, and denoted by

$\overline{}$.

The magnitude of the _____ is the length of the segment and the direction characterizes the displacement of B relative to A: how much one should move the point A to 'carry' it to the point B.

Many algebraic operations on real numbers have close analogues for vectors.

a. 15 theorem
b. Linear partial differential operator
c. Vector
d. BDDC

15. _____ is a type of motion in which the velocity of an object changes equal amounts in equal time periods. An example of an object having _____ would be a ball rolling down a ramp. The object picks up velocity as it goes down the ramp with equal changes in time.

a. ALGOR
b. AUSM
c. ACTRAN
d. Uniform Acceleration

16. This article will state and prove the _____ for differentiation, and then use it to prove these two formulas.

The _____ for differentiation states that for every natural number n, the derivative of $f(x) = x^n$ is $f'(x) = nx^{n-1}$, that is,

$$(x^n)' = nx^{n-1}.$$

The _____ for integration

$$\int x^n \, dx = \frac{x^{n+1}}{n+1} + C$$

for natural n is then an easy consequence. One just needs to take the derivative of this equality and use the _____ and linearity of differentiation on the right-hand side.

a. Leibniz rule
b. Functional integration
c. Test for Divergence
d. Power Rule

Chapter 2. Section Project: Graphs and Limits of Trigonometric Functions

17. In calculus, the _____ allows you to take constants outside a derivative and concentrate on differentiating the function of x itself. This is a part of the linearity of differentiation.

Suppose you have a function

$$g(x) = k \cdot f(x).$$

where k is a constant.

Use the formula for differentiation from first principles to obtain:

$$g'(x) = \lim_{h \to 0} \frac{g(x+h) - g(x)}{h}$$
$$g'(x) = \lim_{h \to 0} \frac{k \cdot f(x+h) - k \cdot f(x)}{h}$$
$$g'(x) = \lim_{h \to 0} \frac{k(f(x+h) - f(x))}{h}$$
$$g'(x) = k \lim_{h \to 0} \frac{f(x+h) - f(x)}{h} \quad (*)$$
$$g'(x) = k \cdot f'(x).$$

This is the statement of the _____, in Lagrange's notation for differentiation.

a. Reciprocal Rule
c. Quotient Rule

b. Product rule
d. Constant factor rule in differentiation

18. The _____ of an angle is the ratio of the length of the adjacent side to the length of the hypotenuse. In our case

$$\cos A = \frac{\text{adjacent}}{\text{hypotenuse}} = \frac{b}{h}.$$

The tangent of an angle is the ratio of the length of the opposite side to the length of the adjacent side. In our case

$$\tan A = \frac{\text{opposite}}{\text{adjacent}} = \frac{a}{b}.$$

The remaining three functions are best defined using the above three functions.

a. Trigonometric functions
c. Trigonometric

b. Sine integral
d. Cosine

Chapter 2. Section Project: Graphs and Limits of Trigonometric Functions

19. A _____ is one of the most curvilinear basic geometric shapes:It has two faces, zero vertices, and zero edges. The surface formed by the points at a fixed distance from a given straight line, the axis of the _____. The solid enclosed by this surface and by two planes perpendicular to the axis is also called a _____.
   - a. 15 theorem
   - b. BDDC
   - c. Right circular cylinder
   - d. Cylinder

20. A _____ is a lens which focuses light which passes through onto a line instead of onto a point, as a spherical lens would. The curved face or faces of a _____ are sections of a cylinder, and focus the image passing through it onto a line parallel to the intersection of the surface of the lens and a plane tangent to it. The lens compresses the image in the direction perpendicular to this line, and leaves it unaltered in the direction parallel to it (in the tangent plane.)
   - a. BDDC
   - b. 15 theorem
   - c. BIBO stability
   - d. Cylindrical lens

21. Let f be a differentiable function, and let f'(x) be its derivative. The derivative of f'(x) (if it has one) is written f''(x) and is called the _____ of f. Similarly, the derivative of a _____, if it exists, is written f'''(x) and is called the third derivative of f.
   - a. Slant asymptote
   - b. Stationary phase approximation
   - c. Vertical asymptote
   - d. Second derivative

22. In physics, _____ is defined as the rate of change of position. it is vector physical quantity; both speed and direction are required to define it. In the SI (metric) system, it is measured in meters per second: (m/s) or ms^{-1}.
   - a. BDDC
   - b. 15 theorem
   - c. BIBO stability
   - d. Velocity

23. In calculus, the _____ is a formula used to find the derivatives of products of functions. It may be stated thus:

$$(f \cdot g)' = f' \cdot g + f \cdot g'$$

or in the Leibniz notation thus:

$$\frac{d}{dx}(u \cdot v) = u \cdot \frac{dv}{dx} + v \cdot \frac{du}{dx}.$$

Discovery of this rule is credited to Gottfried Leibniz, who demonstrated it using differentials. Here is Leibniz's argument: Let u and v be two differentiable functions of x.

   - a. Quotient Rule
   - b. Constant factor rule in differentiation
   - c. Differentiation rules
   - d. Product Rule

24. In calculus, the _____ is a method of finding the derivative of a function that is the quotient of two other functions for which derivatives exist.

Chapter 2. Section Project: Graphs and Limits of Trigonometric Functions

If the function one wishes to differentiate, f(x), can be written as

$$f(x) = \frac{g(x)}{h(x)}$$

and h(x) ≠ 0, then the rule states that the derivative of g(x) / h(x) is equal to:

$$\frac{d}{dx}f(x) = f'(x) = \frac{g'(x)h(x) - g(x)h'(x)}{[h(x)]^2}.$$

Or, more precisely, if all x in some open set containing the number a satisfy h(x) ≠ 0; and g'(a) and h'(a) both exist; then, f'(a) exists as well and:

$$f'(a) = \frac{g'(a)h(a) - g(a)h'(a)}{[h(a)]^2}.$$

The derivative of (4x − 2) / (x² + 1) is:

$$\frac{d}{dx}\left[\frac{(4x-2)}{x^2+1}\right] = \frac{(x^2+1)(4) - (4x-2)(2x)}{(x^2+1)^2}$$

$$= \frac{(4x^2+4) - (8x^2 - 4x)}{(x^2+1)^2} \qquad = \frac{-4x^2 + 4x + 4}{(x^2+1)^2}$$

In the example above, the choices

g(x) = 4x − 2
h(x) = x² + 1

were made. Analogously, the derivative of sin(x) / x² (when x ≠ 0) is:

$$\frac{\cos(x)x^2 - \sin(x)2x}{x^4}$$

Another example is:

$$f(x) = \frac{2x^2}{x^3}$$

whereas g(x) = 2x^2 and h(x) = x^3, and g'(x) = 4x and h'(x) = 3x^2.

    a. Constant factor rule in differentiation
    b. Differentiation rules
    c. Reciprocal Rule
    d. Quotient Rule

25. In mathematics, a _____ is a function which preserves the given order. This concept first arose in calculus, and was later generalized to the more abstract setting of order theory.

In calculus, a function f defined on a subset of the real numbers with real values is called monotonic (also monotonically increasing or non-decreasing), if for all x and y such that x >≤ y one has f(x) >≤ f(y), so f preserves the order.

    a. Monotonic function
    b. Pseudo-differential operator
    c. 15 theorem
    d. Pettis integral

26. Integration is an important concept in mathematics, specifically in the field of calculus and, more broadly, mathematical analysis. Given a function f of a real variable x and an interval [a, b] of the real line, the _____

$$\int_a^b f(x)\,dx,$$

is defined informally to be the net signed area of the region in the xy-plane bounded by the graph of f, the x-axis, and the vertical lines x = a and x = b.

The term '_____' may also refer to the notion of antiderivative, a function F whose derivative is the given function f.

    a. Integral
    b. Integrand
    c. Integral test for convergence
    d. Indefinite integral

27. In mathematics, the _____ for convergence is a method used to test infinite series of non-negative terms for convergence. An early form of the test of convergence was developed in India by Madhava in the 14th century, and by his followers at the Kerala School. In Europe, it was later developed by Maclaurin and Cauchy and is sometimes known as the Maclaurin-Cauchy test.
    a. Integral Test
    b. ACTRAN
    c. AUSM
    d. ALGOR

28. In mathematics, a function on the real numbers is called a _____ (or staircase function) if it can be written as a finite linear combination of indicator functions of intervals. Informally speaking, a _____ is a piecewise constant function having only finitely many pieces.
    a. Square root function
    b. Multiplicative inverse
    c. Hyperbolic sine
    d. Step function

Chapter 2. Section Project: Graphs and Limits of Trigonometric Functions

29. In mathematics, a _____ (or just conic) is a curve obtained by intersecting a cone (more precisely, a circular conical surface) with a plane. A _____ is therefore a restriction of a quadric surface to the plane. The conic sections were named and studied as long ago as 200 BC, when Apollonius of Perga undertook a systematic study of their properties.
    a. 15 theorem
    b. BDDC
    c. Latus rectum
    d. Conic section

30. Trigonometry is a branch of mathematics that deals with triangles, particularly those plane triangles in which one angle has 90 degrees (right triangles.) Trigonometry deals with relationships between the sides and the angles of triangles and with the _____ functions, which describe those relationships.

    Trigonometry has applications in both pure mathematics and in applied mathematics, where it is essential in many branches of science and technology.

    a. Trigonometric
    b. Sine
    c. Trigonometric integrals
    d. Trigonometric functions

31. In mathematics, the _____ are functions of an angle. They are important in the study of triangles and modeling periodic phenomena, among many other applications. _____ are commonly defined as ratios of two sides of a right triangle containing the angle, and can equivalently be defined as the lengths of various line segments from a unit circle.
    a. Sine integral
    b. Trigonometric integrals
    c. Trigonometric
    d. Trigonometric functions

32. In physics, and more specifically kinematics, _____ is the change in velocity over time. Because velocity is a vector, it can change in two ways: a change in magnitude and/or a change in direction. In one dimension, _____ is the rate at which something speeds up or slows down.
    a. ACTRAN
    b. AUSM
    c. Acceleration
    d. ALGOR

33. In mathematics, the _____ is a criterion for the convergence (a convergence test) of an infinite series

$$\sum_{n=1}^{\infty} a_n.$$

It is particularly useful in connection with power series.

The _____ was developed first by Cauchy and so is sometimes known as the Cauchy _____ or Cauchy's radical test.
The _____ uses the number

$$C = \limsup_{n \to \infty} \sqrt[n]{|a_n|},$$

where 'lim sup' denotes the limit superior, possibly ∞.

a. Related rates
b. Mean Value Theorem
c. Racetrack principle
d. Root Test

34. Let f be a differentiable function, and let f'(x) be its derivative. The derivative of f'(x) (if it has one) is written f''(x) and is called the second derivative of f. Similarly, the derivative of a second derivative, if it exists, is written f'''(x) and is called the _____ of f.

a. Differential coefficient
b. Mountain pass theorem
c. Third derivative
d. Derivative

35. In a totally ordered set all elements are mutually comparable, so such a set can have at most one minimal element and at most one maximal element. Then, due to mutual comparability, the minimal element will also be the least element and the maximal element will also be the greatest element. Thus in a totally ordered set we can simply use the terms minimum and _____.

a. Racetrack principle
b. Nth term
c. Leibniz rule
d. Maximum

36. In calculus, the _____ is a formula for the derivative of the composite of two functions.

In intuitive terms, if a variable, y, depends on a second variable, u, which in turn depends on a third variable, x, then the rate of change of y with respect to x can be computed as the rate of change of y with respect to u multiplied by the rate of change of u with respect to x. Schematically,

$$\frac{dy}{dx} = \frac{dy}{du} \cdot \frac{du}{dx}.$$

a. Reciprocal Rule
b. Product rule
c. Differentiation rules
d. Chain Rule

37. A _____ officer is an officer of high military rank. The term or equivalent is used by nearly every country in the world. _____ can be used as a generic term for all grades of _____ officer, or it can specifically refer to a single rank that is just called _____.

a. BDDC
b. BIBO stability
c. 15 theorem
d. General

38. This is a summary of _____, that is, rules for computing the derivative of a function in calculus.

Unless otherwise stated, all functions will be functions from R to R, although more generally, the formulae below make sense wherever they are well defined.

For any functions f and g and any real numbers a and b.

a. Quotient Rule
b. Product rule
c. Constant factor rule in differentiation
d. Differentiation rules

39. The largest and the smallest element of a set are called extreme values, absolute extrema, or extreme records.

Chapter 2. Section Project: Graphs and Limits of Trigonometric Functions

For a differentiable function f, if $f(x_0)$ is an _____ for the set of all values f(x), and if x_0 is in the interior of the domain of f, then x_0 is a critical point, by Fermat's theorem.

In the case of a general partial order one should not confuse a least element (smaller than all other) and a minimal element (nothing is smaller.)

a. Infinitesimal
b. Integration by substitution
c. Extreme Value Theorem
d. Extreme Value

40. In calculus, the _____ states that if a real-valued function f is continuous in the closed and bounded interval [a,b], then f must attain its maximum and minimum value, each at least once. That is, there exist numbers c and d in [a,b] such that:

$$f(c) \geq f(x) \geq f(d) \quad \text{for all } x \in [a, b].$$

A related theorem is the boundedness theorem which states that a continuous function f in the closed interval [a,b] is bounded on that interval. That is, there exist real numbers m and M such that:

$$m \leq f(x) \leq M \quad \text{for all } x \in [a, b].$$

The _____ enriches the boundedness theorem by saying that not only is the function bounded, but it also attains its least upper bound as its maximum and its greatest lower bound as its minimum.

a. Integral of secant cubed
b. Uniform convergence
c. Infinitesimal
d. Extreme Value Theorem

41. In calculus, a method called _____ can be applied to implicitly defined functions. This method is an application of the chain rule allowing one to calculate the derivative of a function given implicitly.

As explained in the introduction, y can be given as a function of x implicitly rather than explicitly. When we have an equation R (x,y) = 0, we may be able to solve it for y and then differentiate. However, sometimes it is simpler to differentiate R(x,y) with respect to x and then solve for dy / dx.

a. Ordinary differential equation
b. Implicit function
c. Automatic differentiation
d. Implicit differentiation

42. In geometry, the _____ or Gutschoven's curve is a two-dimensional algebraic curve resembling the Greek letter κ (kappa.)

Using the Cartesian coordinate system it can be expressed as:

$$x^2(x^2 + y^2) = a^2 y^2$$

or, using parametric equations:

$$x = a\cos t \cot t$$
$$y = a\cos t$$

In polar coordinates its equation is even simpler:

r = atanθ

It has two vertical asymptotes at $x = \pm a$, shown as dashed blue lines in the figure at right.

The _____'s curvature:

$$\kappa(\theta) = \frac{8\left(3 - \sin^2\theta\right)\sin^4\theta}{a\left[\sin^2(2\theta) + 4\right]^{\frac{3}{2}}}$$

Tangential angle:

$$\phi(\theta) = -\arctan\left[\frac{1}{2}\sin(2\theta)\right]$$

The _____ was first studied by Gérard van Gutschoven around 1662.

a. Tractrix
b. Witch of Agnesi
c. Prolate cycloid
d. Kappa curve

43. In mathematics, a (topological) _____ is defined as follows: let I be an interval of real numbers (i.e. a non-empty connected subset of $\mathbb{R}$); then a _____ γ is a continuous mapping $\gamma : I \to X$, where X is a topological space. The _____ γ is said to be simple if it is injective, i.e. if for all x, y in I, we have $\gamma(x) = \gamma(y) \implies x = y$. If I is a closed bounded interval $[a, b]$, we also allow the possibility $\gamma(a) = \gamma(b)$ (this convention makes it possible to talk about closed simple _____.)

a. Closed curve
b. Tractrix
c. Prolate cycloid
d. Curve

44.

In differential calculus, _____ problems involve finding a rate that a quantity changes by relating the population of the earth. The rate of change is usually with respect to people who have died.

a. Visual Calculus	b. Related rates
c. Standard part function	d. Mean Value Theorem

45. A _____ $y_s(x)$ of an ordinary differential equation is a solution that is tangent to every solution from the family of general solutions. By tangent we mean that there is a point x where $y_s(x) = y_c(x)$ and $y'_s(x) = y'_c(x)$ where y_c is any general solution.

Usually, singular solutions appear in differential equations when there is a need to divide in a term that might be equal to zero.

a. Conserved quantity	b. Method of undetermined coefficients
c. Method of matched asymptotic expansions	d. Singular solution

46. In calculus, _____ gives a sequence of approximations of a differentiable function around a given point by polynomials (the Taylor polynomials of that function) whose coefficients depend only on the derivatives of the function at that point. The theorem also gives precise estimates on the size of the error in the approximation. The theorem is named after the mathematician Brook Taylor, who stated it in 1712, though the result was first discovered 41 years earlier in 1671 by James Gregory.

a. Fresnel integrals	b. Related rates
c. Local minimum	d. Taylor's theorem

Chapter 3. Applications of Differentiation

1. In mathematics, two vectors are _____ if they are perpendicular, i.e., they form a right angle. For example, a subway and the street above, although they do not physically intersect, are _____ if they cross at a right angle.
   a. AUSM
   b. Orthogonal
   c. ACTRAN
   d. ALGOR

2. The largest and the smallest element of a set are called extreme values, absolute extrema, or extreme records.

   For a differentiable function f, if f(x_0) is an _____ for the set of all values f(x), and if x_0 is in the interior of the domain of f, then x_0 is a critical point, by Fermat's theorem.

   In the case of a general partial order one should not confuse a least element (smaller than all other) and a minimal element (nothing is smaller.)

   a. Infinitesimal
   b. Integration by substitution
   c. Extreme Value Theorem
   d. Extreme value

3. _____ is a type of motion in which the velocity of an object changes equal amounts in equal time periods. An example of an object having _____ would be a ball rolling down a ramp. The object picks up velocity as it goes down the ramp with equal changes in time.
   a. AUSM
   b. ACTRAN
   c. ALGOR
   d. Uniform Acceleration

4. Continuous functions are of utmost importance in mathematics and applications. However, not all functions are continuous. If a function is not continuous at a point in its domain, one says that it has a _____ there. The set of all points of _____ of a function may be a discrete set, a dense set, or even the entire domain of the function.
   a. BDDC
   b. 15 theorem
   c. Vector
   d. Discontinuity

5. The function $\log_b(x)$ depends on both b and x, but the term _____ in standard usage refers to a function of the form $\log_b(x)$ in which the base b is fixed and so the only argument is x. Thus there is one _____ for each value of the base b (which must be positive and must differ from 1.) Viewed in this way, the base-b _____ is the inverse function of the exponential function b^x.
   a. BDDC
   b. BIBO stability
   c. Logarithm function
   d. 15 theorem

6. In a totally ordered set all elements are mutually comparable, so such a set can have at most one minimal element and at most one maximal element. Then, due to mutual comparability, the minimal element will also be the least element and the maximal element will also be the greatest element. Thus in a totally ordered set we can simply use the terms minimum and _____.
   a. Leibniz rule
   b. Racetrack principle
   c. Nth term
   d. Maximum

7. In a totally ordered set all elements are mutually comparable, so such a set can have at most one minimal element and at most one maximal element. Then, due to mutual comparability, the minimal element will also be the least element and the maximal element will also be the greatest element. Thus in a totally ordered set we can simply use the terms _____ and maximum.

Chapter 3. Applications of Differentiation 43

a. Nth term
b. Maximum
c. Ghosts of departed quantities
d. Minimum

8. In elementary mathematics, physics, and engineering, a _____ is a geometric object that has both a magnitude (or length), direction and sense, (i.e., orientation along the given direction.) A _____ is frequently represented by a line segment with a definite direction, or graphically as an arrow, connecting an initial point A with a terminal point B, and denoted by

$\overrightarrow{AB}$.

The magnitude of the _____ is the length of the segment and the direction characterizes the displacement of B relative to A: how much one should move the point A to 'carry' it to the point B.

Many algebraic operations on real numbers have close analogues for vectors.

a. 15 theorem
b. Vector
c. Linear partial differential operator
d. BDDC

9. _____ is used to describe the steepness, incline, gradient, or grade of a straight line. A higher _____ value indicates a steeper incline. The _____ is defined as the ratio of the 'rise' divided by the 'run' between two points on a line, or in other words, the ratio of the altitude change to the horizontal distance between any two points on the line.

a. Y-intercept
b. 15 theorem
c. Sequence
d. Slope

10. In calculus, a branch of mathematics, the _____ is a measurement of how a function changes when its input changes. Loosely speaking, a _____ can be thought of as how much a quantity is changing at some given point. For example, the _____ of the position (or distance) of a vehicle with respect to time is the instantaneous velocity (respectively, instantaneous speed) at which the vehicle is traveling.

The process of finding a _____ is called differentiation. The fundamental theorem of calculus states that differentiation is the reverse process to integration.

a. Stationary phase approximation
b. Bounded function
c. Semi-differentiability
d. Derivative

11. In mathematics, a _____ (or critical number) is a point on the domain of a function where:

- one dimension: the derivative (or slope of the line when visualized) is equal to zero or a point where the function ceases to be differentiable.
- in general: there are two distinct concepts: either the derivative (Jacobian) vanishes, or it is not of full rank (or, in either case, the function is not differentiable); these agree in one dimension.

Note that in one dimension, a critical value or critical number x of function f is the domain element at which the derivative is zero or undefined, whereas the associated ordered pair (x, y) is the _____. In higher dimensions a critical value is in the range whereas a _____ is in the domain.

There are two situations in which a point becomes a _____ of a function of one variable. The first of which is that the value of the first derivative is equal to zero.

a. Differentiation operator
c. Total derivative

b. Critical point
d. Multivariable calculus

12. In geometry, an _____ is a plane curve produced by tracing the path of a chosen point of a circle -- called epicycle -- which rolls without slipping around a fixed circle. It is a particular kind of roulette.

If the smaller circle has radius r, and the larger circle has radius R = kr, then the parametric equations for the curve can be given by either:

$$x(\theta) = (R+r)\cos\theta - r\cos\left(\frac{R+r}{r}\theta\right)$$
$$y(\theta) = (R+r)\sin\theta - r\sin\left(\frac{R+r}{r}\theta\right),$$

or:

$$x(\theta) = r(k+1)\cos\theta - r\cos((k+1)\theta)$$
$$y(\theta) = r(k+1)\sin\theta - r\sin((k+1)\theta).$$

If k is an integer, then the curve is closed, and has k cusps (i.e., sharp corners, where the curve is not differentiable.)

a. Asymptotic curve
c. ACTRAN

b. ALGOR
d. Epicycloid

13. In probability theory and statistics, the _____ (or expectation value or mean and for continuous random variables with a density function it is the probability density -weighted integral of the possible values.

The term '_____' can be misleading.

a. Expected value
c. AUSM

b. ALGOR
d. ACTRAN

14. In calculus, the _____ states, roughly, that given a section of a smooth curve, there is at least one point on that section at which the derivative (slope) of the curve is equal (parallel) to the 'average' derivative of the section. It is used to prove theorems that make global conclusions about a function on an interval starting from local hypotheses about derivatives at points of the interval.

This theorem can be understood concretely by applying it to motion: If a car travels one hundred miles in one hour, so its average speed during that time was 100 miles per hour.

a. Hyperbolic angle
c. Limits of integration
b. Periodic function
d. Mean Value Theorem

15. In calculus, the _____ is a formula used to find the derivatives of products of functions. It may be stated thus:

$$(f \cdot g)' = f' \cdot g + f \cdot g'$$

or in the Leibniz notation thus:

$$\frac{d}{dx}(u \cdot v) = u \cdot \frac{dv}{dx} + v \cdot \frac{du}{dx}.$$

Discovery of this rule is credited to Gottfried Leibniz, who demonstrated it using differentials. Here is Leibniz's argument: Let u and v be two differentiable functions of x.

a. Constant factor rule in differentiation
c. Quotient Rule
b. Differentiation rules
d. Product Rule

16. In mathematics, a _____ is a function which preserves the given order. This concept first arose in calculus, and was later generalized to the more abstract setting of order theory.

In calculus, a function f defined on a subset of the real numbers with real values is called monotonic (also monotonically increasing or non-decreasing), if for all x and y such that x >≤ y one has f(x) >≤ f(y), so f preserves the order.

a. 15 theorem
c. Pseudo-differential operator
b. Monotonic function
d. Pettis integral

17. In mathematics, an _____, is the apparent shape of a circle viewed obliquely from outside it, as distinct from a hyperbola which is the shape seen from inside. It is the finite or bounded case of a conic section as a shape cut in a cone by a plane, the unbounded cases being the parabola, which like the _____ remains connected, and the hyperbola, which separates into two connected components or branches.

Equivalently an _____ can be defined as the locus of points, or path traced out, in a plane such that the sum of the distances from the moving point to two fixed points remains constant.

a. ACTRAN
c. AUSM
b. Ellipse
d. ALGOR

18. Trigonometry is a branch of mathematics that deals with triangles, particularly those plane triangles in which one angle has 90 degrees (right triangles.) Trigonometry deals with relationships between the sides and the angles of triangles and with the _____ functions, which describe those relationships.

Trigonometry has applications in both pure mathematics and in applied mathematics, where it is essential in many branches of science and technology.

   a. Sine
   b. Trigonometric integrals
   c. Trigonometric functions
   d. Trigonometric

19. In mathematics, the _____ are functions of an angle. They are important in the study of triangles and modeling periodic phenomena, among many other applications. _____ are commonly defined as ratios of two sides of a right triangle containing the angle, and can equivalently be defined as the lengths of various line segments from a unit circle.

   a. Trigonometric integrals
   b. Trigonometric
   c. Sine integral
   d. Trigonometric functions

20. In calculus, the _____ determines whether a given critical point of a function is a maximum, a minimum, or neither.

Suppose that f is a function and we want to determine if f has a maximum or minimum at x. If f is increasing to the left of x and decreasing to the right of x, then x is a local maximum of f.

   a. Continuous function
   b. Test for Divergence
   c. Partial sum
   d. First Derivative Test

21. A _____ is a type of manifold that is locally similar enough to Euclidean space to allow one to do calculus Any manifold can be described by a collection of charts, also known as an atlas.

   a. Minimal surface
   b. Sphere
   c. Tangent line
   d. Differentiable manifold

22. In mathematics, a (topological) _____ is defined as follows: let I be an interval of real numbers (i.e. a non-empty connected subset of $\mathbb{R}$); then a _____ γ is a continuous mapping $\gamma : I \to X$, where X is a topological space. The _____ γ is said to be simple if it is injective, i.e. if for all x, y in I, we have $\gamma(x) = \gamma(y) \implies x = y$. If I is a closed bounded interval $[a, b]$, we also allow the possibility $\gamma(a) = \gamma(b)$ (this convention makes it possible to talk about closed simple _____.)

   a. Tractrix
   b. Closed curve
   c. Curve
   d. Prolate cycloid

23. _____ (including exponential decay) occurs when the growth rate of a mathematical function is proportional to the function's current value. In the case of a discrete domain of definition with equal intervals it is also called geometric growth or geometric decay (the function values form a geometric progression.)

_____ is said to follow an exponential law; the simple-_____ model is known as the Malthusian growth model.

Chapter 3. Applications of Differentiation

a. Exponential growth
c. Inseparable differential equation

b. Oscillating
d. Isomonodromic deformation

24. In mathematics, a concave function is the negative of a convex function. A concave function is also synonymously called _____, concave down, convex cap or upper convex.

Formally, a real-valued function f defined on an interval (or on any convex set C of some vector space) is called concave, if for any two points x and y in its domain C and any t in [0,1], we have

$$f(tx + (1-t)y) \geq tf(x) + (1-t)f(y).$$

Also, f(x) is concave on [a, b] if and only if the function −f(x) is convex on [a, b].

a. Stationary phase approximation
c. Ramp function

b. Concave downwards
d. Concave upwards

25. In mathematics, a real-valued function f defined on an interval (or on any convex subset of some vector space) is called convex, _____, concave up or convex cup, if for any two points x and y in its domain C and any t in [0,1], we have

$$f(tx + (1-t)y) \leq tf(x) + (1-t)f(y).$$

Convex function on an interval.

In other words, a function is convex if and only if its epigraph (the set of points lying on or above the graph) is a convex set.

Pictorially, a function is called 'convex' if the function lies below the straight line segment connecting two points, for any two points in the interval.

A function is called strictly convex if

$$f(tx + (1-t)y) < tf(x) + (1-t)f(y)$$

for any t in (0,1) and $x \neq y$.

A function f is said to be concave if − f is convex.

a. Mountain pass theorem
c. Vertical asymptote

b. Third derivative
d. Concave upwards

26. In mathematics, the _____ is a criterion for the convergence (a convergence test) of an infinite series

$$\sum_{n=1}^{\infty} a_n.$$

It is particularly useful in connection with power series.

The _____ was developed first by Cauchy and so is sometimes known as the Cauchy _____ or Cauchy's radical test. The _____ uses the number

$$C = \limsup_{n \to \infty} \sqrt[n]{|a_n|},$$

where 'lim sup' denotes the limit superior, possibly ∞.

    a. Mean Value Theorem   b. Root Test
    c. Racetrack principle   d. Related rates

27. In differential calculus, an inflection point, or _____ (or inflexion) is a point on a curve at which the curvature changes sign. The curve changes from being concave upwards (positive curvature) to concave downwards (negative curvature), or vice versa. If one imagines driving a vehicle along the curve, it is a point at which the steering-wheel is momentarily 'straight', being turned from left to right or vice versa.

    a. Derivative of a constant   b. Logarithmic derivative
    c. Lin-Tsien equation   d. Point of inflection

28. Let f be a differentiable function, and let f'(x) be its derivative. The derivative of f'(x) (if it has one) is written f''(x) and is called the _____ of f. Similarly, the derivative of a _____, if it exists, is written f'''(x) and is called the third derivative of f.

    a. Second Derivative   b. Stationary phase approximation
    c. Vertical asymptote   d. Slant asymptote

29. In calculus, a branch of mathematics, the _____ is a criterion often useful for determining whether a given stationary point of a function is a local maximum or a local minimum.

The test states: If the function f is twice differentiable at a stationary point x, meaning that $f'(x) = 0$, then:

- If $f''(x) < 0$ then f has a local maximum at x.
- If $f''(x) > 0$ then f has a local minimum at x.
- If $f''(x) = 0$, the _____ says nothing about the point x, has a possible inflection point.

In the last case, the function may have a local maximum or minimum there, but the function is sufficiently 'flat' that this is undetected by the second derivative. In this case one has to examine the third derivative. Such an example is f(x) = x^4.

Chapter 3. Applications of Differentiation 49

a. Second Derivative Test
b. Stationary point
c. Symmetric derivative
d. Linearity of differentiation

30. In mathematics, the hyperbolic functions are analogs of the ordinary trigonometric functions. The basic hyperbolic functions are the _____ 'sinh', and the hyperbolic cosine 'cosh', from which are derived the hyperbolic tangent 'tanh', etc., in analogy to the derived trigonometric functions. The inverse hyperbolic functions are the area _____ 'arsinh' (also called 'asinh', or sometimes by the misnomer of 'arcsinh') and so on.

a. Square root function
b. Signum function
c. Hyperbolic tangent
d. Hyperbolic sine

31. The _____ of an object is the extra energy which it possesses due to its motion. It is defined as the work needed to accelerate a body of a given mass from rest to its current velocity. Having gained this energy during its acceleration, the body maintains this _____ unless its speed changes.

a. Kinetic energy
b. Law of Conservation of Energy
c. BDDC
d. 15 theorem

32. In mathematics, the concept of a '_____' is used to describe the behavior of a function as its argument or input either 'gets close' to some point, or as the argument becomes arbitrarily large; or the behavior of a sequence's elements as their index increases indefinitely. Limits are used in calculus and other branches of mathematical analysis to define derivatives and continuity.

In formulas, _____ is usually abbreviated as lim

a. Limit
b. BIBO stability
c. 15 theorem
d. BDDC

33. The _____ of an angle is the ratio of the length of the opposite side to the length of the hypotenuse. In our case

$$\sin A = \frac{\text{opposite}}{\text{hypotenuse}} = \frac{a}{h}.$$

Note that this ratio does not depend on size of the particular right triangle chosen, as long as it contains the angle A, since all such triangles are similar.

The cosine of an angle is the ratio of the length of the adjacent side to the length of the hypotenuse.

a. Trigonometric
b. Sine integral
c. Trigonometric functions
d. Sine

34. An _____ of a real-valued function y = f(x) is a curve which describes the behavior of f as either x or y tends to infinity.

In other words, as one moves along the graph of f(x) in some direction, the distance between it and the _____ eventually becomes smaller than any distance that one may specify.

a. AUSM
b. ACTRAN
c. ALGOR
d. Asymptote

35. Suppose f is a function. Then the line y = a is a _____ for f if

$$\lim_{x \to \infty} f(x) = a \text{ or } \lim_{x \to -\infty} f(x) = a.$$

Intuitively, this means that f(x) can be made as close as desired to a by making x big enough. How big is big enough depends on how close one wishes to make f(x) to a.

a. Second derivative
b. Third derivative
c. Mountain pass theorem
d. Horizontal asymptote

36. In mathematics, the _____ are analogs of the ordinary trigonometric or circular functions. The basic _____ are the hyperbolic sine 'sinh', and the hyperbolic cosine 'cosh', from which are derived the hyperbolic tangent 'tanh', etc., in analogy to the derived trigonometric functions. The inverse _____ are the area hyperbolic sine 'arsinh' (also called 'asinh', or sometimes by the misnomer of 'arcsinh') and so on.

a. Multiplicative inverse
b. Signum function
c. Hyperbolic cosine
d. Hyperbolic functions

37. When a linear asymptote is not parallel to the x- or y-axis, it is called either an oblique asymptote or equivalently a _____. The function f(x) is asymptotic to y = mx + b if

$$\lim_{x \to \infty} f(x) - (mx + b) = 0 \text{ or } \lim_{x \to -\infty} f(x) - (mx + b) = 0$$

Note that y = mx + b is never a vertical asymptote, but can be a horizontal asymptote if m=0 (in which case it is not an oblique asymptote.)

An example is $f(x)=(x^2-1)/x$ which has an oblique asymptote of y=x (m=1, b=0) as seen in the limit

$$\lim_{x \to \infty} f(x) - x$$
$$= \lim_{x \to \infty} \frac{x^2 - 1}{x} - x$$
$$= \lim_{x \to \infty} (x - 1/x) - x$$
$$= \lim_{x \to \infty} -1/x = 0$$

Computationally identifying an oblique asymptote can be more difficult than a horizontal or vertical asymptote, in particular because the m and b might not be known.

a. Stationary phase approximation
b. Geometric function theory
c. Slant asymptote
d. Second derivative

Chapter 3. Applications of Differentiation 51

38. In geometry, the _____ (also semimajor axis) is used to describe the dimensions of ellipses and hyperbolae.

The major axis of an ellipse is its longest diameter, a line that runs through the centre and both foci, its ends being at the widest points of the shape. The _____ is one half of the major axis, and thus runs from the centre, through a focus, and to the edge of the ellipse.

a. 15 theorem
b. BDDC
c. BIBO stability
d. Semi-major axis

39. In mathematics, a _____ (or just conic) is a curve obtained by intersecting a cone (more precisely, a circular conical surface) with a plane. A _____ is therefore a restriction of a quadric surface to the plane. The conic sections were named and studied as long ago as 200 BC, when Apollonius of Perga undertook a systematic study of their properties.

a. Latus rectum
b. BDDC
c. 15 theorem
d. Conic section

40. In integral calculus we would want to write a fractional algebraic expression as the sum of its _____ in order to take the integral of each simple fraction separately. Once the original denominator, D_0, has been factored we set up a fraction for each factor in the denominator. We may use a subscripted D to represent the denominator of the respective _____ which are the factors in D_0.

a. Left inverse
b. Multinomial theorem
c. Closed-form expression
d. Partial fractions

41. In mathematics, a _____ is an ordered list of objects (or events). Like a set, it contains members (also called elements or terms), and the number of terms (possibly infinite) is called the length of the _____. Unlike a set, order matters, and the exact same elements can appear multiple times at different positions in the _____.

a. Sequence
b. Slope
c. 15 theorem
d. Y-intercept

42. In mathematics, a _____ is an approximation of a general function using a linear function (more precisely, an affine function.)

Given a differentiable function f of one real variable, Taylor's theorem for n=1 states that

$$f(x) = f(a) + f\,'(a)(x-a) + R_2$$

where R_2 is the remainder term. The _____ is obtained by dropping the remainder:

$$f(x) \approx f(a) + f\,'(a)(x-a)$$

which is true for x close to a.

a. Point of inflection
b. Linear approximation
c. Smooth function
d. Lin-Tsien equation

Chapter 3. Applications of Differentiation

43. In geometry, the _____ (or simply the tangent) to a curve at a given point is the straight line that 'just touches' the curve at that point (in the sense explained more precisely below.) As it passes through the point of tangency, the _____ is 'going in the same direction' as the curve, and in this sense it is the best straight-line approximation to the curve at that point. The same definition applies to space curves and curves in n-dimensional Euclidean space.

    a. Minimal surface
    b. Lie derivative
    c. North pole
    d. Tangent line

44. In complex analysis, a mathematical discipline, a _____ of a meromorphic function is a certain type of singularity that behaves like the singularity of $\frac{1}{z^n}$ at z = 0. This means that, in particular, a _____ of the function f(z) is a point z = a such that f(z) approaches infinity uniformly as z approaches a.

Formally, suppose U is an open subset of the complex plane C, a is an element of U and f : U {a} → C is a function which is holomorphic over its domain.

    a. Complex logarithm
    b. Lacunary function
    c. Pole
    d. Bieberbach conjecture

45. In mathematics, a _____ is any function which can be written as the ratio of two polynomial functions.

$$y = \frac{x^2 - 3x - 2}{x^2 - 4}$$

In the case of one variable, x, a _____ is a function of the form

$$f(x) = \frac{P(x)}{Q(x)}$$

where P and Q are polynomial function in x and Q is not the zero polynomial. The domain of f is the set of all points x for which the denominator Q(x) is not zero.

    a. 15 theorem
    b. BIBO stability
    c. BDDC
    d. Rational function

46. In statistics, _____ is the effect of variables' uncertainties (or errors) on the uncertainty of a function based on them. When the variables are the values of experimental measurements they have uncertainties due to measurement limitations (e.g. instrument precision) which propagate to the combination of variables in the function.

The uncertainty is usually defined by the absolute error.

    a. Large eddy simulation
    b. Spectral methods
    c. Galerkin methods
    d. Propagation of uncertainty

Chapter 3. Applications of Differentiation

47. One commonly distinguishes between the _____ and the absolute error. The absolute error is the magnitude of the difference between the exact value and the approximation. The _____ is the absolute error divided by the magnitude of the exact value.

   a. Series acceleration   b. Meshfree methods
   c. Numerical integration   d. Relative error

48. In mathematics, the _____, sometimes called the direct _____ is a criterion for convergence or divergence of a series whose terms are real or complex numbers. The test determines convergence by comparing the terms of the series in question with those of a series whose convergence properties are known.

The _____ states that if the series

$$\sum_{n=1}^{\infty} b_n$$

is an absolutely convergent series and

$$|a_n| \leq |b_n|$$

for sufficiently large n , then the series

$$\sum_{n=1}^{\infty} a_n$$

converges absolutely.

   a. Ratio test   b. Conditionally convergent
   c. Telescoping series   d. Comparison Test

49. In calculus, _____, was originally the use of expressions such as dx and dy and to represent 'infinitely small' (or infinitesimal) increments of quantities x and y, just as >Δx and >Δy represent finite increments of x and y respectively. So for y being a function of x, or

[x]>

the derivative of y with respect to x, which later came to be viewed as

[x]>

was, according to Leibniz, the quotient of an infinitesimal increment of y by an infinitesimal increment of x, or

where the right hand side is Lagrange's notation for the derivative of f at x.

Similarly, although mathematicians usually now view an integral

as a limit

where >Δx is an interval containing x_i, Leibniz viewed it as the sum (the integral sign denoting summation) of infinitely many infinitesimal quantities f(x) dx.

a. Stationary point
c. Time derivative
b. Smooth function
d. Leibniz's notation

50. In infinitesimal calculus, a _____ is traditionally an infinitesimally small change in a variable. For example, if x is a variable, then a change in the value of x is often denoted Δx (or δx when this change is considered to be small.) The _____ dx represents such a change, but is infinitely small.

a. Local maximum
c. Dirichlet integral
b. The Method of Mechanical Theorems
d. Differential

51. A _____ is a mathematical equation for an unknown function of one or several variables that relates the values of the function itself and of its derivatives of various orders. they play a prominent role in engineering, physics, economics and other disciplines.

A simplified real world example of a _____ is modeling the acceleration of a ball falling through the air (considering only gravity and air resistance.)

a. Phase line
c. Differential equation
b. Structural stability
d. Caloric polynomial

Chapter 4. The Wankel Rotary Engine and Area

1. In calculus, an _____, primitive or indefinite integral of a function f is a function F whose derivative is equal to f, i.e., F >' = f. The process of solving for antiderivatives is antidifferentiation (or indefinite integration.) Antiderivatives are related to definite integrals through the fundamental theorem of calculus: the definite integral of a function over an interval is equal to the difference between the values of an _____ evaluated at the endpoints of the interval.
   a. Order of integration
   b. Indefinite integral
   c. Antiderivative
   d. Integrand

2. The _____ is a function in mathematics. The application of this function to a value x is written as exp(x). Equivalently, this can be written in the form e^x, where e is a mathematical constant, the base of the natural logarithm, which equals approximately 2.718281828, and is also known as Euler's number.
   a. ACTRAN
   b. Integral part
   c. Exponential function
   d. Area hyperbolic functions

3. _____ is a type of motion in which the velocity of an object changes equal amounts in equal time periods. An example of an object having _____ would be a ball rolling down a ramp. The object picks up velocity as it goes down the ramp with equal changes in time.
   a. Uniform Acceleration
   b. AUSM
   c. ACTRAN
   d. ALGOR

4. In calculus, the indefinite integral of a given function (i.e. the set of all antiderivatives of the function) is always written with a constant, the _____. This constant expresses an ambiguity inherent in the construction of antiderivatives. If a function f(x) is defined on an interval and F(x) is an antiderivative of f(x), then the set of all antiderivatives of f(x) is given by the functions F(x) + C, where C is an arbitrary constant.
   a. Nonelementary integral
   b. Sum rule in integration
   c. Disk integration
   d. Constant of integration

5. In infinitesimal calculus, a _____ is traditionally an infinitesimally small change in a variable. For example, if x is a variable, then a change in the value of x is often denoted Δx (or δx when this change is considered to be small.) The _____ dx represents such a change, but is infinitely small.
   a. Dirichlet integral
   b. The Method of Mechanical Theorems
   c. Differential
   d. Local maximum

6. A _____ is a mathematical equation for an unknown function of one or several variables that relates the values of the function itself and of its derivatives of various orders. they play a prominent role in engineering, physics, economics and other disciplines.

A simplified real world example of a _____ is modeling the acceleration of a ball falling through the air (considering only gravity and air resistance.)

   a. Phase line
   b. Structural stability
   c. Caloric polynomial
   d. Differential equation

7. A _____ officer is an officer of high military rank. The term or equivalent is used by nearly every country in the world. _____ can be used as a generic term for all grades of _____ officer, or it can specifically refer to a single rank that is just called _____.

a. BIBO stability
b. BDDC
c. 15 theorem
d. General

8. In mathematics, a _____ to an ordinary or partial differential equation is a function for which the derivatives appearing in the equation may not all exist but which is nonetheless deemed to satisfy the equation in some precisely defined sense. There are many different definitions of _____, appropriate for different classes of equations. One of the most important is based on the notion of distributions.

a. Weak solution
b. Structural stability
c. Conserved quantity
d. Singular perturbation

9. In calculus, an antiderivative, primitive or _____ of a function f is a function F whose derivative is equal to f, i.e., F ' = f. The process of solving for antiderivatives is antidifferentiation (or indefinite integration.) Antiderivatives are related to definite integrals through the fundamental theorem of calculus: the definite integral of a function over an interval is equal to the difference between the values of an antiderivative evaluated at the endpoints of the interval.

a. Indefinite integral
b. Integration by parts operator
c. Integral test for convergence
d. Arc length

10. In mathematics, the _____ of a function y = f(x) is a function that, in some fashion, 'undoes' the effect of f The _____ of f is denoted f^{-1}. The statements y=f(x) and x=f^{-1}(y) are equivalent.

a. AUSM
b. ACTRAN
c. Inverse
d. ALGOR

11. In mathematics, if f is a function from A to B then an _____ for f is a function in the opposite direction, from B to A, with the property that a round trip (a composition) from A to B to A (or from B to A to B) returns each element of the initial set to itself. Thus, if an input x into the function f produces an output y, then inputting y into the _____ f^{-1} (read f inverse, not to be confused with exponentiation) produces the output x. Not every function has an inverse; those that do are called invertible.

a. Inverse function
b. Augustin-Jean Fresnel
c. Aristotle
d. Augustin Louis Cauchy

12. Integration is an important concept in mathematics, specifically in the field of calculus and, more broadly, mathematical analysis. Given a function f of a real variable x and an interval [a, b] of the real line, the _____

$$\int_a^b f(x)\,dx,$$

is defined informally to be the net signed area of the region in the xy-plane bounded by the graph of f, the x-axis, and the vertical lines x = a and x = b.

The term '_____' may also refer to the notion of antiderivative, a function F whose derivative is the given function f.

a. Indefinite integral
b. Integrand
c. Integral test for convergence
d. Integral

Chapter 4. The Wankel Rotary Engine and Area

13. A curve γ is said to be closed or a loop if $I = [a, b]$ and if $\gamma(a) = \gamma(b)$. A _____ is thus a continuous mapping of the circle S^1; a simple _____ is also called a Jordan curve or a Jordan arc. The Jordan curve theorem states that such curves divide the plane into an 'interior' and an 'exterior'.

   a. Bullet-nose curve
   b. Kappa curve
   c. Closed curve
   d. Curve

14. In economics, the _____ functional form of production functions is widely used to represent the relationship of an output to inputs. It was proposed by Knut Wicksell (1851-1926), and tested against statistical evidence by Charles Cobb and Paul Douglas in 1900-1928.

For production, the function is

   $Y = AL^{\alpha}K^{\beta}$,

where:

- Y = total production (the monetary value of all goods produced in a year)
- L = labor input
- K = capital input
- A = total factor productivity
- α and β are the output elasticities of labor and capital, respectively. These values are constants determined by available technology.

Output elasticity measures the responsiveness of output to a change in levels of either labor or capital used in production, ceteris paribus. For example if α = 0.15, a 1% increase in labor would lead to approximately a 0.15% increase in output.

   a. 15 theorem
   b. BDDC
   c. Cobb-Douglas
   d. BIBO stability

15. In mathematics, the hyperbolic functions are analogs of the ordinary trigonometric functions. The basic hyperbolic functions are the _____ 'sinh', and the hyperbolic cosine 'cosh', from which are derived the hyperbolic tangent 'tanh', etc., in analogy to the derived trigonometric functions. The inverse hyperbolic functions are the area _____ 'arsinh' (also called 'asinh', or sometimes by the misnomer of 'arcsinh') and so on.

   a. Square root function
   b. Hyperbolic tangent
   c. Signum function
   d. Hyperbolic sine

16. In mathematics, a (topological) _____ is defined as follows: let I be an interval of real numbers (i.e. a non-empty connected subset of $\mathbb{R}$); then a _____ γ is a continuous mapping $\gamma : I \to X$, where X is a topological space. The _____ γ is said to be simple if it is injective, i.e. if for all x, y in I, we have $\gamma(x) = \gamma(y) \implies x = y$. If I is a closed bounded interval $[a, b]$, we also allow the possibility $\gamma(a) = \gamma(b)$ (this convention makes it possible to talk about closed simple _____.)

a. Prolate cycloid
c. Tractrix

b. Curve
d. Closed curve

17. The _____ of an angle is the ratio of the length of the opposite side to the length of the hypotenuse. In our case

$$\sin A = \frac{\text{opposite}}{\text{hypotenuse}} = \frac{a}{h}.$$

Note that this ratio does not depend on size of the particular right triangle chosen, as long as it contains the angle A, since all such triangles are similar.

The cosine of an angle is the ratio of the length of the adjacent side to the length of the hypotenuse.

a. Trigonometric functions
c. Trigonometric

b. Sine integral
d. Sine

18. In mathematics, in the field of differential equations, an initial value problem is an ordinary differential equation together with specified value, called the _____, of the unknown function at a given point in the domain of the solution. In physics or other sciences, modeling a system frequently amounts to solving an initial value problem; in this context, the differential equation is an evolution equation specifying how, given initial conditions, the system will evolve with time.

An initial value problem is a differential equation

$$y'(t) = f(t, y(t)) \quad \text{with} \quad f : \mathbb{R} \times \mathbb{R} \to \mathbb{R}$$

together with a point in the domain of f

$$(t_0, y_0) \in \mathbb{R} \times \mathbb{R},$$

called the _____.

a. Initial condition
c. AUSM

b. ACTRAN
d. ALGOR

19. In mathematics, especially in order theory, an upper bound of a subset S of some partially ordered set (P, ≤) is an element of P which is greater than or equal to every element of S. The term _____ is defined dually as an element of P which is lesser than or equal to every element of S. A set with an upper bound is said to be bounded from above by that bound, a set with a _____ is said to be bounded from below by that bound.

A subset S of a partially ordered set P may fail to have any bounds or may have many different upper and lower bounds. By transitivity, any element greater than or equal to an upper bound of S is again an upper bound of S, and any element lesser than or equal to any _____ of S is again a _____ of S. This leads to the consideration of least upper bounds: (or suprema) and greatest lower bounds (or infima.)

a. BIBO stability	b. 15 theorem
c. BDDC	d. Lower bound

20. _____ is the addition of a set of numbers; the result is their sum or total. An interim or present total of a _____ process is termed the running total. The 'numbers' to be summed may be natural numbers, complex numbers, matrices, or still more complicated objects.

a. 15 theorem	b. BIBO stability
c. BDDC	d. Summation

21. In mathematics, especially in order theory, an _____ of a subset S of some partially ordered set (P, >≤) is an element of P which is greater than or equal to every element of S. The term lower bound is defined dually as an element of P which is lesser than or equal to every element of S. A set with an _____ is said to be bounded from above by that bound, a set with a lower bound is said to be bounded from below by that bound.

A subset S of a partially ordered set P may fail to have any bounds or may have many different upper and lower bounds. By transitivity, any element greater than or equal to an _____ of S is again an _____ of S, and any element lesser than or equal to any lower bound of S is again a lower bound of S. This leads to the consideration of least upper bounds: (or suprema) and greatest lower bounds (or infima.)

a. ALGOR	b. Upper bound
c. AUSM	d. ACTRAN

22. In calculus, a _____ is either of the two limits of a function f(x) of a real variable x as x approaches a specified point either from below or from above. One should write either:

$$\lim_{x \to a^+} f(x) \text{ or } \lim_{x \downarrow a} f(x)$$

for the limit as x decreases in value approaching a (x approaches a 'from above' or 'from the right'), and similarly

$$\lim_{x \to a^-} f(x) \text{ or } \lim_{x \uparrow a} f(x)$$

for the limit as x increases in value approaching a (x approaches a 'from below' or 'from the left'.)

The two one-sided limits exist and are equal if and only if the limit of f(x) as x approaches a exists.

a. ACTRAN	b. One-sided limit
c. AUSM	d. ALGOR

23. In mathematics, the concept of a '_____' is used to describe the behavior of a function as its argument or input either 'gets close' to some point, or as the argument becomes arbitrarily large; or the behavior of a sequence's elements as their index increases indefinitely. Limits are used in calculus and other branches of mathematical analysis to define derivatives and continuity.

In formulas, _____ is usually abbreviated as lim

a. BDDC
b. 15 theorem
c. BIBO stability
d. Limit

24. A _____, in mathematics, is a polynomial function of the form $f(x) = ax^2 + bx + c$, where $a \neq 0$. The graph of a _____ is a parabola whose major axis is parallel to the y-axis.

The expression ax² + bx + c in the definition of a _____ is a polynomial of degree 2 or a 2nd degree polynomial, because the highest exponent of x is 2.

a. Discriminant
b. Quadratic function
c. Leading coefficient
d. Resultant

25. In mathematics, a _____ is a method for approximating the total area underneath a curve on a graph, otherwise known as an integral. It may also be used to define the integration operation.

Consider a function $f: D \rightarrow R$, where D is a subset of the real numbers R, and let $I = [a, b]$ be a closed interval contained in D. A finite set of points $\{x_0, x_1, x_2, ... x_n\}$ such that $a = x_0 < x_1 < x_2 ... < x_n = b$ creates a partition

$P = \{[x_0, x_1), [x_1, x_2), ... [x_{n-1}, x_n]\}$

of I.

a. Solid of revolution
b. Risch algorithm
c. Riemann sum
d. Signed measure

26. In differential calculus, an inflection point, or _____ (or inflexion) is a point on a curve at which the curvature changes sign. The curve changes from being concave upwards (positive curvature) to concave downwards (negative curvature), or vice versa. If one imagines driving a vehicle along the curve, it is a point at which the steering-wheel is momentarily 'straight', being turned from left to right or vice versa.

a. Lin-Tsien equation
b. Logarithmic derivative
c. Derivative of a constant
d. Point of inflection

27. A _____ is a statement of the meaning of a word or phrase. The term to be defined is known as the definiendum. The words which define it are known as the definiens.

a. BIBO stability
b. Definition
c. BDDC
d. 15 theorem

28. In calculus, a branch of mathematics, the _____ is a measurement of how a function changes when its input changes. Loosely speaking, a _____ can be thought of as how much a quantity is changing at some given point. For example, the _____ of the position (or distance) of a vehicle with respect to time is the instantaneous velocity (respectively, instantaneous speed) at which the vehicle is traveling.

The process of finding a _____ is called differentiation. The fundamental theorem of calculus states that differentiation is the reverse process to integration.

a. Derivative
b. Semi-differentiability
c. Stationary phase approximation
d. Bounded function

29. In mathematics, the _____ is a two-dimensional coordinate system in which each point on a plane is determined by an angle and a distance. The _____ is especially useful in situations where the relationship between two points is most easily expressed in terms of angles and distance; in the more familiar Cartesian or rectangular coordinate system, such a relationship can only be found through trigonometric formulation.

As the coordinate system is two-dimensional, each point is determined by two polar coordinates: the radial coordinate and the angular coordinate.

a. 15 theorem
b. BIBO stability
c. BDDC
d. Polar coordinate system

30. In mathematics and its applications, a _____ system is a system for assigning an n-tuple of numbers or scalars to each point in an n-dimensional space. This concept is part of the theory of manifolds. 'Scalars' in many cases means real numbers, but, depending on context, can mean complex numbers or elements of some other commutative ring.

a. Cylindrical coordinate system
b. Coordinate
c. Spherical coordinate system
d. 15 theorem

31. _____ is any physical or virtual entity that is owned by an individual or jointly by a group of individuals. An owner of _____ has the right to consume, sell, rent, mortgage, transfer and exchange his or her _____. Important widely-recognized types of _____ include real _____, personal _____ (other physical possessions), and intellectual _____ (rights over artistic creations, inventions, etc.), although the latter is not always as widely recognized or enforced.

a. 15 theorem
b. BDDC
c. BIBO stability
d. Property

32. The _____ specifies the relationship between the two central operations of calculus, differentiation and integration.

The first part of the theorem, sometimes called the first _____, shows that an indefinite integration can be reversed by a differentiation.

The second part, sometimes called the second _____, allows one to compute the definite integral of a function by using any one of its infinitely many antiderivatives.

a. Fundamental Theorem of Calculus
b. Periodic function
c. Leibniz formula
d. Limits of integration

33. Continuous functions are of utmost importance in mathematics and applications. However, not all functions are continuous. If a function is not continuous at a point in its domain, one says that it has a _____ there. The set of all points of _____ of a function may be a discrete set, a dense set, or even the entire domain of the function.

a. Vector
b. 15 theorem
c. BDDC
d. Discontinuity

34. An _____ is a type of quadric surface that is a higher dimensional analogue of an ellipse. The equation of a standard axis-aligned _____ body in an xyz-Cartesian coordinate system is

$$\frac{x^2}{a^2} + \frac{y^2}{b^2} + \frac{z^2}{c^2} = 1$$

where a and b are the equatorial radii (along the x and y axes) and c is the polar radius (along the z-axis), all of which are fixed positive real numbers determining the shape of the _____.

More generally, a not-necessarily-axis-aligned _____ is defined by the equation

$$\mathbf{x}^T A \mathbf{x} = 1$$

where A is a symmetric positive definite matrix and x is a vector.

a. ALGOR
b. ACTRAN
c. AUSM
d. Ellipsoid

35. The _____ a(t) is a function defined in terms of time t expressing the ratio of the value at time t (future value) and the initial investment (present value.) It is used in interest theory.

Thus a(0)=1 and the value at time t is given by:

$$A(t) = k \cdot a(t)$$

a. AUSM
b. ACTRAN
c. ALGOR
d. Accumulation function

36. In mathematics, a _____ is a function of the form

$$f(x) = ax^3 + bx^2 + cx + d,$$

where a is nonzero; or in other words, a polynomial of degree three. The derivative of a _____ is a quadratic function. The integral of a _____ is a quartic function.

a. Quadratic formula
b. Quartic function
c. Linear equation
d. Cubic function

37. In mathematics, a _____ represents the application of one function to the results of another. For instance, the functions f: X → Y and g: Y → Z can be composed by first computing f(x) and then applying a function g to the output of f(x.)

Thus one obtains a function g ∘ f: X → Z defined by (g ∘ f)(x) = g(f(x)) for all x in X. The notation g ∘ f is read as 'g circle f', or 'g composed with f', 'g after f', 'g following f', or just 'g of f'.

a. Surjective
b. Piecewise-defined function
c. Constant function
d. Composite function

38. In calculus, _____ is a tool for finding antiderivatives and integrals. Using the fundamental theorem of calculus often requires finding an antiderivative. For this and other reasons, _____ is a relatively important tool for mathematicians.
a. Odd function
b. Integration by Substitution
c. Extreme value
d. Integral of secant cubed

39. In complex analysis, a mathematical discipline, a _____ of a meromorphic function is a certain type of singularity that behaves like the singularity of $\frac{1}{z^n}$ at z = 0. This means that, in particular, a _____ of the function f(z) is a point z = a such that f(z) approaches infinity uniformly as z approaches a.

Formally, suppose U is an open subset of the complex plane C, a is an element of U and f : U {a} → C is a function which is holomorphic over its domain.

a. Lacunary function
b. Complex logarithm
c. Bieberbach conjecture
d. Pole

40. The formula is used to transform one integral into another integral that is easier to compute. Thus, the formula can be used from left to right or from right to left in order to simplify a given integral. When used in the former manner, it is sometimes known as _____.
a. U-substitution
b. Extreme Value Theorem
c. Extreme value
d. Integration by substitution

41. In mathematics, a _____ is a basic technique used to simplify problems in which the original variables are replaced with new ones; the new and old variables being related in some specified way. The intent is that the problem expressed in new variables may be simpler, or else equivalent to a better understood problem.

A very simple example of a useful variable change can be seen in the problem of finding the roots of the eighth order polynomial:

$$x^8 + 3x^4 + 2 = 0$$

Eighth order polynomial equations are generally impossible to solve in terms of elementary functions.

a. Linear equation
b. Quadratic formula
c. Cubic function
d. Change of variables

42. This article will state and prove the _____ for differentiation, and then use it to prove these two formulas.

The _____ for differentiation states that for every natural number n, the derivative of $f(x) = x^n$ is $f'(x) = nx^{n-1}$, that is,

$$(x^n)' = nx^{n-1}.$$

The _____ for integration

$$\int x^n \, dx = \frac{x^{n+1}}{n+1} + C$$

for natural n is then an easy consequence. One just needs to take the derivative of this equality and use the _____ and linearity of differentiation on the right-hand side.

a. Leibniz rule
b. Test for Divergence
c. Functional integration
d. Power Rule

43. In mathematics, an _____ is a function built from a finite number of exponentials, logarithms, constants, one variable, and nth roots through composition and combinations using the four elementary operations (+ - × ÷.) The trigonometric functions and their inverses are assumed to be included in the elementary functions by using complex variables and the relations between the trigonometric functions and the exponential and logarithm functions.

Elementary functions are considered a subset of special functions.

a. ACTRAN
b. Elementary function
c. ALGOR
d. AUSM

44. In mathematics, even functions and odd functions are functions which satisfy particular symmetry relations, with respect to taking additive inverses. They are important in many areas of mathematical analysis, especially the theory of power series and Fourier series. They are named for the parity of the powers of the power functions which satisfy each condition: the function f(x) = x^n is an even function if n is an even integer, and it is an _____ if n is an odd integer.

a. Integral of secant cubed
b. Odd function
c. Even function
d. Integration by substitution

45. In numerical analysis, _____ constitutes a broad family of algorithms for calculating the numerical value of a definite integral, and by extension, the term is also sometimes used to describe the numerical solution of differential equations The term numerical quadrature is more or less a synonym for _____, especially as applied to one-dimensional integrals.

a. Meshfree methods
b. Multigrid method
c. Galerkin methods
d. Numerical integration

46. In mathematics, the _____ is a way to approximately calculate the definite integral

$$\int_a^b f(x)\,dx.$$

The _____ works by approximating the region under the graph of the function f by a trapezoid and calculating its area. It follows that

$$\int_a^b f(x)\,dx \approx (b-a)\frac{f(a)+f(b)}{2}.$$

To calculate this integral more accurately, one first splits the interval of integration [a,b] into n smaller subintervals, and then applies the _____ on each of them. One obtains the composite _____:

$$\int_a^b f(x)\,dx \approx \frac{b-a}{n}\left[\frac{f(a)+f(b)}{2} + \sum_{k=1}^{n-1} f\left(a+k\frac{b-a}{n}\right)\right].$$

This can alternatively be written as:

$$\int_a^b f(x)\,dx \approx \frac{b-a}{2n}\left(f(x_0) + 2f(x_1) + 2f(x_2) + \cdots + 2f(x_{n-1}) + f(x_n)\right)$$

where

$$x_k = a + k\frac{b-a}{n}, \text{ for } k = 0, 1, \ldots, n$$

(one can also use a non-uniform grid.)

a. BIBO stability

b. BDDC

c. 15 theorem

d. Trapezoidal Rule

Chapter 4. The Wankel Rotary Engine and Area

47. In the various subfields of physics, there exist two common usages of the term _____, both with rigorous mathematical frameworks.

   - In the study of transport phenomena (heat transfer, mass transfer and fluid dynamics), _____ is defined as the amount that flows through a unit area per unit time. _____ in this definition is a vector.
   - In the field of electromagnetism and mathematics, _____ is usually the integral of a vector quantity over a finite surface. The result of this integration is a scalar quantity. The magnetic _____ is thus the integral of the magnetic vector field B over a surface, and the electric _____ is defined similarly. Using this definition, the _____ of the Poynting vector over a specified surface is the rate at which electromagnetic energy flows through that surface. Confusingly, the Poynting vector is sometimes called the power _____, which is an example of the first usage of _____, above. It has units of watts per square metre (W·m^{-2})

One could argue, based on the work of James Clerk Maxwell, that the transport definition precedes the more recent way the term is used in electromagnetism. The specific quote from Maxwell is 'In the case of fluxes, we have to take the integral, over a surface, of the _____ through every element of the surface. The result of this operation is called the surface integral of the _____.

a. 15 theorem
b. BDDC
c. BIBO stability
d. Flux

Chapter 5. Plastics and Cooling

1. In mathematics, two vectors are _____ if they are perpendicular, i.e., they form a right angle. For example, a subway and the street above, although they do not physically intersect, are _____ if they cross at a right angle.
   a. AUSM
   b. ACTRAN
   c. Orthogonal
   d. ALGOR

2. The function $\log_b(x)$ depends on both b and x, but the term _____ in standard usage refers to a function of the form $\log_b(x)$ in which the base b is fixed and so the only argument is x. Thus there is one _____ for each value of the base b (which must be positive and must differ from 1.) Viewed in this way, the base-b _____ is the inverse function of the exponential function b^x.
   a. 15 theorem
   b. BDDC
   c. BIBO stability
   d. Logarithm function

3. In mathematics, a _____ (or direction field) is a graphical representation of the solutions of a first-order differential equation. It is achieved without solving the differential equation analytically, and thence it is useful. The representation may be used to qualitatively visualise solutions, or to numerically approximate them.
   a. Visual Calculus
   b. Leibniz function
   c. Continuous function
   d. Slope field

4. In a totally ordered set all elements are mutually comparable, so such a set can have at most one minimal element and at most one maximal element. Then, due to mutual comparability, the minimal element will also be the least element and the maximal element will also be the greatest element. Thus in a totally ordered set we can simply use the terms minimum and _____.
   a. Nth term
   b. Leibniz rule
   c. Racetrack principle
   d. Maximum

5. _____ is used to describe the steepness, incline, gradient, or grade of a straight line. A higher _____ value indicates a steeper incline. The _____ is defined as the ratio of the 'rise' divided by the 'run' between two points on a line, or in other words, the ratio of the altitude change to the horizontal distance between any two points on the line.
   a. Slope
   b. 15 theorem
   c. Sequence
   d. Y-intercept

6. _____ is a type of motion in which the velocity of an object changes equal amounts in equal time periods. An example of an object having _____ would be a ball rolling down a ramp. The object picks up velocity as it goes down the ramp with equal changes in time.
   a. ACTRAN
   b. AUSM
   c. ALGOR
   d. Uniform Acceleration

7. The _____, formerly known as the hyperbolic logarithm, is the logarithm to the base e, where e is an irrational constant approximately equal to 2.718281828. It is also sometimes referred to as the Napierian logarithm, although the original meaning of this term is slightly different. In simple terms, the _____ of a number x is the power to which e would have to be raised to equal x -- for example the natural log of e itself is 1 because $e^1 = e$, while the _____ of 1 would be 0, since $e^0 = 1$.
   a. 15 theorem
   b. BIBO stability
   c. BDDC
   d. Natural logarithm

8. In mathematics, the _____ is an operation which takes two vectors over the real numbers R and returns a real-valued scalar quantity. It is the standard inner product of the orthonormal Euclidean space. It contrasts with the cross product which produces a vector result.
- a. Scalar multiplication
- b. Homogeneous function
- c. Vector-valued function
- d. Dot product

9. In calculus, a branch of mathematics, the _____ is a measurement of how a function changes when its input changes. Loosely speaking, a _____ can be thought of as how much a quantity is changing at some given point. For example, the _____ of the position (or distance) of a vehicle with respect to time is the instantaneous velocity (respectively, instantaneous speed) at which the vehicle is traveling.

The process of finding a _____ is called differentiation. The fundamental theorem of calculus states that differentiation is the reverse process to integration.

- a. Bounded function
- b. Semi-differentiability
- c. Stationary phase approximation
- d. Derivative

10. In mathematics, specifically in calculus and complex analysis, the _____ of a function f is defined by the formula

$$\frac{f'}{f}$$

where f ' is the derivative of f.

When f is a function f(x) of a real variable x, and takes real, strictly positive values, this is indeed the formula for (log f)′, that is, the derivative of the natural logarithm of f, as follows directly from the chain rule.

Many properties of the real logarithm also apply to the _____, even when the function does not take values in the positive reals.

- a. Directional derivative
- b. Lin-Tsien equation
- c. Point of inflection
- d. Logarithmic derivative

11. In mathematics, the _____ (or modulus) of a real number is its numerical value without regard to its sign. So, for example, 3 is the _____ of both 3 and −3.

The _____ of a number a is denoted by $|a|$.

- a. ACTRAN
- b. Exponential function
- c. Area hyperbolic functions
- d. Absolute value

12. Cantor defined two kinds of _____ numbers, the ordinal numbers and the cardinal numbers. Ordinal numbers may be identified with well-ordered sets, or counting carried on to any stopping point, including points after an _____ number have already been counted. Generalizing finite and the ordinary _____ sequences which are maps from the positive integers leads to mappings from ordinal numbers, and transfinite sequences.

a. ALGOR
b. ACTRAN
c. AUSM
d. Infinite

13. Continuous functions are of utmost importance in mathematics and applications. However, not all functions are continuous. If a function is not continuous at a point in its domain, one says that it has a _____ there. The set of all points of _____ of a function may be a discrete set, a dense set, or even the entire domain of the function.
    a. Discontinuity
    b. Vector
    c. BDDC
    d. 15 theorem

14. Integration is an important concept in mathematics, specifically in the field of calculus and, more broadly, mathematical analysis. Given a function f of a real variable x and an interval [a, b] of the real line, the _____

$$\int_a^b f(x)\,dx,$$

is defined informally to be the net signed area of the region in the xy-plane bounded by the graph of f, the x-axis, and the vertical lines x = a and x = b.

The term '_____' may also refer to the notion of antiderivative, a function F whose derivative is the given function f.

   a. Indefinite integral
   b. Integral
   c. Integral test for convergence
   d. Integrand

15. In mathematics, the hyperbolic functions are analogs of the ordinary trigonometric functions. The basic hyperbolic functions are the hyperbolic sine 'sinh', and the hyperbolic cosine 'cosh', from which are derived the _____ 'tanh', etc., in analogy to the derived trigonometric functions. The inverse hyperbolic functions are the area hyperbolic sine 'arsinh' (also called 'asinh', or sometimes by the misnomer of 'arcsinh') and so on.
    a. Step function
    b. Hyperbolic tangent
    c. Hyperbolic sine
    d. Signum function

16. In geometry, the _____ (or simply the tangent) to a curve at a given point is the straight line that 'just touches' the curve at that point (in the sense explained more precisely below.) As it passes through the point of tangency, the _____ is 'going in the same direction' as the curve, and in this sense it is the best straight-line approximation to the curve at that point. The same definition applies to space curves and curves in n-dimensional Euclidean space.
    a. North pole
    b. Minimal surface
    c. Lie derivative
    d. Tangent line

17. Trigonometry is a branch of mathematics that deals with triangles, particularly those plane triangles in which one angle has 90 degrees (right triangles.) Trigonometry deals with relationships between the sides and the angles of triangles and with the _____ functions, which describe those relationships.

Trigonometry has applications in both pure mathematics and in applied mathematics, where it is essential in many branches of science and technology.

a. Sine
b. Trigonometric functions
c. Trigonometric integrals
d. Trigonometric

18. In mathematics, the _____ are functions of an angle. They are important in the study of triangles and modeling periodic phenomena, among many other applications. _____ are commonly defined as ratios of two sides of a right triangle containing the angle, and can equivalently be defined as the lengths of various line segments from a unit circle.
a. Trigonometric
b. Sine integral
c. Trigonometric integrals
d. Trigonometric functions

19. A curve γ is said to be closed or a loop if $I = [a, b]$ and if $\gamma(a) = \gamma(b)$. A _____ is thus a continuous mapping of the circle S^1; a simple _____ is also called a Jordan curve or a Jordan arc. The Jordan curve theorem states that such curves divide the plane into an 'interior' and an 'exterior'.
a. Curve
b. Closed curve
c. Bullet-nose curve
d. Kappa curve

20. In economics, the _____ functional form of production functions is widely used to represent the relationship of an output to inputs. It was proposed by Knut Wicksell (1851-1926), and tested against statistical evidence by Charles Cobb and Paul Douglas in 1900-1928.

For production, the function is

$Y = AL^{\alpha}K^{\beta}$,

where:

- Y = total production (the monetary value of all goods produced in a year)
- L = labor input
- K = capital input
- A = total factor productivity
- α and β are the output elasticities of labor and capital, respectively. These values are constants determined by available technology.

Output elasticity measures the responsiveness of output to a change in levels of either labor or capital used in production, ceteris paribus. For example if α = 0.15, a 1% increase in labor would lead to approximately a 0.15% increase in output.

a. BIBO stability
b. Cobb-Douglas
c. BDDC
d. 15 theorem

21. Let f be a differentiable function, and let f'(x) be its derivative. The derivative of f'(x) (if it has one) is written f''(x) and is called the _____ of f. Similarly, the derivative of a _____, if it exists, is written f'''(x) and is called the third derivative of f.
a. Stationary phase approximation
b. Vertical asymptote
c. Slant asymptote
d. Second Derivative

Chapter 5. Plastics and Cooling 71

22. In calculus, a branch of mathematics, the _____ is a criterion often useful for determining whether a given stationary point of a function is a local maximum or a local minimum.

The test states: If the function f is twice differentiable at a stationary point x, meaning that $f'(x) = 0$, then:

- If $f''(x) < 0$ then f has a local maximum at x.
- If $f''(x) > 0$ then f has a local minimum at x.
- If $f''(x) = 0$, the _____ says nothing about the point x, has a possible inflection point.

In the last case, the function may have a local maximum or minimum there, but the function is sufficiently 'flat' that this is undetected by the second derivative. In this case one has to examine the third derivative. Such an example is f(x) = x⁴.

a. Second Derivative Test
b. Symmetric derivative
c. Stationary point
d. Linearity of differentiation

23. In mathematics, a (topological) _____ is defined as follows: let I be an interval of real numbers (i.e. a non-empty connected subset of $\mathbb{R}$); then a _____ γ is a continuous mapping $\gamma : I \to X$, where X is a topological space. The _____ γ is said to be simple if it is injective, i.e. if for all x, y in I, we have $\gamma(x) = \gamma(y) \implies x = y$. If I is a closed bounded interval $[a, b]$, we also allow the possibility $\gamma(a) = \gamma(b)$ (this convention makes it possible to talk about closed simple _____.)

a. Curve
b. Closed curve
c. Tractrix
d. Prolate cycloid

24. In complex analysis, a mathematical discipline, a _____ of a meromorphic function is a certain type of singularity that behaves like the singularity of $\frac{1}{z^n}$ at z = 0. This means that, in particular, a _____ of the function f(z) is a point z = a such that f(z) approaches infinity uniformly as z approaches a.

Formally, suppose U is an open subset of the complex plane C, a is an element of U and f : U {a} → C is a function which is holomorphic over its domain.

a. Lacunary function
b. Pole
c. Complex logarithm
d. Bieberbach conjecture

25. In mathematics, the _____ of a function y = f(x) is a function that, in some fashion, 'undoes' the effect of f The _____ of f is denoted f⁻¹. The statements y=f(x) and x=f⁻¹(y) are equivalent.

a. Inverse
b. AUSM
c. ACTRAN
d. ALGOR

26. In mathematics, if ƒ is a function from A to B then an _____ for ƒ is a function in the opposite direction, from B to A, with the property that a round trip (a composition) from A to B to A (or from B to A to B) returns each element of the initial set to itself. Thus, if an input x into the function ƒ produces an output y, then inputting y into the _____ f^{-1} (read f inverse, not to be confused with exponentiation) produces the output x. Not every function has an inverse; those that do are called invertible.
   a. Inverse function
   b. Augustin-Jean Fresnel
   c. Aristotle
   d. Augustin Louis Cauchy

27. _____ is any physical or virtual entity that is owned by an individual or jointly by a group of individuals. An owner of _____ has the right to consume, sell, rent, mortgage, transfer and exchange his or her _____. Important widely-recognized types of _____ include real _____, personal _____ (other physical possessions), and intellectual _____ (rights over artistic creations, inventions, etc.), although the latter is not always as widely recognized or enforced.
   a. BIBO stability
   b. BDDC
   c. 15 theorem
   d. Property

28. In mathematics, the _____ is a test used to determine if a function is injective, surjective or bijective.

Suppose there is a function f : X → Y with a graph., and you have a horizontal line of X x Y :
$$y_0 \in Y, \{(x, y_0) : x \in X\} = (X \times y_0).$$

- If the function is injective, then it can be visualized as one whose graph is never intersected by any horizontal line more than once.
- If and only if f is surjective, any horizontal line will intersect the graph at least at one point (when the horizontal line is in the codomain.)
- If f is bijective, any horizontal line will intersect the graph at exactly one point.

This test is also used to find whether or not the inverse of the function is indeed a function as well. This is due to the reflective properties of the function over y=x.

   a. 15 theorem
   b. BIBO stability
   c. BDDC
   d. Horizontal line test

29. In mathematics, the _____ is a criterion for the convergence (a convergence test) of an infinite series

$$\sum_{n=1}^{\infty} a_n.$$

It is particularly useful in connection with power series.

The _____ was developed first by Cauchy and so is sometimes known as the Cauchy _____ or Cauchy's radical test. The _____ uses the number

$$C = \limsup_{n \to \infty} \sqrt[n]{|a_n|},$$

where 'lim sup' denotes the limit superior, possibly ∞.

a. Racetrack principle
b. Related rates
c. Root Test
d. Mean Value Theorem

30. In mathematics, a _____ (or just conic) is a curve obtained by intersecting a cone (more precisely, a circular conical surface) with a plane. A _____ is therefore a restriction of a quadric surface to the plane. The conic sections were named and studied as long ago as 200 BC, when Apollonius of Perga undertook a systematic study of their properties.
a. BDDC
b. Latus rectum
c. 15 theorem
d. Conic section

31. An _____ is a type of quadric surface that is a higher dimensional analogue of an ellipse. The equation of a standard axis-aligned _____ body in an xyz-Cartesian coordinate system is

$$\frac{x^2}{a^2} + \frac{y^2}{b^2} + \frac{z^2}{c^2} = 1$$

where a and b are the equatorial radii (along the x and y axes) and c is the polar radius (along the z-axis), all of which are fixed positive real numbers determining the shape of the _____.

More generally, a not-necessarily-axis-aligned _____ is defined by the equation

$$\mathbf{x}^T A \mathbf{x} = 1$$

where A is a symmetric positive definite matrix and x is a vector.

a. ALGOR
b. Ellipsoid
c. ACTRAN
d. AUSM

32. The largest and the smallest element of a set are called extreme values, absolute extrema, or extreme records.

For a differentiable function f, if $f(x_0)$ is an _____ for the set of all values f(x), and if x_0 is in the interior of the domain of f, then x_0 is a critical point, by Fermat's theorem.

In the case of a general partial order one should not confuse a least element (smaller than all other) and a minimal element (nothing is smaller.)

a. Infinitesimal
b. Integration by substitution
c. Extreme Value Theorem
d. Extreme Value

33. In calculus, the _____ states that if a real-valued function f is continuous in the closed and bounded interval [a,b], then f must attain its maximum and minimum value, each at least once. That is, there exist numbers c and d in [a,b] such that:

$$f(c) \geq f(x) \geq f(d) \quad \text{for all } x \in [a, b].$$

A related theorem is the boundedness theorem which states that a continuous function f in the closed interval [a,b] is bounded on that interval. That is, there exist real numbers m and M such that:

$$m \leq f(x) \leq M \quad \text{for all } x \in [a, b].$$

The _____ enriches the boundedness theorem by saying that not only is the function bounded, but it also attains its least upper bound as its maximum and its greatest lower bound as its minimum.

a. Extreme Value Theorem
b. Integral of secant cubed
c. Infinitesimal
d. Uniform convergence

34. The _____ is a function in mathematics. The application of this function to a value x is written as exp(x). Equivalently, this can be written in the form e^x, where e is a mathematical constant, the base of the natural logarithm, which equals approximately 2.718281828, and is also known as Euler's number.

a. Integral part
b. ACTRAN
c. Area hyperbolic functions
d. Exponential function

35. In mathematics, the hyperbolic functions are analogs of the ordinary trigonometric functions. The basic hyperbolic functions are the _____ 'sinh', and the hyperbolic cosine 'cosh', from which are derived the hyperbolic tangent 'tanh', etc., in analogy to the derived trigonometric functions. The inverse hyperbolic functions are the area _____ 'arsinh' (also called 'asinh', or sometimes by the misnomer of 'arcsinh') and so on.

a. Signum function
b. Hyperbolic tangent
c. Square root function
d. Hyperbolic sine

36. The _____ of an angle is the ratio of the length of the opposite side to the length of the hypotenuse. In our case

$$\sin A = \frac{\text{opposite}}{\text{hypotenuse}} = \frac{a}{h}.$$

Note that this ratio does not depend on size of the particular right triangle chosen, as long as it contains the angle A, since all such triangles are similar.

The cosine of an angle is the ratio of the length of the adjacent side to the length of the hypotenuse.

a. Sine
b. Trigonometric functions
c. Sine integral
d. Trigonometric

37. In mathematics, the _____ for convergence is a method used to test infinite series of non-negative terms for convergence. An early form of the test of convergence was developed in India by Madhava in the 14th century, and by his followers at the Kerala School. In Europe, it was later developed by Maclaurin and Cauchy and is sometimes known as the Maclaurin-Cauchy test.

a. AUSM
c. ACTRAN

b. Integral Test
d. ALGOR

38. In geometry, the _____ or Gutschoven's curve is a two-dimensional algebraic curve resembling the Greek letter κ (kappa.)

Using the Cartesian coordinate system it can be expressed as:

$x^2(x^2 + y^2) = a^2y^2$

or, using parametric equations:

$$x = a \cos t \cot t$$
$$y = a \cos t$$

In polar coordinates its equation is even simpler:

r = atanθ

It has two vertical asymptotes at $x = \pm a$, shown as dashed blue lines in the figure at right.

The _____'s curvature:

$$\kappa(\theta) = \frac{8\left(3 - \sin^2\theta\right)\sin^4\theta}{a\left[\sin^2(2\theta) + 4\right]^{\frac{3}{2}}}$$

Tangential angle:

$$\phi(\theta) = -\arctan\left[\frac{1}{2}\sin(2\theta)\right]$$

The _____ was first studied by Gérard van Gutschoven around 1662.

a. Witch of Agnesi
c. Kappa curve

b. Tractrix
d. Prolate cycloid

39. For some curves there is a smallest number L that is an upper bound on the length of any polygonal approximation. If such a number exists, then the curve is said to be rectifiable and the curve is defined to have _____ L.

Let C be a curve in Euclidean (or, generally, a metric) space X = R^n, so C is the image of a continuous function f : [a, b] → X of the interval [a, b] into X.

a. Integrand
b. Arc length
c. Integration by parametric derivatives
d. Order of integration

40. _____ is the long dimension of any object. The _____ of a thing is the distance between its ends, its linear extent as measured from end to end. This may be distinguished from height, which is vertical extent, and width or breadth, which are the distance from side to side, measuring across the object at right angles to the _____.
   a. BIBO stability
   b. 15 theorem
   c. Length
   d. BDDC

41. _____ is the concept of adding accumulated interest back to the principal, so that interest is earned on interest from that moment on. The act of declaring interest to be principal is called compounding (i.e., interest is compounded.) A loan, for example, may have its interest compounded every month: in this case, a loan with $100 principal and 1% interest per month would have a balance of $101 at the end of the first month.
   a. BDDC
   b. 15 theorem
   c. BIBO stability
   d. Compound interest

42. In infinitesimal calculus, a _____ is traditionally an infinitesimally small change in a variable. For example, if x is a variable, then a change in the value of x is often denoted Δx (or δx when this change is considered to be small.) The _____ dx represents such a change, but is infinitely small.
   a. Differential
   b. Dirichlet integral
   c. The Method of Mechanical Theorems
   d. Local maximum

43. A _____ is a mathematical equation for an unknown function of one or several variables that relates the values of the function itself and of its derivatives of various orders. they play a prominent role in engineering, physics, economics and other disciplines.

A simplified real world example of a _____ is modeling the acceleration of a ball falling through the air (considering only gravity and air resistance.)

   a. Structural stability
   b. Phase line
   c. Caloric polynomial
   d. Differential equation

44. is called the proportionality constant or _____.

- If an object travels at a constant speed, then the distance traveled is proportional to the time spent travelling, with the speed being the _____.

- The circumference of a circle is proportional to its diameter, with the _____ equal to π.

- On a map drawn to scale, the distance between any two points on the map is proportional to the distance between the two locations that the points represent, with the _____ being the scale of the map.

- The force acting on a certain object due to gravity is proportional to the object's mass; the _____ between the the mass and the force is known as gravitational acceleration.

Since

$$y = kx$$

is equivalent to

$$x = \left(\frac{1}{k}\right) y,$$

it follows that if y is proportional to x, with (nonzero) proportionality constant k, then x is also proportional to y with proportionality constant 1/k.

If y is proportional to x, then the graph of y as a function of x will be a straight line passing through the origin with the slope of the line equal to the _____: it corresponds to linear growth.

a. BDDC
b. 15 theorem
c. Constant of proportionality
d. Reduction

45. A quantity is said to be subject to _____ if it decreases at a rate proportional to its value. Symbolically, this can be expressed as the following differential equation, where N is the quantity and λ is a positive number called the decay constant.

$$\frac{dN}{dt} = -\lambda N.$$

The solution to this equation is:

$$N(t) = N_0 e^{-\lambda t}.$$

Here N(t) is the quantity at time t, and N_0 = N(0) is the initial quantity, i.e. the quantity at time t = 0.

a. ACTRAN
b. ALGOR
c. Exponential sum
d. Exponential decay

46. _____ (including exponential decay) occurs when the growth rate of a mathematical function is proportional to the function's current value. In the case of a discrete domain of definition with equal intervals it is also called geometric growth or geometric decay (the function values form a geometric progression.)

_____ is said to follow an exponential law; the simple-_____ model is known as the Malthusian growth model.

a. Inseparable differential equation
b. Oscillating
c. Isomonodromic deformation
d. Exponential growth

47. The _____ of a quantity whose value decreases with time is the interval required for the quantity to decay to half of its initial value. The concept originated in describing how long it takes atoms to undergo radioactive decay but also applies in a wide variety of other situations.

The term '_____' dates to 1907.

a. Half-life
b. BDDC
c. 15 theorem
d. BIBO stability

48. In vector calculus, the _____ is an operator that measures the magnitude of a vector field's source or sink at a given point; the _____ of a vector field is a (signed) scalar. For example, consider air as it is heated or cooled. The relevant vector field for this example is the velocity of the moving air at a point.
a. Triple product
b. Gradient theorem
c. Green's theorem
d. Divergence

49. In vector calculus, the _____ Ostrogradskye;s theorem the _____ states that the outward flux of a vector field through a surface is equal to the triple integral of the divergence on the region inside the surface. Intuitively, it states that the sum of all sources minus the sum of all sinks gives the net flow out of a region.
a. Divergence
b. Del
c. Green's theorem
d. Divergence Theorem

50. A _____ officer is an officer of high military rank. The term or equivalent is used by nearly every country in the world. _____ can be used as a generic term for all grades of _____ officer, or it can specifically refer to a single rank that is just called _____.
a. General
b. 15 theorem
c. BIBO stability
d. BDDC

51. In mathematics, a _____ to an ordinary or partial differential equation is a function for which the derivatives appearing in the equation may not all exist but which is nonetheless deemed to satisfy the equation in some precisely defined sense. There are many different definitions of _____, appropriate for different classes of equations. One of the most important is based on the notion of distributions.
a. Singular perturbation
b. Conserved quantity
c. Structural stability
d. Weak solution

52. A _____ $y_s(x)$ of an ordinary differential equation is a solution that is tangent to every solution from the family of general solutions. By tangent we mean that there is a point x where $y_s(x) = y_c(x)$ and $y'_s(x) = y'_c(x)$ where y_c is any general solution.

Usually, singular solutions appear in differential equations when there is a need to divide in a term that might be equal to zero.

a. Method of undetermined coefficients
c. Singular solution
b. Method of matched asymptotic expansions
d. Conserved quantity

53. In mathematics, in the field of differential equations, an initial value problem is an ordinary differential equation together with specified value, called the _____, of the unknown function at a given point in the domain of the solution. In physics or other sciences, modeling a system frequently amounts to solving an initial value problem; in this context, the differential equation is an evolution equation specifying how, given initial conditions, the system will evolve with time.

An initial value problem is a differential equation

$$y'(t) = f(t, y(t)) \quad \text{with} \quad f : \mathbb{R} \times \mathbb{R} \to \mathbb{R}$$

together with a point in the domain of f

$$(t_0, y_0) \in \mathbb{R} \times \mathbb{R},$$

called the _____.

a. ALGOR
c. Initial condition
b. AUSM
d. ACTRAN

54. In mathematics, a _____ differential equation may refer to one of two related things, both of which are differential equations that can be attacked by a method of separation of variables.

- For ordinary differential equations, it describes a class of equations that can be separated into a pair of integrals. See: Examples of differential equations

- For partial differential equations, it describes a class of equations that can be broken down into differential equations in fewer independent variables. See _____ partial differential equation.

a. Method of undetermined coefficients
c. Lax pair
b. Differential equation
d. Separable

55. In mathematics, _____ is any of several methods for solving ordinary and partial differential equations, in which algebra allows one to rewrite an equation so that each of two variables occurs on a different side of the equation.

Suppose a differential equation can be written in the form

$$\frac{d}{dx} f(x) = g(x) h(f(x)), \qquad (1)$$

which we can write more simply by letting y = f(x):

$$\frac{dy}{dx} = g(x)h(y).$$

As long as h(y) ≠ 0, we can rearrange terms to obtain:

$$\frac{dy}{h(y)} = g(x)dx,$$

so that the two variables x and y have been separated.

Some who dislike Leibniz's notation may prefer to write this as

$$\frac{1}{h(y)}\frac{dy}{dx} = g(x),$$

but that fails to make it quite as obvious why this is called '_____'.

   a. Damping ratio   b. Separation of variables
   c. Sturm separation theorem   d. Power series method

56. A _____ has several distinct meanings.

One meaning is that a first-order ordinary differential equation is homogeneous if it has the form

$$\frac{dy}{dx} = F(y/x).$$

To solve such equations, one makes the change of variables u = y/x, which will transform such an equation into separable one.

Another meaning is a linear _____, which is a differential equation of the form

$$Ly = 0$$

where the differential operator L is a linear operator, and y is the unknown function.

   a. Structural stability   b. Differential algebraic equations
   c. Nahm equations   d. Homogeneous differential equation

57. In mathematics, a _____ is a function with multiplicative scaling behaviour: if the argument is multiplied by a factor, then the result is multiplied by some power of this factor.

Suppose that $f : V \to W$ is a function between two vector spaces over a field F.

We say that f is homogeneous of degree k if

$$f(\alpha \mathbf{v}) = \alpha^k f(\mathbf{v})$$

for all nonzero $\alpha \in F$ and $\mathbf{v} \in V$.

a. Dot product
b. Direction vector
c. Homogeneous function
d. Direction cosines

58. This article will state and prove the _____ for differentiation, and then use it to prove these two formulas.

The _____ for differentiation states that for every natural number n, the derivative of $f(x) = x^n$ is $f'(x) = nx^{n-1}$, that is,

$$(x^n)' = nx^{n-1}.$$

The _____ for integration

$$\int x^n \, dx = \frac{x^{n+1}}{n+1} + C$$

for natural n is then an easy consequence. One just needs to take the derivative of this equality and use the _____ and linearity of differentiation on the right-hand side.

a. Functional integration
b. Power Rule
c. Test for Divergence
d. Leibniz rule

59. In mathematics, a _____ of a function of several variables is its derivative with respect to one of those variables with the others held constant (as opposed to the total derivative, in which all variables are allowed to vary.) Partial derivatives are useful in vector calculus and differential geometry.

The _____ of a function f with respect to the variable x is written as f'$_x$, $\partial_x f$, or ∂f/∂x.

a. Differentiation operator
b. Level curve
c. Partial derivative
d. Jacobian

60. In mathematics, a _____ is a basic technique used to simplify problems in which the original variables are replaced with new ones; the new and old variables being related in some specified way. The intent is that the problem expressed in new variables may be simpler, or else equivalent to a better understood problem.

A very simple example of a useful variable change can be seen in the problem of finding the roots of the eighth order polynomial:

$$x^8 + 3x^4 + 2 = 0$$

Eighth order polynomial equations are generally impossible to solve in terms of elementary functions.

a. Cubic function
b. Quadratic formula
c. Linear equation
d. Change of variables

61. A _____ is the path a moving object follows through space. The object might be a projectile or a satellite, for example. It thus includes the meaning of orbit - the path of a planet, an asteroid or a comet as it travels around a central mass.

a. 15 theorem
b. BDDC
c. BIBO stability
d. Trajectory

62. In geometry, a disk (also spelled disc) is the region in a plane bounded by a circle.

A disk is said to be closed or open according to whether or not it contains the circle that constitutes its boundary. In Cartesian coordinates, the open disk of center (a,b) and radius R is given by the formula

$$D = \{(x, y) \in \mathbb{R}^2 : (x - a)^2 + (y - b)^2 < R^2\}$$

while the _____ of the same center and radius is given by

$$\overline{D} = \{(x, y) \in \mathbb{R}^2 : (x - a)^2 + (y - b)^2 \leq R^2\}.$$

The area of a closed or open disk of radius R is πR^2

a. BIBO stability
b. Closed disk
c. 15 theorem
d. BDDC

63. In mathematics, a _____ is a constant multiplicative factor of a certain object. For example, in the expression 9x^2, the _____ of x^2 is 9.

The object can be such things as a variable, a vector, a function, etc.

a. Degree of the polynomial
b. Coefficient
c. Resultant
d. Binomial type

Chapter 5. Plastics and Cooling

64. The method of _____ or ordinary _____ is used to solve overdetermined systems. _____ is often applied in statistical contexts, particularly regression analysis.

_____ can be interpreted as a method of fitting data. The best fit in the _____ sense is that instance of the model for which the sum of squared residuals has its least value, a residual being the difference between an observed value and the value given by the model.

a. 15 theorem
b. Least squares
c. BDDC
d. BIBO stability

65. In mathematics, the concept of a '_____' is used to describe the behavior of a function as its argument or input either 'gets close' to some point, or as the argument becomes arbitrarily large; or the behavior of a sequence's elements as their index increases indefinitely. Limits are used in calculus and other branches of mathematical analysis to define derivatives and continuity.

In formulas, _____ is usually abbreviated as lim

a. BDDC
b. 15 theorem
c. BIBO stability
d. Limit

66. The _____ of an angle is the ratio of the length of the adjacent side to the length of the hypotenuse. In our case

$$\cos A = \frac{\text{adjacent}}{\text{hypotenuse}} = \frac{b}{h}.$$

The tangent of an angle is the ratio of the length of the opposite side to the length of the adjacent side. In our case

$$\tan A = \frac{\text{opposite}}{\text{adjacent}} = \frac{a}{b}.$$

The remaining three functions are best defined using the above three functions.

a. Trigonometric
b. Cosine
c. Sine integral
d. Trigonometric functions

67. The concept of _____ in mathematics evolved from the concept of _____ in physics. The nth _____ of a real-valued function f(x) of a real variable about a value c is

$$\mu'_n = \int_{-\infty}^{\infty} (x-c)^n f(x)\,dx.$$

It is possible to define moments for random variables in a more general fashion than moments for real values. See Moments in metric spaces.

a. Poisson distribution
c. Median

b. Geometric mean
d. Moment

68. In mathematics, the _____, sometimes called the direct _____ is a criterion for convergence or divergence of a series whose terms are real or complex numbers. The test determines convergence by comparing the terms of the series in question with those of a series whose convergence properties are known.

The _____ states that if the series

$$\sum_{n=1}^{\infty} b_n$$

is an absolutely convergent series and

$$|a_n| \leq |b_n|$$

for sufficiently large n , then the series

$$\sum_{n=1}^{\infty} a_n$$

converges absolutely.

a. Ratio test
c. Telescoping series

b. Conditionally convergent
d. Comparison Test

69. In calculus, an _____ is the limit of a definite integral as an endpoint of the interval of integration approaches either a specified real number or ∞ or −∞ or, in some cases, as both endpoints approach limits.

Specifically, an _____ is a limit of the form

$$\lim_{b \to \infty} \int_a^b f(x)\,dx, \qquad \lim_{a \to -\infty} \int_a^b f(x)\,dx,$$

or of the form

$$\lim_{c \to b^-} \int_a^c f(x)\,dx, \qquad \lim_{c \to a^+} \int_c^b f(x)\,dx,$$

in which one takes a limit in one or the other (or sometimes both) endpoints . Improper integrals may also occur at an interior point of the domain of integration, or at multiple such points.

Chapter 5. Plastics and Cooling

a. AUSM
b. ALGOR
c. ACTRAN
d. Improper integral

70. In calculus, _____, was originally the use of expressions such as dx and dy and to represent 'infinitely small' (or infinitesimal) increments of quantities x and y, just as >Δx and >Δy represent finite increments of x and y respectively. So for y being a function of x, or

the derivative of y with respect to x, which later came to be viewed as

was, according to Leibniz, the quotient of an infinitesimal increment of y by an infinitesimal increment of x, or

where the right hand side is Lagrange's notation for the derivative of f at x.

Similarly, although mathematicians usually now view an integral

as a limit

where >Δx is an interval containing x_i, Leibniz viewed it as the sum (the integral sign denoting summation) of infinitely many infinitesimal quantities f(x) dx.

a. Stationary point
b. Smooth function
c. Time derivative
d. Leibniz's notation

71. _____ is a quantity used to predict an object's ability to resist torsion, in objects (or segments of objects) with an invariant circular cross-section and no significant warping or out-of-plane deformation. It is used to calculate the angular displacement of an object subjected to a torque. It is analogous to the area moment of inertia, which characterizes an object's ability to resist bending and is required to calculate displacement.

a. Spring equation
b. Navier-Stokes equations
c. Spring constant
d. Polar moment of inertia

72. In mathematics, the _____ or cyclometric functions are the inverse functions of the trigonometric functions. The principal inverses are listed in the following table.

If x is allowed to be a complex number, then the range of y applies only to its real part.

a. ACTRAN
b. Inverse trigonometric functions
c. AUSM
d. ALGOR

73. _____, also called mass _____ or the angular mass, (SI units kg m^2) is a measure of an object's resistance to changes in its rotation rate. It is the rotational analog of mass. That is, it is the inertia of a rigid rotating body with respect to its rotation.

a. Moment of inertia
b. Klein-Gordon equation
c. Dirac equation
d. Wave equation

74. In mathematics, the _____ (or replacement set) of a given function is the set of 'input' values for which the function is defined. For instance, the _____ of cosine would be all real numbers, while the _____ of the square root would be only numbers greater than or equal to 0 (ignoring complex numbers in both cases.) In a representation of a function in a xy Cartesian coordinate system, the _____ is represented on the x axis (or abscissa.)

a. BDDC
b. 15 theorem
c. BIBO stability
d. Domain

75. For the largest k where $a_k \neq 0$, a_k is called the _____ of P because most often, polynomials are written starting from the left with the largest power of x. So for example the _____ of the polynomial

$$4x^5 + x^3 + 2x^2$$

is 4.

The coefficients of polynomial also may be in the other order:

$$Q(x) = a_0 x^k + a_1 x^{k-1} + \cdots + a_{k-1} x^1 + a_k$$

and must be $a_0 \neq 0$ and a_0 is the _____ of Q.

a. Symmetric function
b. Resultant
c. Discriminant
d. Leading coefficient

76. In mathematics, an _____ on a real vector space is a choice of which ordered bases are 'positively' oriented and which are 'negatively' oriented. In the three-dimensional Euclidean space, the two possible basis orientations are called right-handed and left-handed (or right-chiral and left-chiral), respectively. However, the choice of _____ is independent of the handedness or chirality of the bases (although right-handed bases are typically declared to be positively oriented, they may also be assigned a negative _____.)

a. ALGOR
b. Unit vector
c. ACTRAN
d. Orientation

Chapter 5. Plastics and Cooling

77. In physics, _____ is defined as the rate of change of position. it is vector physical quantity; both speed and direction are required to define it. In the SI (metric) system, it is measured in meters per second: (m/s) or ms⁻¹.
    a. 15 theorem
    b. Velocity
    c. BIBO stability
    d. BDDC

78. This is a summary of _____, that is, rules for computing the derivative of a function in calculus.

Unless otherwise stated, all functions will be functions from R to R, although more generally, the formulae below make sense wherever they are well defined.

For any functions f and g and any real numbers a and b.

    a. Differentiation rules
    b. Product rule
    c. Quotient Rule
    d. Constant factor rule in differentiation

79. In mathematics, an _____ is a function built from a finite number of exponentials, logarithms, constants, one variable, and nth roots through composition and combinations using the four elementary operations (+ - × ÷.) The trigonometric functions and their inverses are assumed to be included in the elementary functions by using complex variables and the relations between the trigonometric functions and the exponential and logarithm functions.

Elementary functions are considered a subset of special functions.

    a. ALGOR
    b. Elementary function
    c. AUSM
    d. ACTRAN

80. In mathematics, _____ refers to any of a number of loosely related concepts in different areas of geometry. Intuitively, _____ is the amount by which a geometric object deviates from being flat, or straight in the case of a line, but this is defined in different ways depending on the context. There is a key distinction between extrinsic _____, which is defined for objects embedded in another space (usually a Euclidean space) in a way that relates to the radius of _____ of circles that touch the object, and intrinsic _____, which is defined at each point in a differential manifold.
    a. Curvature
    b. Minimal surface
    c. Sphere
    d. Lie derivative

81. In elementary algebra, _____ is a technique for converting a quadratic polynomial of the form

$$ax^2 + bx + c$$

to the form

$$a(\cdots\cdots)^2 + \text{constant}.$$

The expression inside the parenthesis is of the form x − constant. Thus one converts ax² + bx + c to

$$a(x - h)^2 + k$$

and one must find h and k.

_____ is used in

- solving quadratic equations,
- graphing quadratic functions,
- evaluating integrals in calculus,
- finding Laplace transforms.

In mathematics, _____ is considered a basic algebraic operation, and is often applied without remark in any computation involving quadratic polynomials.

There is a simple formula in elementary algebra for computing the square of a binomial:

$$(x + p)^2 = x^2 + 2px + p^2.$$

For example:

$$(x + 3)^2 = x^2 + 6x + 9 \qquad (p = 3)$$
$$(x - 5)^2 = x^2 - 10x + 25 \qquad (p = -5).$$

In any perfect square, the number p is always half the coefficient of x, and then the constant term is equal to p².

a. Closed-form expression
b. Hurwitz quaternion order
c. Multinomial theorem
d. Completing the square

82. In calculus, an antiderivative, primitive or _____ of a function f is a function F whose derivative is equal to f, i.e., F ′ = f. The process of solving for antiderivatives is antidifferentiation (or indefinite integration.) Antiderivatives are related to definite integrals through the fundamental theorem of calculus: the definite integral of a function over an interval is equal to the difference between the values of an antiderivative evaluated at the endpoints of the interval.

a. Integration by parts operator
b. Indefinite integral
c. Arc length
d. Integral test for convergence

Chapter 5. Plastics and Cooling

83. In the various subfields of physics, there exist two common usages of the term _____, both with rigorous mathematical frameworks.

- In the study of transport phenomena (heat transfer, mass transfer and fluid dynamics), _____ is defined as the amount that flows through a unit area per unit time. _____ in this definition is a vector.
- In the field of electromagnetism and mathematics, _____ is usually the integral of a vector quantity over a finite surface. The result of this integration is a scalar quantity. The magnetic _____ is thus the integral of the magnetic vector field B over a surface, and the electric _____ is defined similarly. Using this definition, the _____ of the Poynting vector over a specified surface is the rate at which electromagnetic energy flows through that surface. Confusingly, the Poynting vector is sometimes called the power _____, which is an example of the first usage of _____, above. It has units of watts per square metre (W·m^{-2})

One could argue, based on the work of James Clerk Maxwell, that the transport definition precedes the more recent way the term is used in electromagnetism. The specific quote from Maxwell is 'In the case of fluxes, we have to take the integral, over a surface, of the _____ through every element of the surface. The result of this operation is called the surface integral of the _____.

   a. Flux
   c. BIBO stability
   b. 15 theorem
   d. BDDC

84. In mathematics, the hyperbolic functions are analogs of the ordinary trigonometric functions. The basic hyperbolic functions are the hyperbolic sine 'sinh', and the _____ 'cosh', from which are derived the hyperbolic tangent 'tanh', etc., in analogy to the derived trigonometric functions. The inverse hyperbolic functions are the area hyperbolic sine 'arsinh' (also called 'asinh', or sometimes by the misnomer of 'arcsinh') and so on.
   a. Square root function
   c. Hyperbolic tangent
   b. Step function
   d. Hyperbolic cosine

85. In mathematics, the _____ are analogs of the ordinary trigonometric or circular functions. The basic _____ are the hyperbolic sine 'sinh', and the hyperbolic cosine 'cosh', from which are derived the hyperbolic tangent 'tanh', etc., in analogy to the derived trigonometric functions. The inverse _____ are the area hyperbolic sine 'arsinh' (also called 'asinh', or sometimes by the misnomer of 'arcsinh') and so on.
   a. Signum function
   c. Hyperbolic cosine
   b. Multiplicative inverse
   d. Hyperbolic functions

86. The terms of the series are often produced according to a certain rule, such as by a formula, by an algorithm, by a sequence of measurements, or even by a random number generator. As there are an infinite number of terms, this notion is often called an _____. Unlike finite summations, series need tools from mathematical analysis to be fully understood and manipulated.
   a. Infinite series
   c. Extreme Value Theorem
   b. Integration by substitution
   d. Extreme value

87. _____ is the addition of a set of numbers; the result is their sum or total. An interim or present total of a _____ process is termed the running total. The 'numbers' to be summed may be natural numbers, complex numbers, matrices, or still more complicated objects.

a. BIBO stability
b. BDDC
c. 15 theorem
d. Summation

88. The terms 'dependent variable' and '_____' are used in similar but subtly different ways in mathematics and statistics as part of the standard terminology in those subjects. They are used to distinguish between two types of quantities being considered, separating them into those available at the start of a process and those being created by it, where the latter (dependent variables) are dependent on the former (independent variables.)

In traditional calculus, a function is defined as a relation between two terms called variables because their values vary.

a. ACTRAN
b. ALGOR
c. AUSM
d. Independent variable

89. In calculus and other branches of mathematical analysis, an _____ is an algebraic expression obtained in the context of limits. Limits involving algebraic operations are often performed by replacing subexpressions by their limits; if the expression obtained after this substitution does not give enough information to determine the original limit, it is known as an _____. The indeterminate forms include 0^0, $0/0$, 1^∞, $\infty - \infty$, ∞/∞, $0 \times \infty$, and ∞^0.

a. ALGOR
b. AUSM
c. ACTRAN
d. Indeterminate form

90. In differential calculus, an inflection point, or _____ (or inflexion) is a point on a curve at which the curvature changes sign. The curve changes from being concave upwards (positive curvature) to concave downwards (negative curvature), or vice versa. If one imagines driving a vehicle along the curve, it is a point at which the steering-wheel is momentarily 'straight', being turned from left to right or vice versa.

a. Logarithmic derivative
b. Lin-Tsien equation
c. Derivative of a constant
d. Point of inflection

91. In mathematics, _____ are equalities that involve trigonometric functions that are true for every single value of the occurring variables. These identities are useful whenever expressions involving trigonometric functions need to be simplified. An important application is the integration of non-trigonometric functions: a common technique involves first using the substitution rule with a trigonometric function, and then simplifying the resulting integral with a trigonometric identity.

a. BDDC
b. BIBO stability
c. 15 theorem
d. Trigonometric identities

92. In physics and geometry, the _____ is the theoretical shape of a hanging flexible chain or cable when supported at its ends and acted upon by a uniform gravitational force (its own weight) and in equilibrium. The curve has a U shape that is similar in appearance to the parabola, though it is a different curve.

a. 15 theorem
b. BDDC
c. Catenary
d. BIBO stability

93. The inverses of the hyperbolic functions are the _____. The names hint at the fact that they compute the area of a sector of the unit hyperbola $x^2 - y^2 = 1$ in the same way that the inverse trigonometric functions compute the arclength of a sector on the unit circle $x^2 + y^2 = 1$. The usual abbreviations for them in mathematics are arsinh, arcsinh (in the USA) or asinh (in computer science.)

Chapter 5. Plastics and Cooling

a. Integral part
b. ACTRAN
c. Area hyperbolic functions
d. Exponential function

94. The _____ is the chord parallel to the directrix and passing through the focus (or one of the two foci.)

The semi-_____ (l) is half the _____.

The focal parameter (p) is the distance from the focus (or one of the two foci) to the directrix.

a. 15 theorem
b. Latus rectum
c. Foci
d. BDDC

95. In mathematics, even functions and odd functions are functions which satisfy particular symmetry relations, with respect to taking additive inverses. They are important in many areas of mathematical analysis, especially the theory of power series and Fourier series. They are named for the parity of the powers of the power functions which satisfy each condition: the function $f(x) = x^n$ is an even function if n is an even integer, and it is an _____ if n is an odd integer.

a. Even function
b. Odd function
c. Integral of secant cubed
d. Integration by substitution

96. The _____ is a mathematical curve and one of the earliest fractal curves to have been described. It appeared in a 1904 paper titled 'On a continuous curve without tangents, constructible from elementary geometry' by the Swedish mathematician Helge von Koch. The Koch curve is a special case of the Césaro curve where $a = \frac{1}{2} + \frac{i}{\sqrt{12}}$, which is in turn a special case of the de Rham curve.

a. BIBO stability
b. BDDC
c. 15 theorem
d. Koch snowflake

97. In differential geometry there are a number of second-order, linear, elliptic differential operators bearing the name _____.

The connection _____ is a differential operator acting on the various tensor bundles of a manifold, defined in terms of a Riemmanian- or pseudo-Riemannian metric.

a. Semi-elliptic operator
b. Dirac operator
c. Peetre theorem
d. Laplacian

98. The _____ states that the total amount of energy in an isolated system remains constant. A consequence of this law is that energy cannot be created or destroyed. The only thing that can happen with energy in an isolated system is that it can change form, that is to say for instance kinetic energy can become thermal energy.

a. 15 theorem
b. BDDC
c. Potential energy
d. Law of Conservation of Energy

99. _____ is the curve along which a small object moves, under the influence of friction, when pulled on a horizontal plane by a piece of thread and a puller that moves at a right angle to the initial line between the object and the puller at an infinitesimal speed. It is therefore a curve of pursuit. It was first introduced by Claude Perrault in 1670, and later studied by Sir Isaac Newton and Christian Huygens (1692.)

   a. Tractrix
   b. Curve
   c. Bullet-nose curve
   d. Folium of Descartes

Chapter 6. Constructing an Arch Dam

1. The _____ specifies the relationship between the two central operations of calculus, differentiation and integration.

   The first part of the theorem, sometimes called the first _____, shows that an indefinite integration can be reversed by a differentiation.

   The second part, sometimes called the second _____, allows one to compute the definite integral of a function by using any one of its infinitely many antiderivatives.

   a. Fundamental Theorem of Calculus
   b. Periodic function
   c. Leibniz formula
   d. Limits of integration

2. In mathematics, a (topological) _____ is defined as follows: let I be an interval of real numbers (i.e. a non-empty connected subset of $\mathbb{R}$); then a _____ γ is a continuous mapping $\gamma : I \to X$, where X is a topological space. The _____ γ is said to be simple if it is injective, i.e. if for all x, y in I, we have $\gamma(x) = \gamma(y) \implies x = y$. If I is a closed bounded interval $[a, b]$, we also allow the possibility $\gamma(a) = \gamma(b)$ (this convention makes it possible to talk about closed simple _____.)

   a. Closed curve
   b. Tractrix
   c. Curve
   d. Prolate cycloid

3. Integration is an important concept in mathematics, specifically in the field of calculus and, more broadly, mathematical analysis. Given a function f of a real variable x and an interval [a, b] of the real line, the _____

   $$\int_a^b f(x)\, dx,$$

   is defined informally to be the net signed area of the region in the xy-plane bounded by the graph of f, the x-axis, and the vertical lines x = a and x = b.

   The term '_____' may also refer to the notion of antiderivative, a function F whose derivative is the given function f.

   a. Integral
   b. Integrand
   c. Integral test for convergence
   d. Indefinite integral

4. The function difference divided by the point difference is known as the _____, it is also known as Newton's quotient):

   $$\frac{\Delta F(P)}{\Delta P} = \frac{F(P + \Delta P) - F(P)}{\Delta P} = \frac{\nabla F(P + \Delta P)}{\Delta P}.$$

94 *Chapter 6. Constructing an Arch Dam*

If ΔP is infinitesimal, then the _____ is a derivative, otherwise it is a divided difference:

$$\text{If } |\Delta P| = \iota o t a : \quad \frac{\Delta F(P)}{\Delta P} = \frac{dF(P)}{dP} = F'(P) = G(P);$$

$$\text{If } |\Delta P| > \iota o t a : \quad \frac{\Delta F(P)}{\Delta P} = \frac{DF(P)}{DP} = F[P, P + \Delta P].$$

Regardless if ΔP is infinitesimal or finite, there is (at least--in the case of the derivative--theoretically) a point range, where the boundaries are P ± (.5)ΔP (depending on the orientation--ΔF(P), δF(P) or ∇F(P)):

LB = Lower Boundary; UB = Upper Boundary;

Anyone familiar with derivatives knows that they can be regarded as functions themselves, harboring their own derivatives. Thus each function is home to sequential degrees ('higher orders') of derivation, or differentiation. This property can be generalized to all difference quotients. As this sequencing requires a corresponding boundary splintering, it is practical to break up the point range into smaller, equi-sized sections, with each section being marked by an intermediary point ('P_i'), where LB = P_0 and UB = P_{A_n}, the nth point, equaling the degree/order:

LB = P_0 = P_0 + 0Δ_1P = P_{A_n} - (Åf-0)Δ_1P; P_1 = P_0 + 1Δ_1P = P_{A_n} - (Åf-1)Δ_1P; P_2 = P_0 + 2Δ_1P = P_{A_n} - (Åf-2)Δ_1P; P_3 = P_0 + 3Δ_1P = P_{A_n} - (Åf-3)Δ_1P; ↓↓↓↓ P_{A_n-3} = P_0 + (Åf-3)Δ_1P = P_{A_n} - 3Δ_1P; P_{A_n-2} = P_0 + (Åf-2)Δ_1P = P_{A_n} - 2Δ_1P; P_{A_n-1} = P_0 + (Åf-1)Δ_1P = P_{A_n} - 1Δ_1P; UB = P_{A_n-0} = P_0 + (Åf-0)Δ_1P = P_{A_n} - 0Δ_1P = P_{A_n};

ΔP = Δ_1P = P_1 - P_0 = P_2 - P_1 = P_3 - P_2 = ...

a. Notation for differentiation
c. Directional derivative

b. Continuously differentiable
d. Difference quotient

5. In mathematics, engineering, and manufacturing, a _____ is a solid figure obtained by rotating a plane curve around some straight line (the axis) that lies on the same plane.

Assuming that the curve does not cross the axis, the solid's volume is equal to the length of the circle described by the figure's centroid, times the figure's area (Pappus's second centroid Theorem.)

Rotating a curve

A representative disk is a three-dimensional volume element of a _____.

a. Riemann sum
c. Solid of revolution

b. Surface of revolution
d. Trigonometric substitution

6. In mathematics, the _____ of two monic polynomials P and Q over a field k is defined as the product

$$\mathrm{res}(P,Q) = \prod_{(x,y):\, P(x)=0,\, Q(y)=0} (x-y),$$

of the differences of their roots, where x and y take on values in the algebraic closure of k. For non-monic polynomials with leading coefficients p and q, respectively, the above product is multiplied by

$$p^{\deg Q} q^{\deg P}.$$

- The _____ is the determinant of the Sylvester matrix (and of the Bezout matrix.)

- When Q is separable, the above product can be rewritten to

$$\mathrm{res}(P,Q) = \prod_{P(x)=0} Q(x)$$

and this expression remains unchanged if Q is reduced modulo P. Note that, when non-monic, this includes the factor $q^{\deg P}$ but still needs the factor $p^{\deg Q}$.

- Let $P' = P \mod Q$. The above idea can be continued by swapping the roles of P' and Q. However, P' has a set of roots different from that of P. This can be resolved by writing $\prod_{Q(y)=0} P'(y)$ as a determinant again, where P' has leading zero coefficients. This determinant can now be simplified by iterative expansion with respect to the column, where only the leading coefficient q of Q appears.

$$\mathrm{res}(P,Q) = q^{\deg P - \deg P'} \cdot \mathrm{res}(P',Q)$$

Continuing this procedure ends up in a variant of the Euclidean algorithm. This procedure needs quadratic runtime.

a. Leading coefficient
c. Difference polynomial

b. Resultant
d. Quadratic function

7. A _____, $F_{net} = F_1 + F_2 + …$ (also known as a resultant force) is a vector produced when two or more forces { F_1, F_2, … } act upon a single object. It is calculated by vector addition of the force vectors acting upon the object. A _____ can also be defined as the overall force acting on an object, when all the individual forces acting on the object are added together.

a. Net force
b. 15 theorem
c. BIBO stability
d. BDDC

8. In elementary mathematics, physics, and engineering, a _____ is a geometric object that has both a magnitude (or length), direction and sense, (i.e., orientation along the given direction.) A _____ is frequently represented by a line segment with a definite direction, or graphically as an arrow, connecting an initial point A with a terminal point B, and denoted by

>

The magnitude of the _____ is the length of the segment and the direction characterizes the displacement of B relative to A: how much one should move the point A to 'carry' it to the point B.

Many algebraic operations on real numbers have close analogues for vectors.

a. 15 theorem
b. BDDC
c. Vector
d. Linear partial differential operator

9. In mathematics a _____ is a construction in vector calculus which associates a vector to every point in a (locally) Euclidean space.

Vector fields are often used in physics to model, for example, the speed and direction of a moving fluid throughout space, or the strength and direction of some force, such as the magnetic or gravitational force, as it changes from point to point.

In the rigorous mathematical treatment, (tangent) vector fields are defined on manifolds as sections of a manifold's tangent bundle.

a. BDDC
b. 15 theorem
c. BIBO stability
d. Vector field

10. The _____ of any solid, liquid, plasma, vacuum or theoretical object is how much three-dimensional space it occupies, often quantified numerically. One-dimensional figures (such as lines) and two-dimensional shapes (such as squares) are assigned zero _____ in the three-dimensional space. _____ is commonly presented in units such as mL or cm^3 (milliliters or cubic centimeters.)

a. Klein-Gordon equation
b. Vector potential
c. Dirac equation
d. Volume

11. _____ is a means of calculating the volume of a solid of revolution, when integrating along the axis of revolution. This method models the generated 3 dimensional shape as a 'stack' of an infinite number of disks of infinitesimal thickness. It is possible to use 'washers' instead of 'disks' (the washer method) to obtain 'hollow' solids of revolutions, and uses the same principles that underlie _____.

a. Disk integration
b. Quadratic integral
c. Length of an irregular arc
d. Double integral

12. In calculus, a branch of mathematics, the _____ is a measurement of how a function changes when its input changes. Loosely speaking, a _____ can be thought of as how much a quantity is changing at some given point. For example, the _____ of the position (or distance) of a vehicle with respect to time is the instantaneous velocity (respectively, instantaneous speed) at which the vehicle is traveling.

The process of finding a _____ is called differentiation. The fundamental theorem of calculus states that differentiation is the reverse process to integration.

   a. Semi-differentiability
   b. Derivative
   c. Bounded function
   d. Stationary phase approximation

13. _____ is any physical or virtual entity that is owned by an individual or jointly by a group of individuals. An owner of _____ has the right to consume, sell, rent, mortgage, transfer and exchange his or her _____. Important widely-recognized types of _____ include real _____, personal _____ (other physical possessions), and intellectual _____ (rights over artistic creations, inventions, etc.), although the latter is not always as widely recognized or enforced.

   a. BDDC
   b. 15 theorem
   c. BIBO stability
   d. Property

14. For some curves there is a smallest number L that is an upper bound on the length of any polygonal approximation. If such a number exists, then the curve is said to be rectifiable and the curve is defined to have _____ L.

Let C be a curve in Euclidean (or, generally, a metric) space X = R^n, so C is the image of a continuous function f : [a, b] → X of the interval [a, b] into X.

   a. Integrand
   b. Order of integration
   c. Integration by parametric derivatives
   d. Arc length

15. _____ is a type of motion in which the velocity of an object changes equal amounts in equal time periods. An example of an object having _____ would be a ball rolling down a ramp. The object picks up velocity as it goes down the ramp with equal changes in time.

   a. Uniform Acceleration
   b. AUSM
   c. ALGOR
   d. ACTRAN

16. In calculus, the indefinite integral of a given function (i.e. the set of all antiderivatives of the function) is always written with a constant, the _____. This constant expresses an ambiguity inherent in the construction of antiderivatives. If a function f(x) is defined on an interval and F(x) is an antiderivative of f(x), then the set of all antiderivatives of f(x) is given by the functions F(x) + C, where C is an arbitrary constant.

   a. Nonelementary integral
   b. Disk integration
   c. Constant of integration
   d. Sum rule in integration

17. To put it differently, the class C^0 consists of all continuous functions. The class C^1 consists of all differentiable functions whose derivative is continuous; such functions are called _____. Thus, a C^1 function is exactly a function whose derivative exists and is of class C^0.

   a. Linear approximation
   b. Lin-Tsien equation
   c. Point of inflection
   d. Continuously differentiable

Chapter 6. Constructing an Arch Dam

18. A _____ is a type of manifold that is locally similar enough to Euclidean space to allow one to do calculus Any manifold can be described by a collection of charts, also known as an atlas.

    a. Tangent line
    b. Sphere
    c. Minimal surface
    d. Differentiable manifold

19. _____ is the long dimension of any object. The _____ of a thing is the distance between its ends, its linear extent as measured from end to end. This may be distinguished from height, which is vertical extent, and width or breadth, which are the distance from side to side, measuring across the object at right angles to the _____.

    a. BIBO stability
    b. Length
    c. BDDC
    d. 15 theorem

20. A _____ is a surface created by rotating a curve lying on some plane (the generatrix) around a straight line (the axis of rotation) that lies on the same plane.

Examples of surfaces generated by a straight line are the cylindrical and conical surfaces. A circle that is rotated about a (coplanar) axis through the center generates a sphere.

    a. Constant of integration
    b. Shell integration
    c. Surface of revolution
    d. Riemann sum

21. In physics, the _____ is a unit of force specified in the centimetre-gram-second (CGS) system of units, a predecessor of the modern SI. One _____ is equal to exactly 10 micronewtons. Equivalently, the _____ is defined as 'the force required to accelerate a mass of one gram at a rate of one centimetre per second squared':

1 dyn = 1 gÂ·cm/s² = 10⁻⁵ kgÂ·m/s² = 10 ÂµN

The _____ per centimetre is the unit usually associated with measuring surface tension.

    a. Dyne
    b. BIBO stability
    c. 15 theorem
    d. BDDC

22. The _____ is the derived unit of energy in the International System of Units. It is defined as:

$$1\,\mathrm{J} = 1\,\mathrm{kg} \cdot \mathrm{m}^2 \cdot \mathrm{s}^{-2}$$

One _____ is the amount of energy required to perform the following physical actions:

- The work done by a force of one newton travelling through a distance of one metre;
- The work required to move an electric charge of one coulomb through an electrical potential difference of one volt; or one coulomb volt, with the symbol CÂ·V;
- The work done to produce the power of one watt continuously for one second; or one watt second (compare kilowatt hour), with the symbol WÂ·s. Thus a kilowatt hour is 3,600,000 joules or 3.6 megajoules;

Chapter 6. Constructing an Arch Dam 99

1 _____ is equal to:

- 1×10⁷ ergs (exactly)
- 1.6022×10¹⁹ eV (electronvolts)
- 0.2390 cal (gram calories or small calories)
- 2.3901×10⁻⁴ kcal (kilocalories, kilogram calories, large calories or food calories)
- 9.4782×10⁻⁴ BTU (British thermal unit)
- 0.7376 ftÂ·lbf (foot-pound force)
- 23.7 ftÂ·pdl (foot-poundals)
- 2.7778×10⁻⁷ kilowatt-hour
- 2.7778×10⁻⁴ watt-hour
- 9.8692×10⁻³ litre-atmosphere
- 1×10⁻⁴⁴ Foe (exactly)

Units defined in terms of the _____ include:

- 1 thermochemical calorie = 4.184 J
- 1 International Table calorie = 4.1868 J
- 1 watt hour = 3600 J
- 1 kilowatt hour = 3.6 × 10⁶ J (or 3.6 MJ)
- 1 ton TNT exploding = 4.184 GJ

Useful to remember:

- 1 _____ = 1 newton × 1 meter = 1 watt × 1 second

One _____ in everyday life is approximately:

- the energy required to lift a small apple one metre straight up.
- the energy released when that same apple falls one meter to the ground.
- the energy released as heat by a quiet person, every hundredth of a second.
- the energy required to heat one gram of dry, cool air by 1 degree Celsius.
- one hundredth of the energy a person can receive by drinking a drop of beer.
- the kinetic energy of an adult human moving a distance of about a handspan every second.

- Conversion of units
- Orders of magnitude (energy)
- Fluence

a. BIBO stability
c. Joule
b. 15 theorem
d. BDDC

23. In computer science and information science, _____ could also be a method or an algorithm. Again, an example will illustrate: There are systems of counting, as with Roman numerals, and various systems for filing papers, or catalogues, and various library systems, of which the Dewey Decimal _____ is an example. This still fits with the definition of components which are connected together (in this case in order to facilitate the flow of information.)

a. 15 theorem
c. BIBO stability
b. BDDC
d. System

24. In geometry, _____ of a curve is found at a point that is at a distance equal to the radius of curvature lying on the normal vector. It is the point at infinity if the curvature is zero. The osculating circle to the curve is centered at the _____.

a. Kampyle of Eudoxus
c. Strophoid
b. Center of curvature
d. Dolbeault operator

25. In vector calculus a conservative vector field is a vector field which is the gradient of a scalar potential. There are two closely related concepts: path independence and _____ vector fields. Every conservative vector field has zero curl (and is thus _____), and every conservative vector field has the path independence property.

a. ALGOR
c. ACTRAN
b. AUSM
d. Irrotational

26. In mathematics, especially in order theory, an upper bound of a subset S of some partially ordered set (P, ≤) is an element of P which is greater than or equal to every element of S. The term _____ is defined dually as an element of P which is lesser than or equal to every element of S. A set with an upper bound is said to be bounded from above by that bound, a set with a _____ is said to be bounded from below by that bound.

A subset S of a partially ordered set P may fail to have any bounds or may have many different upper and lower bounds. By transitivity, any element greater than or equal to an upper bound of S is again an upper bound of S, and any element lesser than or equal to any _____ of S is again a _____ of S. This leads to the consideration of least upper bounds: (or suprema) and greatest lower bounds (or infima.)

a. BDDC
c. BIBO stability
b. 15 theorem
d. Lower bound

27. The concept of _____ in mathematics evolved from the concept of _____ in physics. The nth _____ of a real-valued function f(x) of a real variable about a value c is

$$\mu'_n = \int_{-\infty}^{\infty} (x - c)^n f(x)\, dx.$$

It is possible to define moments for random variables in a more general fashion than moments for real values. See Moments in metric spaces.

a. Geometric mean
b. Median
c. Moment
d. Poisson distribution

28. In calculus, interchange of the _____ is a methodology that transforms multiple integrations of functions into other, hopefully simpler, integrals by changing the order in which the integrations are performed.

The problem for examination is evaluation of an integral of the form:

$$\iint_D dxdy\ f(x,y),$$

where D is some two-dimensional area in the xy-plane. For some functions f straightforward integration is feasible, but where that is not true, the integral can sometimes be reduced to simpler form by changing the _____.

a. Order of integration
b. Indefinite integral
c. Arc length
d. Integration by parts

29. In geometry, a _____ is a three-dimensional figure formed by six parallelograms. It is to a parallelogram as a cube is to a square: Euclidean geometry supports all four notions but affine geometry admits only parallelograms and parallelepipeds. Three equivalent definitions of _____ are

- a polyhedron with six faces (hexahedron), each of which is a parallelogram,
- a hexahedron with three pairs of parallel faces, and
- a prism of which the base is a parallelogram.

The cuboid (six rectangular faces), cube (six square faces), and the rhombohedron (six rhombus faces) are all specific cases of _____.

Parallelepipeds are a subclass of the prismatoids.

a. BIBO stability
b. BDDC
c. 15 theorem
d. Parallelepiped

30. In mathematics, _____ refers to any of a number of loosely related concepts in different areas of geometry. Intuitively, _____ is the amount by which a geometric object deviates from being flat, or straight in the case of a line, but this is defined in different ways depending on the context. There is a key distinction between extrinsic _____, which is defined for objects embedded in another space (usually a Euclidean space) in a way that relates to the radius of _____ of circles that touch the object, and intrinsic _____, which is defined at each point in a differential manifold.

a. Lie derivative
b. Sphere
c. Minimal surface
d. Curvature

31. In mathematics, a _____ is an ordered list of objects (or events). Like a set, it contains members (also called elements or terms), and the number of terms (possibly infinite) is called the length of the _____. Unlike a set, order matters, and the exact same elements can appear multiple times at different positions in the _____.

Chapter 6. Constructing an Arch Dam

a. Slope
b. 15 theorem
c. Y-intercept
d. Sequence

32. _____ is the tendency of a force to rotate an object about an axis (or fulcrum or pivot.) Just as a force is a push or a pull, a _____ can be thought of as a twist. The symbol for _____ is τ, the Greek letter tau.
   a. BIBO stability
   b. BDDC
   c. 15 theorem
   d. Torque

33. In physics, and more specifically kinematics, _____ is the change in velocity over time. Because velocity is a vector, it can change in two ways: a change in magnitude and/or a change in direction. In one dimension, _____ is the rate at which something speeds up or slows down.
   a. Acceleration
   b. ALGOR
   c. AUSM
   d. ACTRAN

34. In mathematics, the concept of a '_____' is used to describe the behavior of a function as its argument or input either 'gets close' to some point, or as the argument becomes arbitrarily large; or the behavior of a sequence's elements as their index increases indefinitely. Limits are used in calculus and other branches of mathematical analysis to define derivatives and continuity.

   In formulas, _____ is usually abbreviated as lim

   a. Limit
   b. BDDC
   c. 15 theorem
   d. BIBO stability

35. _____ is the addition of a set of numbers; the result is their sum or total. An interim or present total of a _____ process is termed the running total. The 'numbers' to be summed may be natural numbers, complex numbers, matrices, or still more complicated objects.
   a. BIBO stability
   b. Summation
   c. 15 theorem
   d. BDDC

36. The _____ of a material is defined as its mass per unit volume. The symbol of _____ is ρ '>rho.)

Mathematically:

$$d = \frac{m}{V}$$

where:

   d is the _____,
   m is the mass,
   V is the volume.

   a. BIBO stability
   b. BDDC
   c. 15 theorem
   d. Density

Chapter 6. Constructing an Arch Dam

37. In mathematics, an _____ on a real vector space is a choice of which ordered bases are 'positively' oriented and which are 'negatively' oriented. In the three-dimensional Euclidean space, the two possible basis orientations are called right-handed and left-handed (or right-chiral and left-chiral), respectively. However, the choice of _____ is independent of the handedness or chirality of the bases (although right-handed bases are typically declared to be positively oriented, they may also be assigned a negative _____.)
   a. Unit vector
   b. ALGOR
   c. ACTRAN
   d. Orientation

38. In mathematics, a _____ is a closed surface of mass M and surface density $\sigma(x,y)$ such that:

$$M = \int\int \sigma(x,y)\, dx\, dy$$

, over the closed surface.

Planar laminas can be used to determine moments of inertia, or center of mass.

   a. 15 theorem
   b. Locally integrable function
   c. BDDC
   d. Planar lamina

39. In geometry, the _____, geometric center, or barycenter of a plane figure X is the intersection of all straight lines that divide X into two parts of equal moment about the line. Informally, it is the 'average' of all points of X. The definition extends to any object X in n-dimensional space: its _____ is the intersection of all hyperplanes that divide X into two parts of equal moment.
   a. BIBO stability
   b. Centroid
   c. BDDC
   d. 15 theorem

40. In geometry, a _____ (pl. tori) is a surface of revolution generated by revolving a circle in three dimensional space about an axis coplanar with the circle, which does not touch the circle. Examples of tori include the surfaces of doughnuts and inner tubes.
   a. Prolate
   b. Hyperbolic paraboloid
   c. Paraboloid
   d. Torus

1. In mathematics, a _____ is a curve in a Euclidian plane (cf. space curve.) The most frequently studied cases are smooth plane curves (including piecewise smooth plane curves), and algebraic plane curves.
   a. Plane curve
   b. Vector area
   c. Lipschitz domain
   d. Gyroid

2. In mathematics, a (topological) _____ is defined as follows: let I be an interval of real numbers (i.e. a non-empty connected subset of $\mathbb{R}$); then a _____ γ is a continuous mapping $\gamma : I \to X$, where X is a topological space. The _____ γ is said to be simple if it is injective, i.e. if for all x, y in I, we have $\gamma(x) = \gamma(y) \implies x = y$. If I is a closed bounded interval $[a, b]$, we also allow the possibility $\gamma(a) = \gamma(b)$ (this convention makes it possible to talk about closed simple _____.)
   a. Prolate cycloid
   b. Tractrix
   c. Closed curve
   d. Curve

3. Cantor defined two kinds of _____ numbers, the ordinal numbers and the cardinal numbers. Ordinal numbers may be identified with well-ordered sets, or counting carried on to any stopping point, including points after an _____ number have already been counted. Generalizing finite and the ordinary _____ sequences which are maps from the positive integers leads to mappings from ordinal numbers, and transfinite sequences.
   a. AUSM
   b. ALGOR
   c. ACTRAN
   d. Infinite

4. The terms of the series are often produced according to a certain rule, such as by a formula, by an algorithm, by a sequence of measurements, or even by a random number generator. As there are an infinite number of terms, this notion is often called an _____. Unlike finite summations, series need tools from mathematical analysis to be fully understood and manipulated.
   a. Extreme value
   b. Extreme Value Theorem
   c. Integration by substitution
   d. Infinite series

5. In mathematics, the _____ is a representation of a function as an infinite sum of terms calculated from the values of its derivatives at a single point. It may be regarded as the limit of the Taylor polynomials. If the series is centered at zero, the series is also called a Maclaurin series.
   a. 15 theorem
   b. Taylor series
   c. BDDC
   d. BIBO stability

6. Integration is an important concept in mathematics, specifically in the field of calculus and, more broadly, mathematical analysis. Given a function f of a real variable x and an interval [a, b] of the real line, the _____

$$\int_a^b f(x)\,dx,$$

is defined informally to be the net signed area of the region in the xy-plane bounded by the graph of f, the x-axis, and the vertical lines x = a and x = b.

The term '_____' may also refer to the notion of antiderivative, a function F whose derivative is the given function f.

a. Integral	b. Integrand
c. Integral test for convergence	d. Indefinite integral

7. The _____ of an angle is the ratio of the length of the opposite side to the length of the hypotenuse. In our case

$$\sin A = \frac{\text{opposite}}{\text{hypotenuse}} = \frac{a}{h}.$$

Note that this ratio does not depend on size of the particular right triangle chosen, as long as it contains the angle A, since all such triangles are similar.

The cosine of an angle is the ratio of the length of the adjacent side to the length of the hypotenuse.

a. Sine integral	b. Trigonometric functions
c. Sine	d. Trigonometric

8. In mathematics, a _____ is a constant multiplicative factor of a certain object. For example, in the expression 9x², the _____ of x^2 is 9.

The object can be such things as a variable, a vector, a function, etc.

a. Binomial type	b. Degree of the polynomial
c. Resultant	d. Coefficient

9. The _____ specifies the relationship between the two central operations of calculus, differentiation and integration.

The first part of the theorem, sometimes called the first _____, shows that an indefinite integration can be reversed by a differentiation.

The second part, sometimes called the second _____, allows one to compute the definite integral of a function by using any one of its infinitely many antiderivatives.

a. Periodic function	b. Fundamental Theorem of Calculus
c. Leibniz formula	d. Limits of integration

10. In mathematics, the _____ are analogs of the ordinary trigonometric or circular functions. The basic _____ are the hyperbolic sine 'sinh', and the hyperbolic cosine 'cosh', from which are derived the hyperbolic tangent 'tanh', etc., in analogy to the derived trigonometric functions. The inverse _____ are the area hyperbolic sine 'arsinh' (also called 'asinh', or sometimes by the misnomer of 'arcsinh') and so on.

a. Hyperbolic cosine	b. Multiplicative inverse
c. Hyperbolic functions	d. Signum function

11. In metric topology and related fields of mathematics, a set U is called _____ if, intuitively speaking, starting from any point x in U one can move by a small amount in any direction and still be in the set U. In other words, the distance between any point x in U and the edge of U is always greater than zero.

As an example, consider the _____ interval (0, 1) consisting of all real numbers x with 0 < x < 1. Here, the topology is the usual topology on the real line. We can look at this in two ways.

a. Open
b. AUSM
c. ACTRAN
d. ALGOR

12. The _____ of an angle is the ratio of the length of the adjacent side to the length of the hypotenuse. In our case

$$\cos A = \frac{\text{adjacent}}{\text{hypotenuse}} = \frac{b}{h}.$$

The tangent of an angle is the ratio of the length of the opposite side to the length of the adjacent side. In our case

$$\tan A = \frac{\text{opposite}}{\text{adjacent}} = \frac{a}{b}.$$

The remaining three functions are best defined using the above three functions.

a. Trigonometric functions
b. Cosine
c. Trigonometric
d. Sine integral

13. In mathematics, the concept of a '_____' is used to describe the behavior of a function as its argument or input either 'gets close' to some point, or as the argument becomes arbitrarily large; or the behavior of a sequence's elements as their index increases indefinitely. Limits are used in calculus and other branches of mathematical analysis to define derivatives and continuity.

In formulas, _____ is usually abbreviated as lim

a. BIBO stability
b. Limit
c. 15 theorem
d. BDDC

14. In geometry, the _____ (or simply the tangent) to a curve at a given point is the straight line that 'just touches' the curve at that point (in the sense explained more precisely below.) As it passes through the point of tangency, the _____ is 'going in the same direction' as the curve, and in this sense it is the best straight-line approximation to the curve at that point. The same definition applies to space curves and curves in n-dimensional Euclidean space.

a. Minimal surface
b. Lie derivative
c. North pole
d. Tangent line

15. In mathematics, an _____ space is a vector space with the additional structure of _____. This additional structure associates each pair of vectors in the space with a scalar quantity known as the _____ of the vectors. Inner products allow the rigorous introduction of intuitive geometrical notions such as the length of a vector or the angle between two vectors.

a. Inner product b. AUSM
c. ACTRAN d. ALGOR

16. In mathematics, two vectors are _____ if they are perpendicular, i.e., they form a right angle. For example, a subway and the street above, although they do not physically intersect, are _____ if they cross at a right angle.
a. ALGOR b. AUSM
c. ACTRAN d. Orthogonal

17. In mathematics, the hyperbolic functions are analogs of the ordinary trigonometric functions. The basic hyperbolic functions are the hyperbolic sine 'sinh', and the hyperbolic cosine 'cosh', from which are derived the _____ 'tanh', etc., in analogy to the derived trigonometric functions. The inverse hyperbolic functions are the area hyperbolic sine 'arsinh' (also called 'asinh', or sometimes by the misnomer of 'arcsinh') and so on.
a. Hyperbolic tangent b. Signum function
c. Hyperbolic sine d. Step function

18. Trigonometry is a branch of mathematics that deals with triangles, particularly those plane triangles in which one angle has 90 degrees (right triangles.) Trigonometry deals with relationships between the sides and the angles of triangles and with the _____ functions, which describe those relationships.

Trigonometry has applications in both pure mathematics and in applied mathematics, where it is essential in many branches of science and technology.

a. Trigonometric functions b. Sine
c. Trigonometric d. Trigonometric integrals

19. In mathematics, _____ is the substitution of trigonometric functions for other expressions. One may use the trigonometric identities to simplify certain integrals containing radical expressions:

- If the integrand contains

$$\sqrt{a^2 - x^2},$$

let

$$x = a \sin \theta$$

and use the identity

$$1 - \sin^2\theta = \cos^2\theta.$$

- If the integrand contains

$$\sqrt{a^2 + x^2}$$

let $x = a \tan \theta$
and use the identity

$$1 + \tan^2 \theta = \sec^2 \theta.$$

- If the integrand contains

$$\sqrt{x^2 - a^2}$$

let

$$x = a \sec \theta$$

and use the identity

$$\sec^2 \theta - 1 = \tan^2 \theta.$$

In the integral

$$\int \frac{dx}{\sqrt{a^2 - x^2}}$$

we may use

$$x = a\sin(\theta), \; dx = a\cos(\theta)\, d\theta$$
$$\theta = \arcsin\left(\frac{x}{a}\right)$$

so that the integral becomes

$$\int \frac{dx}{\sqrt{a^2 - x^2}} = \int \frac{a\cos(\theta)\, d\theta}{\sqrt{a^2 - a^2\sin^2(\theta)}} = \int \frac{a\cos(\theta)\, d\theta}{\sqrt{a^2(1 - \sin^2(\theta))}}$$
$$= \int \frac{a\cos(\theta)\, d\theta}{\sqrt{a^2 \cos^2(\theta)}} = \int d\theta = \theta + C = \arcsin\left(\frac{x}{a}\right) + C$$

Note that the above step requires that a > 0 and cos(θ) > 0; we can choose the a to be the positive square root of a^2; and we impose the restriction on θ to be −π/2 < θ < π/2 by using the arcsin function.

For a definite integral, one must figure out how the bounds of integration change. For example, as x goes from 0 to a/2, then sin (θ) goes from 0 to 1/2, so θ goes from 0 to π/6.

a. Trigonometric substitution
c. Riemann sum
b. Rectangle method
d. Surface of revolution

20. _____ is a type of motion in which the velocity of an object changes equal amounts in equal time periods. An example of an object having _____ would be a ball rolling down a ramp. The object picks up velocity as it goes down the ramp with equal changes in time.

a. ACTRAN
b. ALGOR
c. AUSM
d. Uniform Acceleration

21. In integral calculus we would want to write a fractional algebraic expression as the sum of its _____ in order to take the integral of each simple fraction separately. Once the original denominator, D_0, has been factored we set up a fraction for each factor in the denominator. We may use a subscripted D to represent the denominator of the respective _____ which are the factors in D_0.
   a. Closed-form expression
   b. Multinomial theorem
   c. Left inverse
   d. Partial fractions

22. In mathematics, _____ refers to the rewriting of an expression into a simpler form. For example, the process of rewriting a fraction into one with the smallest whole-number denominator possible (while keeping the numerator an integer) is called 'reducing a fraction'. Rewriting a radical (or 'root') expression with the smallest possible whole number under the radical symbol is called 'reducing a radical'.
   a. BDDC
   b. 15 theorem
   c. Reduction
   d. Quartic

23. A _____ is an algebraic equation in which each term is either a constant or the product of a constant and (the first power of) a single variable. Linear equations can have one, two, three or more variables. Linear equations occur with great regularity in applied mathematics.
   a. Linear equation
   b. Quadratic formula
   c. Cubic function
   d. Quartic function

24. The function $\log_b(x)$ depends on both b and x, but the term _____ in standard usage refers to a function of the form $\log_b(x)$ in which the base b is fixed and so the only argument is x. Thus there is one _____ for each value of the base b (which must be positive and must differ from 1.) Viewed in this way, the base-b _____ is the inverse function of the exponential function b^x.
   a. BIBO stability
   b. BDDC
   c. 15 theorem
   d. Logarithm function

25. In complex analysis, a mathematical discipline, a _____ of a meromorphic function is a certain type of singularity that behaves like the singularity of $\frac{1}{z^n}$ at z = 0. This means that, in particular, a _____ of the function f(z) is a point z = a such that f(z) approaches infinity uniformly as z approaches a.

Formally, suppose U is an open subset of the complex plane C, a is an element of U and f : U {a} → C is a function which is holomorphic over its domain.
   a. Pole
   b. Complex logarithm
   c. Bieberbach conjecture
   d. Lacunary function

26. In mathematics, a _____ is any function which can be written as the ratio of two polynomial functions.

$$y = \frac{x^2 - 3x - 2}{x^2 - 4}$$

In the case of one variable, x, a _____ is a function of the form

$$f(x) = \frac{P(x)}{Q(x)}$$

where P and Q are polynomial function in x and Q is not the zero polynomial. The domain of f is the set of all points x for which the denominator Q(x) is not zero.

a. BIBO stability
b. 15 theorem
c. BDDC
d. Rational function

27. In calculus and other branches of mathematical analysis, an _____ is an algebraic expression obtained in the context of limits. Limits involving algebraic operations are often performed by replacing subexpressions by their limits; if the expression obtained after this substitution does not give enough information to determine the original limit, it is known as an _____. The indeterminate forms include 0^0, $0/0$, 1^∞, $\infty - \infty$, ∞/∞, $0\times\infty$, and ∞^0.

a. AUSM
b. ACTRAN
c. ALGOR
d. Indeterminate form

28. In probability theory and statistics, the _____ (or expectation value or mean and for continuous random variables with a density function it is the probability density-weighted integral of the possible values.

The term '_____' can be misleading.

a. ACTRAN
b. ALGOR
c. AUSM
d. Expected value

29. In calculus, the _____ states, roughly, that given a section of a smooth curve, there is at least one point on that section at which the derivative (slope) of the curve is equal (parallel) to the 'average' derivative of the section. It is used to prove theorems that make global conclusions about a function on an interval starting from local hypotheses about derivatives at points of the interval.

This theorem can be understood concretely by applying it to motion: If a car travels one hundred miles in one hour, so its average speed during that time was 100 miles per hour.

a. Limits of integration
b. Periodic function
c. Mean Value Theorem
d. Hyperbolic angle

30. In a totally ordered set all elements are mutually comparable, so such a set can have at most one minimal element and at most one maximal element. Then, due to mutual comparability, the minimal element will also be the least element and the maximal element will also be the greatest element. Thus in a totally ordered set we can simply use the terms minimum and _____.

a. Racetrack principle
b. Maximum
c. Nth term
d. Leibniz rule

31. In calculus, the _____ is a formula for the derivative of the composite of two functions.

In intuitive terms, if a variable, y, depends on a second variable, u, which in turn depends on a third variable, x, then the rate of change of y with respect to x can be computed as the rate of change of y with respect to u multiplied by the rate of change of u with respect to x. Schematically,

$$\frac{dy}{dx} = \frac{dy}{du} \cdot \frac{du}{dx}.$$

a. Product rule
b. Differentiation rules
c. Chain Rule
d. Reciprocal Rule

32. Continuous functions are of utmost importance in mathematics and applications. However, not all functions are continuous. If a function is not continuous at a point in its domain, one says that it has a _____ there. The set of all points of _____ of a function may be a discrete set, a dense set, or even the entire domain of the function.

a. 15 theorem
b. Vector
c. BDDC
d. Discontinuity

33. In vector calculus, the _____ is an operator that measures the magnitude of a vector field's source or sink at a given point; the _____ of a vector field is a (signed) scalar. For example, consider air as it is heated or cooled. The relevant vector field for this example is the velocity of the moving air at a point.

a. Green's theorem
b. Gradient theorem
c. Triple product
d. Divergence

34. In calculus, an _____ is the limit of a definite integral as an endpoint of the interval of integration approaches either a specified real number or ∞ or −∞ or, in some cases, as both endpoints approach limits.

Specifically, an _____ is a limit of the form

$$\lim_{b \to \infty} \int_a^b f(x)\, dx, \qquad \lim_{a \to -\infty} \int_a^b f(x)\, dx,$$

or of the form

$$\lim_{c \to b^-} \int_a^c f(x)\, dx, \qquad \lim_{c \to a^+} \int_c^b f(x)\, dx,$$

in which one takes a limit in one or the other (or sometimes both) endpoints. Improper integrals may also occur at an interior point of the domain of integration, or at multiple such points.

a. Improper integral
b. AUSM
c. ACTRAN
d. ALGOR

35. In mathematics, the _____ of a function y = f(x) is a function that, in some fashion, 'undoes' the effect of f The _____ of f is denoted f⁻¹. The statements y=f(x) and x=f⁻¹(y) are equivalent.
   a. ACTRAN
   b. ALGOR
   c. AUSM
   d. Inverse

36. In mathematics, if f is a function from A to B then an _____ for f is a function in the opposite direction, from B to A, with the property that a round trip (a composition) from A to B to A (or from B to A to B) returns each element of the initial set to itself. Thus, if an input x into the function f produces an output y, then inputting y into the _____ f^{-1} (read f inverse, not to be confused with exponentiation) produces the output x. Not every function has an inverse; those that do are called invertible.
   a. Inverse function
   b. Augustin Louis Cauchy
   c. Aristotle
   d. Augustin-Jean Fresnel

37. In calculus and mathematical analysis the _____ of the integral

$$\int_a^b f(x)\,dx$$

of a Riemann integrable function f defined on a closed and bounded interval [a, b] are the real numbers a and b.

_____ can also be defined for improper integrals, with the _____ of both

$$\lim_{z \to a^+} \int_z^b f(x)\,dx$$

and

$$\lim_{z \to b^-} \int_a^z f(x)\,dx$$

again being a and b. For an improper integral

$$\int_a^\infty f(x)\,dx$$

or

$$\int_{-\infty}^b f(x)\,dx$$

the _____ are a and ∞, or −∞ and b, respectively.

a. Differential
c. Maxima
b. Test for Divergence
d. Limits of integration

38. In mathematics, the _____ of a non-negative integer n, denoted by n!, is the product of all positive integers less than or equal to n. For example,

$$5! = 1 \times 2 \times 3 \times 4 \times 5 = 120$$

and

$$6! = 1 \times 2 \times 3 \times 4 \times 5 \times 6 = 720.$$

The notation n! was introduced by Christian Kramp in 1808.

The _____ function is formally defined by

$$n! = \prod_{k=1}^{n} k \qquad \forall n \in \mathbb{N}$$

or recursively defined by

$$n! = \begin{cases} n \leq 1 & 1 \\ n > 1 & n(n-1)! \end{cases} \qquad \forall n \in \mathbb{N}.$$

Both of the above definitions incorporate the instance

$$0! = 1$$

as an instance of the fact that the product of no numbers at all is 1.

a. Constraint counting
c. BDDC
b. Factorial
d. 15 theorem

39. In mathematics, the _____ is an extension of the factorial function to real and complex numbers. For a complex number z with positive real part the _____ is defined by

$$\Gamma(z) = \int_0^\infty t^{z-1} e^{-t} \, dt \ .$$

This definition can be extended to the rest of the complex plane, excepting the non-positive integers.

If n is a positive integer, then

$$\Gamma(n) = (n - 1)!,$$

showing the connection to the factorial function.

a. Pochhammer k-symbol
b. Multivariate gamma function
c. Gamma function
d. Digamma function

40. _____ is a way of expressing knowledge or belief that an event will occur or has occurred. In mathematics the concept has been given an exact meaning in _____ theory, that is used extensively in such areas of study as mathematics, statistics, finance, gambling, science, and philosophy to draw conclusions about the likelihood of potential events and the underlying mechanics of complex systems.

The word _____ does not have a consistent direct definition.

a. Discrete probability distributions
b. Normal distribution
c. Linear regression
d. Probability

41. In mathematics, a _____ (pdf) is a function that represents a probability distribution in terms of integrals.

Formally, a probability distribution has density f, if f is a non-negative Lebesgue-integrable function $\mathbb{R} \to \mathbb{R}$ such that the probability of the interval [a, b] is given by

$$\int_a^b f(x)\, dx$$

for any two numbers a and b. This implies that the total integral of f must be 1.

a. 15 theorem
b. BDDC
c. Probability density function
d. Factorial moment generating function

42. The _____ of a material is defined as its mass per unit volume. The symbol of _____ is ρ '>rho.)

Mathematically:

$$d = \frac{m}{V}$$

where:

        d is the _____,
        m is the mass,
        V is the volume.

a. 15 theorem
c. BDDC
b. BIBO stability
d. Density

43. In mathematics, a probability _____ is a function that represents a probability distribution in terms of integrals.

Formally, a probability distribution has density f, if f is a non-negative Lebesgue-integrable function $\mathbb{R} \to \mathbb{R}$ such that the probability of the interval [a, b] is given by

$$\int_a^b f(x)\, dx$$

for any two numbers a and b. This implies that the total integral of f must be 1.

a. BDDC
c. Factorial moment generating function
b. 15 theorem
d. Density function

Chapter 8. The Koch Snowflake: Infinite Perimeter?

1. The _____ is a mathematical curve and one of the earliest fractal curves to have been described. It appeared in a 1904 paper titled 'On a continuous curve without tangents, constructible from elementary geometry' by the Swedish mathematician Helge von Koch. The Koch curve is a special case of the Césaro curve where $a = \frac{1}{2} + \frac{i}{\sqrt{12}}$, which is in turn a special case of the de Rham curve.

   a. BIBO stability
   b. BDDC
   c. 15 theorem
   d. Koch snowflake

2. In mathematics, a _____ is an ordered list of objects (or events). Like a set, it contains members (also called elements or terms), and the number of terms (possibly infinite) is called the length of the _____. Unlike a set, order matters, and the exact same elements can appear multiple times at different positions in the _____.

   a. Y-intercept
   b. Slope
   c. 15 theorem
   d. Sequence

3. In a totally ordered set all elements are mutually comparable, so such a set can have at most one minimal element and at most one maximal element. Then, due to mutual comparability, the minimal element will also be the least element and the maximal element will also be the greatest element. Thus in a totally ordered set we can simply use the terms minimum and _____.

   a. Nth term
   b. Racetrack principle
   c. Leibniz rule
   d. Maximum

4. In a totally ordered set all elements are mutually comparable, so such a set can have at most one minimal element and at most one maximal element. Then, due to mutual comparability, the minimal element will also be the least element and the maximal element will also be the greatest element. Thus in a totally ordered set we can simply use the terms _____ and maximum.

   a. Ghosts of departed quantities
   b. Maximum
   c. Nth term
   d. Minimum

5. In mathematics, the _____ test for divergence is a simple test for the divergence of an infinite series:

   - If $\lim_{n \to \infty} a_n \neq 0$ or if the limit does not exist, then $\sum_{n=1}^{\infty} a_n$ diverges.

Many authors do not name this test or give it a shorter name.

Unlike stronger convergence tests, the term test cannot prove by itself that a series converges. In particular, the converse to the test is not true; instead all one can say is:

   - If $\lim_{n \to \infty} a_n = 0$, then $\sum_{n=1}^{\infty} a_n$ may or may not converge. In other words, if $\lim_{n \to \infty} a_n = 0$, the test is inconclusive.

The harmonic series is a classic example of a divergent series whose terms limit to zero. The more general class of p-series,

$$\sum_{n=1}^{\infty} \frac{1}{n^p},$$

exemplifies the possible results of the test:

- If $p \le 0$, then the term test identifies the series as divergent.
- If $0 < p \le 1$, then the term test is inconclusive, but the series is divergent by the integral test for convergence.
- If $1 < p$, then the term test is inconclusive, but the series is convergent, again by the integral test for convergence.

The test is typically proved in contrapositive form:

- If $\sum_{n=1}^{\infty} a_n$ converges, then $\lim_{n \to \infty} a_n = 0$.

If s_n are the partial sums of the series, then the assumption that the series converges means that

$$\lim_{n \to \infty} s_n = s$$

for some number s. Then

$$\lim_{n \to \infty} a_n = \lim_{n \to \infty} (s_n - s_{n-1}) = s - s = 0.$$

The assumption that the series converges means that it passes Cauchy's convergence test: for every $\varepsilon > 0$ there is a number N such that

$$|a_{n+1} + a_{n+2} + \ldots + a_{n+p}| < \varepsilon$$

holds for all n > N and p ≥ 1. Setting p = 1 recovers the definition of the statement

$$\lim_{n \to \infty} a_n = 0.$$

The simplest version of the term test applies to infinite series of real numbers.

a. Nth term
b. Slope field
c. Leibniz differential
d. Minimum

6. In elementary mathematics, physics, and engineering, a _____ is a geometric object that has both a magnitude (or length), direction and sense, (i.e., orientation along the given direction.) A _____ is frequently represented by a line segment with a definite direction, or graphically as an arrow, connecting an initial point A with a terminal point B, and denoted by

>

The magnitude of the _____ is the length of the segment and the direction characterizes the displacement of B relative to A: how much one should move the point A to 'carry' it to the point B.

Many algebraic operations on real numbers have close analogues for vectors.

a. BDDC
b. Linear partial differential operator
c. Vector
d. 15 theorem

7. In mathematics, a _____ (or just conic) is a curve obtained by intersecting a cone (more precisely, a circular conical surface) with a plane. A _____ is therefore a restriction of a quadric surface to the plane. The conic sections were named and studied as long ago as 200 BC, when Apollonius of Perga undertook a systematic study of their properties.

a. BDDC
b. 15 theorem
c. Latus rectum
d. Conic section

8. In calculus, a branch of mathematics, the _____ is a measurement of how a function changes when its input changes. Loosely speaking, a _____ can be thought of as how much a quantity is changing at some given point. For example, the _____ of the position (or distance) of a vehicle with respect to time is the instantaneous velocity (respectively, instantaneous speed) at which the vehicle is traveling.

The process of finding a _____ is called differentiation. The fundamental theorem of calculus states that differentiation is the reverse process to integration.

a. Bounded function
b. Stationary phase approximation
c. Semi-differentiability
d. Derivative

9. In vector calculus, the _____ is an operator that measures the magnitude of a vector field's source or sink at a given point; the _____ of a vector field is a (signed) scalar. For example, consider air as it is heated or cooled. The relevant vector field for this example is the velocity of the moving air at a point.

a. Triple product
b. Gradient theorem
c. Green's theorem
d. Divergence

10. In calculus, the _____ determines whether a given critical point of a function is a maximum, a minimum, or neither.

Suppose that f is a function and we want to determine if f has a maximum or minimum at x. If f is increasing to the left of x and decreasing to the right of x, then x is a local maximum of f.

a. First Derivative Test
b. Partial sum
c. Continuous function
d. Test for Divergence

11. In mathematics, the _____ is a criterion for the convergence (a convergence test) of an infinite series

$$\sum_{n=1}^{\infty} a_n.$$

It is particularly useful in connection with power series.

The _____ was developed first by Cauchy and so is sometimes known as the Cauchy _____ or Cauchy's radical test.
The _____ uses the number

$$C = \limsup_{n \to \infty} \sqrt[n]{|a_n|},$$

where 'lim sup' denotes the limit superior, possibly ∞.

a. Mean Value Theorem
b. Related rates
c. Racetrack principle
d. Root Test

12. _____ is used to describe the steepness, incline, gradient, or grade of a straight line. A higher _____ value indicates a steeper incline. The _____ is defined as the ratio of the 'rise' divided by the 'run' between two points on a line, or in other words, the ratio of the altitude change to the horizontal distance between any two points on the line.

a. Sequence
b. 15 theorem
c. Y-intercept
d. Slope

13. In mathematics, the concept of a '_____' is used to describe the behavior of a function as its argument or input either 'gets close' to some point, or as the argument becomes arbitrarily large; or the behavior of a sequence's elements as their index increases indefinitely. Limits are used in calculus and other branches of mathematical analysis to define derivatives and continuity.

In formulas, _____ is usually abbreviated as lim

a. BDDC
b. Limit
c. 15 theorem
d. BIBO stability

Chapter 8. The Koch Snowflake: Infinite Perimeter?

14. In complex analysis, a mathematical discipline, a _____ of a meromorphic function is a certain type of singularity that behaves like the singularity of $\frac{1}{z^n}$ at z = 0. This means that, in particular, a _____ of the function f(z) is a point z = a such that f(z) approaches infinity uniformly as z approaches a.

Formally, suppose U is an open subset of the complex plane C, a is an element of U and f : U {a} → C is a function which is holomorphic over its domain.

 a. Complex logarithm
 b. Lacunary function
 c. Bieberbach conjecture
 d. Pole

15. Let f be a differentiable function, and let f'(x) be its derivative. The derivative of f'(x) (if it has one) is written f''(x) and is called the _____ of f. Similarly, the derivative of a _____, if it exists, is written f'''(x) and is called the third derivative of f.

 a. Slant asymptote
 b. Vertical asymptote
 c. Stationary phase approximation
 d. Second Derivative

16. In calculus, a branch of mathematics, the _____ is a criterion often useful for determining whether a given stationary point of a function is a local maximum or a local minimum.

The test states: If the function f is twice differentiable at a stationary point x, meaning that $f'(x) = 0$, then:

- If $f''(x) < 0$ then f has a local maximum at x.
- If $f''(x) > 0$ then f has a local minimum at x.
- If $f''(x) = 0$, the _____ says nothing about the point x, has a possible inflection point.

In the last case, the function may have a local maximum or minimum there, but the function is sufficiently 'flat' that this is undetected by the second derivative. In this case one has to examine the third derivative. Such an example is f(x) = x^4.

 a. Second Derivative Test
 b. Stationary point
 c. Symmetric derivative
 d. Linearity of differentiation

17. In mathematics, the _____ of a non-negative integer n, denoted by n!, is the product of all positive integers less than or equal to n. For example,

$$5! = 1 \times 2 \times 3 \times 4 \times 5 = 120$$

and

$$6! = 1 \times 2 \times 3 \times 4 \times 5 \times 6 = 720.$$

The notation n! was introduced by Christian Kramp in 1808.

The _____ function is formally defined by

$$n! = \prod_{k=1}^{n} k \quad \forall n \in \mathbb{N}$$

or recursively defined by

$$n! = \begin{cases} n \leq 1 & 1 \\ n > 1 & n(n-1)! \end{cases} \quad \forall n \in \mathbb{N}.$$

Both of the above definitions incorporate the instance

$$0! = 1$$

as an instance of the fact that the product of no numbers at all is 1.

a. Constraint counting
c. Factorial

b. 15 theorem
d. BDDC

18. In calculus, interchange of the _____ is a methodology that transforms multiple integrations of functions into other, hopefully simpler, integrals by changing the order in which the integrations are performed.

The problem for examination is evaluation of an integral of the form:

$$\iint_D dxdy \, f(x,y),$$

where D is some two-dimensional area in the xy-plane. For some functions f straightforward integration is feasible, but where that is not true, the integral can sometimes be reduced to simpler form by changing the _____.

a. Integration by parts
c. Arc length

b. Order of integration
d. Indefinite integral

19. In calculus, the _____ is a theorem regarding the limit of a function.

The _____ is a technical result which is very important in proofs in calculus and mathematical analysis. It is typically used to confirm the limit of a function via comparison with two other functions whose limits are known or easily computed.

a. Limit of a sequence	b. Table of limits
c. 15 theorem	d. Squeeze Theorem

20. In mathematics, the _____ (or modulus) of a real number is its numerical value without regard to its sign. So, for example, 3 is the _____ of both 3 and −3.

The _____ of a number a is denoted by $|a|$.

a. Absolute Value	b. ACTRAN
c. Area hyperbolic functions	d. Exponential function

21. In mathematics, a _____ is a function which preserves the given order. This concept first arose in calculus, and was later generalized to the more abstract setting of order theory.

In calculus, a function f defined on a subset of the real numbers with real values is called monotonic (also monotonically increasing or non-decreasing), if for all x and y such that x >≤ y one has f(x) >≤ f(y), so f preserves the order.

a. Monotonic function	b. 15 theorem
c. Pseudo-differential operator	d. Pettis integral

22. In mathematics, a function f defined on some set X with real or complex values is a _____ function, if the set of its values is _____. In other words, there exists a number M>0 such that

$$|f(x)| \leq M$$

for all x in X.

Sometimes, if $f(x) \leq A$ for all x in X, then the function is said to be _____ above by A.

a. Stationary phase approximation	b. Concave upwards
c. Differential coefficient	d. Bounded

23. In mathematics, given a subset S of a partially ordered set T, the _____ (sup) of S, if it exists, is the least element of T that is greater than or equal to each element of S. Consequently, the _____ is also referred to as the least upper bound, lub or LUB. If the _____ exists, it may or may not belong to S.

a. 15 theorem	b. BIBO stability
c. BDDC	d. Supremum

24. In mathematics, especially in order theory, an upper bound of a subset S of some partially ordered set (P, ≤) is an element of P which is greater than or equal to every element of S. The term _____ is defined dually as an element of P which is lesser than or equal to every element of S. A set with an upper bound is said to be bounded from above by that bound, a set with a _____ is said to be bounded from below by that bound.

A subset S of a partially ordered set P may fail to have any bounds or may have many different upper and lower bounds. By transitivity, any element greater than or equal to an upper bound of S is again an upper bound of S, and any element lesser than or equal to any _____ of S is again a _____ of S. This leads to the consideration of least upper bounds: (or suprema) and greatest lower bounds (or infima.)

a. 15 theorem
b. BIBO stability
c. Lower bound
d. BDDC

25. One commonly distinguishes between the _____ and the absolute error. The absolute error is the magnitude of the difference between the exact value and the approximation. The _____ is the absolute error divided by the magnitude of the exact value.

a. Series acceleration
b. Relative error
c. Numerical integration
d. Meshfree methods

26. In mathematics, especially in order theory, an _____ of a subset S of some partially ordered set (P, >≤) is an element of P which is greater than or equal to every element of S. The term lower bound is defined dually as an element of P which is lesser than or equal to every element of S. A set with an _____ is said to be bounded from above by that bound, a set with a lower bound is said to be bounded from below by that bound.

A subset S of a partially ordered set P may fail to have any bounds or may have many different upper and lower bounds. By transitivity, any element greater than or equal to an _____ of S is again an _____ of S, and any element lesser than or equal to any lower bound of S is again a lower bound of S. This leads to the consideration of least upper bounds: (or suprema) and greatest lower bounds (or infima.)

a. ALGOR
b. ACTRAN
c. AUSM
d. Upper bound

27. In mathematics and the arts, two quantities are in the _____ if the ratio between the sum of those quantities and the larger one is the same as the ratio between the larger one and the smaller. The _____ is an irrational mathematical constant, approximately 1.6180339887.

At least since the Renaissance, many artists and architects have proportioned their works to approximate the _____ -- especially in the form of the golden rectangle, in which the ratio of the longer side to the shorter is the _____ --believing this proportion to be aesthetically pleasing.

a. BIBO stability
b. BDDC
c. 15 theorem
d. Golden ratio

28. A _____ is an expression which compares quantities relative to each other. The most common examples involve two quantities, but in theory any number of quantities can be compared. In mathematical terms, they are represented by separating each quantity with a colon, for example the _____ 2:3, which is read as the _____ 'two to three'.

a. 15 theorem
b. Y-intercept
c. Ratio
d. Sequence

29. In infinitesimal calculus, a _____ is traditionally an infinitesimally small change in a variable. For example, if x is a variable, then a change in the value of x is often denoted Δx (or δx when this change is considered to be small.) The _____ dx represents such a change, but is infinitely small.
   a. The Method of Mechanical Theorems
   b. Local maximum
   c. Dirichlet integral
   d. Differential

30. In mathematics, the hyperbolic functions are analogs of the ordinary trigonometric functions. The basic hyperbolic functions are the _____ 'sinh', and the hyperbolic cosine 'cosh', from which are derived the hyperbolic tangent 'tanh', etc., in analogy to the derived trigonometric functions. The inverse hyperbolic functions are the area _____ 'arsinh' (also called 'asinh', or sometimes by the misnomer of 'arcsinh') and so on.
   a. Signum function
   b. Hyperbolic sine
   c. Square root function
   d. Hyperbolic tangent

31. In mathematics, the hyperbolic functions are analogs of the ordinary trigonometric functions. The basic hyperbolic functions are the hyperbolic sine 'sinh', and the hyperbolic cosine 'cosh', from which are derived the _____ 'tanh', etc., in analogy to the derived trigonometric functions. The inverse hyperbolic functions are the area hyperbolic sine 'arsinh' (also called 'asinh', or sometimes by the misnomer of 'arcsinh') and so on.
   a. Step function
   b. Hyperbolic tangent
   c. Hyperbolic sine
   d. Signum function

32. Cantor defined two kinds of _____ numbers, the ordinal numbers and the cardinal numbers. Ordinal numbers may be identified with well-ordered sets, or counting carried on to any stopping point, including points after an _____ number have already been counted. Generalizing finite and the ordinary _____ sequences which are maps from the positive integers leads to mappings from ordinal numbers, and transfinite sequences.
   a. ACTRAN
   b. Infinite
   c. AUSM
   d. ALGOR

33. The terms of the series are often produced according to a certain rule, such as by a formula, by an algorithm, by a sequence of measurements, or even by a random number generator. As there are an infinite number of terms, this notion is often called an _____. Unlike finite summations, series need tools from mathematical analysis to be fully understood and manipulated.
   a. Extreme value
   b. Integration by substitution
   c. Infinite series
   d. Extreme Value Theorem

34. Call S_N the _____ to N of the sequence $\{a_n\}$, or _____ of the series. A series is the sequence of partial sums, $\{S_N\}$.

When talking about series, one can refer either to the sequence $\{S_N\}$ of the partial sums, or to the sum of the series,

$$\sum_{n=0}^{\infty} a_n$$

i.e., the limit of the sequence of partial sums - it is clear which one is meant from context.

a. Maxima
c. Dirichlet integral

b. The Method of Mechanical Theorems
d. Partial sum

35. In mathematics, _____ refers to the rewriting of an expression into a simpler form. For example, the process of rewriting a fraction into one with the smallest whole-number denominator possible (while keeping the numerator an integer) is called 'reducing a fraction'. Rewriting a radical (or 'root') expression with the smallest possible whole number under the radical symbol is called 'reducing a radical'.

a. Quartic
c. BDDC

b. 15 theorem
d. Reduction

36. In mathematics, the _____ of two monic polynomials P and Q over a field k is defined as the product

$$\text{res}(P,Q) = \prod_{(x,y):\, P(x)=0,\, Q(y)=0} (x-y),$$

of the differences of their roots, where x and y take on values in the algebraic closure of k. For non-monic polynomials with leading coefficients p and q, respectively, the above product is multiplied by

$$p^{\deg Q} q^{\deg P}.$$

- The _____ is the determinant of the Sylvester matrix (and of the Bezout matrix.)

- When Q is separable, the above product can be rewritten to

$$\text{res}(P,Q) = \prod_{P(x)=0} Q(x)$$

and this expression remains unchanged if Q is reduced modulo P. Note that, when non-monic, this includes the factor $q^{\deg P}$ but still needs the factor $p^{\deg Q}$.

- Let $P' = P \mod Q$. The above idea can be continued by swapping the roles of P' and Q. However, P' has a set of roots different from that of P. This can be resolved by writing $\prod_{Q(y)=0} P'(y)$ as a determinant again, where P' has leading zero coefficients. This determinant can now be simplified by iterative expansion with respect to the column, where only the leading coefficient q of Q appears.

$$\text{res}(P,Q) = q^{\deg P - \deg P'} \cdot \text{res}(P',Q)$$

Continuing this procedure ends up in a variant of the Euclidean algorithm. This procedure needs quadratic runtime.

a. Difference polynomial
c. Quadratic function

b. Leading coefficient
d. Resultant

37. In mathematics, the _____, named after German mathematician Bernhard Riemann, is a prominent function of great significance in number theory because of its relation to the distribution of prime numbers. It also has applications in other areas such as physics, probability theory, and applied statistics.

The Riemann hypothesis, a conjecture about the distribution of the zeros of the _____, is considered by many mathematicians to be the most important unsolved problem in pure mathematics.

a. 15 theorem
b. BIBO stability
c. BDDC
d. Riemann zeta function

38. In physics, and more specifically kinematics, _____ is the change in velocity over time. Because velocity is a vector, it can change in two ways: a change in magnitude and/or a change in direction. In one dimension, _____ is the rate at which something speeds up or slows down.
a. Acceleration
b. ALGOR
c. ACTRAN
d. AUSM

39. In mathematics and its applications, a _____ system is a system for assigning an n-tuple of numbers or scalars to each point in an n-dimensional space. This concept is part of the theory of manifolds. 'Scalars' in many cases means real numbers, but, depending on context, can mean complex numbers or elements of some other commutative ring.
a. Cylindrical coordinate system
b. Coordinate
c. Spherical coordinate system
d. 15 theorem

40. The _____ of an angle is the ratio of the length of the opposite side to the length of the hypotenuse. In our case

$$\sin A = \frac{\text{opposite}}{\text{hypotenuse}} = \frac{a}{h}.$$

Note that this ratio does not depend on size of the particular right triangle chosen, as long as it contains the angle A, since all such triangles are similar.

The cosine of an angle is the ratio of the length of the adjacent side to the length of the hypotenuse.

a. Sine integral
b. Sine
c. Trigonometric functions
d. Trigonometric

41. In geometry, the _____ (or simply the tangent) to a curve at a given point is the straight line that 'just touches' the curve at that point (in the sense explained more precisely below.) As it passes through the point of tangency, the _____ is 'going in the same direction' as the curve, and in this sense it is the best straight-line approximation to the curve at that point. The same definition applies to space curves and curves in n-dimensional Euclidean space.
a. North pole
b. Tangent line
c. Lie derivative
d. Minimal surface

42. In mathematics, a _____ is an informal expression referring to a series whose sum can be found by exploiting the circumstance that nearly every term cancels with either a succeeding or preceding term. Such a technique is also known as the method of differences.

For example, the series

$$\sum_{n=1}^{\infty} \frac{1}{n(n+1)}$$

simplifies as

$$\sum_{n=1}^{\infty} \frac{1}{n(n+1)} = \sum_{n=1}^{\infty} \left(\frac{1}{n} - \frac{1}{n+1}\right)$$
$$= \left(1 - \frac{1}{2}\right) + \left(\frac{1}{2} - \frac{1}{3}\right) + \cdots$$
$$= 1 + \left(-\frac{1}{2} + \frac{1}{2}\right) + \left(-\frac{1}{3} + \frac{1}{3}\right) + \cdots = 1.$$

Although telescoping can be a useful technique, there are pitfalls to watch out for:

$$0 = \sum_{n=1}^{\infty} 0 = \sum_{n=1}^{\infty} (1-1) = 1 + \sum_{n=1}^{\infty} (-1+1) = 1$$

is not correct because regrouping of terms is invalid unless the individual terms converge to 0; see Grandi's series.

a. Converge absolutely
c. Telescoping series

b. Geometric series
d. Sequence transformation

43. In mathematics, the _____, sometimes called the direct _____ is a criterion for convergence or divergence of a series whose terms are real or complex numbers. The test determines convergence by comparing the terms of the series in question with those of a series whose convergence properties are known.

The _____ states that if the series

$$\sum_{n=1}^{\infty} b_n$$

is an absolutely convergent series and

$$|a_n| \leq |b_n|$$

for sufficiently large n , then the series

$$\sum_{n=1}^{\infty} a_n$$

converges absolutely.

a. Ratio test
c. Comparison Test

b. Conditionally convergent
d. Telescoping series

44. In mathematics, a _____ is a function of the form

$$f(x) = ax^3 + bx^2 + cx + d,$$

where a is nonzero; or in other words, a polynomial of degree three. The derivative of a _____ is a quadratic function. The integral of a _____ is a quartic function.

a. Linear equation
c. Quartic function

b. Cubic function
d. Quadratic formula

45. In mathematics, a _____ is a series with a constant ratio between successive terms. For example, the series

$$\frac{1}{2} + \frac{1}{4} + \frac{1}{8} + \frac{1}{16} + \cdots$$

is geometric, because each term is equal to half of the previous term. The sum of this series is 1, as illustrated in the following picture:

_____ are one of the simplest examples of infinite series with finite sums.

a. Sequence transformation
c. Converge absolutely

b. Conditionally convergent
d. Geometric series

46. In geometry, a _____ is a three-dimensional figure formed by six parallelograms. It is to a parallelogram as a cube is to a square: Euclidean geometry supports all four notions but affine geometry admits only parallelograms and parallelepipeds. Three equivalent definitions of _____ are

- a polyhedron with six faces (hexahedron), each of which is a parallelogram,
- a hexahedron with three pairs of parallel faces, and
- a prism of which the base is a parallelogram.

The cuboid (six rectangular faces), cube (six square faces), and the rhombohedron (six rhombus faces) are all specific cases of _____.

Parallelepipeds are a subclass of the prismatoids.

a. BIBO stability
c. Parallelepiped

b. 15 theorem
d. BDDC

47. In mathematics, the nth term _____ is a simple test for the divergence of an infinite series:

- If $\lim_{n \to \infty} a_n \neq 0$ or if the limit does not exist, then $\sum_{n=1}^{\infty} a_n$ diverges.

Many authors do not name this test or give it a shorter name.

Unlike stronger convergence tests, the term test cannot prove by itself that a series converges. In particular, the converse to the test is not true; instead all one can say is:

- If $\lim_{n \to \infty} a_n = 0$, then $\sum_{n=1}^{\infty} a_n$ may or may not converge. In other words, if $\lim_{n \to \infty} a_n = 0$, the test is inconclusive.

The harmonic series is a classic example of a divergent series whose terms limit to zero. The more general class of p-series,

$$\sum_{n=1}^{\infty} \frac{1}{n^p},$$

exemplifies the possible results of the test:

- If $p \leq 0$, then the term test identifies the series as divergent.
- If $0 < p \leq 1$, then the term test is inconclusive, but the series is divergent by the integral test for convergence.
- If $1 < p$, then the term test is inconclusive, but the series is convergent, again by the integral test for convergence.

The test is typically proved in contrapositive form:

- If $\sum_{n=1}^{\infty} a_n$ converges, then $\lim_{n \to \infty} a_n = 0$.

If s_n are the partial sums of the series, then the assumption that the series converges means that

$$\lim_{n \to \infty} s_n = s$$

for some number s. Then

$$\lim_{n \to \infty} a_n = \lim_{n \to \infty} (s_n - s_{n-1}) = s - s = 0.$$

The assumption that the series converges means that it passes Cauchy's convergence test: for every $\varepsilon > 0$ there is a number N such that

$$|a_{n+1} + a_{n+2} + \ldots + a_{n+p}| < \varepsilon$$

holds for all n > N and p ≥ 1. Setting p = 1 recovers the definition of the statement

$$\lim_{n \to \infty} a_n = 0.$$

The simplest version of the term test applies to infinite series of real numbers.

a. Test for Divergence
b. Leibniz differential
c. Fundamental Theorem of Calculus
d. Calculus controversy

48. The _____ of any solid, liquid, plasma, vacuum or theoretical object is how much three-dimensional space it occupies, often quantified numerically. One-dimensional figures (such as lines) and two-dimensional shapes (such as squares) are assigned zero _____ in the three-dimensional space. _____ is commonly presented in units such as mL or cm³ (milliliters or cubic centimeters.)

a. Dirac equation
b. Klein-Gordon equation
c. Vector potential
d. Volume

49. Integration is an important concept in mathematics, specifically in the field of calculus and, more broadly, mathematical analysis. Given a function f of a real variable x and an interval [a, b] of the real line, the _____

$$\int_a^b f(x)\, dx,$$

is defined informally to be the net signed area of the region in the xy-plane bounded by the graph of f, the x-axis, and the vertical lines x = a and x = b.

The term '_____' may also refer to the notion of antiderivative, a function F whose derivative is the given function f.

a. Integral test for convergence
c. Integrand
b. Indefinite integral
d. Integral

50. In mathematics, the _____ for convergence is a method used to test infinite series of non-negative terms for convergence. An early form of the test of convergence was developed in India by Madhava in the 14th century, and by his followers at the Kerala School. In Europe, it was later developed by Maclaurin and Cauchy and is sometimes known as the Maclaurin-Cauchy test.
   a. ALGOR
   b. AUSM
   c. ACTRAN
   d. Integral Test

51. _____ is the concept of adding accumulated interest back to the principal, so that interest is earned on interest from that moment on. The act of declaring interest to be principal is called compounding (i.e., interest is compounded.) A loan, for example, may have its interest compounded every month: in this case, a loan with $100 principal and 1% interest per month would have a balance of $101 at the end of the first month.
   a. BIBO stability
   b. Compound interest
   c. 15 theorem
   d. BDDC

52. A _____ is a mathematical equation for an unknown function of one or several variables that relates the values of the function itself and of its derivatives of various orders. they play a prominent role in engineering, physics, economics and other disciplines.

A simplified real world example of a _____ is modeling the acceleration of a ball falling through the air (considering only gravity and air resistance.)

   a. Structural stability
   b. Differential equation
   c. Phase line
   d. Caloric polynomial

53. A _____ officer is an officer of high military rank. The term or equivalent is used by nearly every country in the world. _____ can be used as a generic term for all grades of _____ officer, or it can specifically refer to a single rank that is just called _____.
   a. BDDC
   b. 15 theorem
   c. BIBO stability
   d. General

54. In acoustics and telecommunication, a _____ of a wave is a component frequency of the signal that is an integer multiple of the fundamental frequency. For example, if the fundamental frequency is f, the harmonics have frequencies f, 2f, 3f, 4f, etc. The harmonics have the property that they are all periodic at the fundamental frequency, therefore the sum of harmonics is also periodic at that frequency.
   a. 15 theorem
   b. Harmonic
   c. BIBO stability
   d. BDDC

55. In mathematics, the _____ is the infinite series

$$\sum_{k=1}^{\infty} \frac{1}{k} = 1 + \frac{1}{2} + \frac{1}{3} + \frac{1}{4} + \cdots.$$

Its name derives from the concept of overtones, or harmonics, in music: the wavelengths of the overtones of a vibrating string are 1/2, 1/3, 1/4, etc., of the string's fundamental wavelength. Every term of the series after the first is the harmonic mean of the neighboring terms; the term harmonic mean likewise derives from music.

The _____ diverges to infinity, albeit rather slowly (the first 10^{43} terms sum to less than 100 .)

a. BDDC
b. 15 theorem
c. BIBO stability
d. Harmonic series

56. In mathematics, a _____ is a method for approximating the total area underneath a curve on a graph, otherwise known as an integral. It may also be used to define the integration operation.

Consider a function $f: D \to \mathbf{R}$, where D is a subset of the real numbers $\mathbf{R}$, and let $I = [a, b]$ be a closed interval contained in D. A finite set of points $\{x_0, x_1, x_2, \ldots x_n\}$ such that $a = x_0 < x_1 < x_2 \ldots < x_n = b$ creates a partition

$$P = \{[x_0, x_1), [x_1, x_2), \ldots [x_{n-1}, x_n]\}$$

of I.

a. Solid of revolution
b. Riemann sum
c. Risch algorithm
d. Signed measure

57. In mathematics, a _____ or rhodonea curve is a sinusoid plotted in polar coordinates. Up to similarity, these curves can all be expressed by a polar equation of the form

$$r = \cos(k\theta).$$

If k is an integer, the curve will be _____ shaped with

- 2k petals if k is even, and
- k petals if k is odd.

When k is even, the entire graph of the _____ will be traced out exactly once when the value of θ changes from 0 to 2π. When k is odd, this will happen on the interval between 0 and π. (More generally, this will happen on any interval of length 2π for k even, and π for k odd.)

a. Cochleoid
b. Curtate cycloid
c. Space curve
d. Rose

Chapter 8. The Koch Snowflake: Infinite Perimeter?

58. In mathematics, a (topological) _____ is defined as follows: let I be an interval of real numbers (i.e. a non-empty connected subset of $\mathbb{R}$); then a _____ γ is a continuous mapping $\gamma : I \to X$, where X is a topological space. The _____ γ is said to be simple if it is injective, i.e. if for all x, y in I, we have $\gamma(x) = \gamma(y) \implies x = y$. If I is a closed bounded interval $[a, b]$, we also allow the possibility $\gamma(a) = \gamma(b)$ (this convention makes it possible to talk about closed simple _____.)

a. Tractrix
b. Curve
c. Prolate cycloid
d. Closed curve

59. In mathematics, an _____ is an infinite series of the form

$$\sum_{n=0}^{\infty}(-1)^n a_n,$$

with $a_n \geq 0$ (or $a_n \leq 0$) for all n. A finite sum of this kind is an alternating sum. An _____ converges if the terms a_n converge to 0 monotonically.

a. Uniform convergence
b. Infinite series
c. Extreme value
d. Alternating Series

60. The _____ is a method used to prove that infinite series of terms converge. It was discovered by Gottfried Leibniz and is sometimes known as Leibniz's test or the Leibniz criterion.

A series of the form

$$\sum_{n=1}^{\infty}(-1)^n a_n$$

where all the a_n are positive or 0, is called an alternating series.

a. Alternating Series Test
b. Eisenstein series
c. ACTRAN
d. Absolute convergence

61. In mathematics, a series (or sometimes also an integral) is said to converge absolutely if the sum (or integral) of the absolute value of the summand or integrand is finite.

More precisely, a real or complex-valued series $\sum_{n=0}^{\infty} a_n$ is said to converge absolutely if $\sum_{n=0}^{\infty}|a_n| < \infty.$

_____ is vitally important to the study of infinite series because on the one hand, it is strong enough that such series retain certain basic properties of finite sums -- the most important ones being rearrangement of the terms and convergence of products of two infinite series -- that are unfortunately not possessed by all convergent series. On the other hand _____ is weak enough to occur very often in practice.

a. Absolute convergence
b. Alternating series test
c. ACTRAN
d. Eisenstein series

62. The _____ converges:

$$\sum_{k=1}^{\infty} \frac{(-1)^{k+1}}{k} = 1 - \frac{1}{2} + \frac{1}{3} - \frac{1}{4} + \cdots = \ln 2 = 0.693\,147\,180\ldots.$$

This equality is a consequence of the Mercator series, the Taylor series for the natural logarithm. Another equality, similar in form to Mercator's series, is:

$$\sum_{k=0}^{\infty} \frac{(-1)^k}{2k+1} = 1 - \frac{1}{3} + \frac{1}{5} - \frac{1}{7} + \cdots = \arctan(1) = \frac{\pi}{4}.$$

This is a consequence of the Taylor series representation of the inverse tangent function (which has a radius of convergence of 1.)

The nth partial sum of the diverging harmonic series,

$$H_n = \sum_{k=1}^{n} \frac{1}{k},$$

is called the nth harmonic number.

a. ALGOR
b. Alternating Harmonic series
c. AUSM
d. ACTRAN

63. In mathematics, the _____ is a test (or 'criterion') for the convergence of a series

$$\sum_{n=0}^{\infty} a_n$$

whose terms are real or complex numbers. The test was first published by Jean le Rond d'Alembert and is sometimes known as d'Alembert's _____. The test makes use of the number

( )

in the cases where this limit exists.

   a. Converge absolutely
   b. Geometric series
   c. Ratio Test
   d. Telescoping series

64. A _____, $F_{net} = F_1 + F_2 + …$ (also known as a resultant force) is a vector produced when two or more forces { F_1, F_2, … } act upon a single object. It is calculated by vector addition of the force vectors acting upon the object. A _____ can also be defined as the overall force acting on an object, when all the individual forces acting on the object are added together.
   a. BIBO stability
   b. 15 theorem
   c. BDDC
   d. Net force

65. In mathematics, a _____ is a quadric surface of special kind. There are two kinds of paraboloids: elliptic and hyperbolic. The elliptic _____ is shaped like an oval cup and can have a maximum or minimum point.
   a. Torus
   b. PDE surfaces
   c. Hyperbolic paraboloid
   d. Paraboloid

66. _____ is a term in geometry and in everyday life that refers to a property in Euclidean space of two or more lines or planes, or a combination of these. The existence and properties of parallel lines are the basis of Euclid's parallel postulate. Two lines parallel would be denoted as ABC DEF.
   a. Parallelism
   b. 15 theorem
   c. BIBO stability
   d. BDDC

67. In calculus, _____ gives a sequence of approximations of a differentiable function around a given point by polynomials (the Taylor polynomials of that function) whose coefficients depend only on the derivatives of the function at that point. The theorem also gives precise estimates on the size of the error in the approximation. The theorem is named after the mathematician Brook Taylor, who stated it in 1712, though the result was first discovered 41 years earlier in 1671 by James Gregory.
   a. Related rates
   b. Fresnel integrals
   c. Local minimum
   d. Taylor's theorem

68. In vector calculus, the _____ Ostrogradskye;s theorem the _____ states that the outward flux of a vector field through a surface is equal to the triple integral of the divergence on the region inside the surface. Intuitively, it states that the sum of all sources minus the sum of all sinks gives the net flow out of a region.
   a. Green's theorem
   b. Del
   c. Divergence
   d. Divergence Theorem

Chapter 8. The Koch Snowflake: Infinite Perimeter?

69. In the various subfields of physics, there exist two common usages of the term _____, both with rigorous mathematical frameworks.

- In the study of transport phenomena (heat transfer, mass transfer and fluid dynamics), _____ is defined as the amount that flows through a unit area per unit time. _____ in this definition is a vector.
- In the field of electromagnetism and mathematics, _____ is usually the integral of a vector quantity over a finite surface. The result of this integration is a scalar quantity. The magnetic _____ is thus the integral of the magnetic vector field B over a surface, and the electric _____ is defined similarly. Using this definition, the _____ of the Poynting vector over a specified surface is the rate at which electromagnetic energy flows through that surface. Confusingly, the Poynting vector is sometimes called the power _____, which is an example of the first usage of _____, above. It has units of watts per square metre (WÂ·m^{-2})

One could argue, based on the work of James Clerk Maxwell, that the transport definition precedes the more recent way the term is used in electromagnetism. The specific quote from Maxwell is 'In the case of fluxes, we have to take the integral, over a surface, of the _____ through every element of the surface. The result of this operation is called the surface integral of the _____.

a. BDDC
c. Flux
b. 15 theorem
d. BIBO stability

70. In geometry, _____ of a curve is found at a point that is at a distance equal to the radius of curvature lying on the normal vector. It is the point at infinity if the curvature is zero. The osculating circle to the curve is centered at the _____.

a. Center of curvature
c. Strophoid
b. Dolbeault operator
d. Kampyle of Eudoxus

71. In mathematics, a _____ (in one variable) is an infinite series of the form

$$f(x) = \sum_{n=0}^{\infty} a_n (x-c)^n = a_0 + a_1(x-c)^1 + a_2(x-c)^2 + a_3(x-c)^3 + \cdots$$

where a$_n$ represents the coefficient of the nth term, c is a constant, and x varies around c (for this reason one sometimes speaks of the series as being centered at c

In many situations c is equal to zero, for instance when considering a Maclaurin series.

a. Power series
c. Differential coefficient
b. Differential calculus
d. Stationary phase approximation

72. In mathematics, _____ refers to any of a number of loosely related concepts in different areas of geometry. Intuitively, _____ is the amount by which a geometric object deviates from being flat, or straight in the case of a line, but this is defined in different ways depending on the context. There is a key distinction between extrinsic _____, which is defined for objects embedded in another space (usually a Euclidean space) in a way that relates to the radius of _____ of circles that touch the object, and intrinsic _____, which is defined at each point in a differential manifold.

a. Sphere
b. Lie derivative
c. Minimal surface
d. Curvature

73. In mathematics, a _____ is a function whose definition is dependent on the value of the independent variable. Mathematically, a real-valued function f of a real variable x is a relationship whose definition is given differently on disjoint subsets of its domain

The word piecewise is also used to describe any property of a _____ that holds for each piece but may not hold for the whole domain of the function.

a. Constant function
b. Range
c. Surjective
d. Piecewise-defined function

74. In mathematics, the _____ of a power series is a non-negative quantity, either a real number or ∞, that represents a domain (within the radius) in which the series will converge. Within the _____, a power series converges absolutely and uniformly on compacta as well. If the series converges, it is the Taylor series of the analytic function to which it converges inside its _____.

a. Branch point
b. Blaschke product
c. Holomorphically separable
d. Radius of convergence

75. A _____ is a type of manifold that is locally similar enough to Euclidean space to allow one to do calculus Any manifold can be described by a collection of charts, also known as an atlas.

a. Tangent line
b. Sphere
c. Differentiable manifold
d. Minimal surface

76. In mathematics, a _____ is a closed surface of mass M and surface density $\sigma(x,y)$ such that:

$$M = \int \int \sigma(x,y)\,dx\,dy$$

, over the closed surface.

Planar laminas can be used to determine moments of inertia, or center of mass.

a. BDDC
b. 15 theorem
c. Locally integrable function
d. Planar lamina

77. A _____ is a surface in the Euclidean space R^3 which is defined by a parametric equation with two parameters. Parametric representation is the most general way to specify a surface. Surfaces that occur in two of the main theorems of vector calculus, Stokes' theorem and divergence theorem, are frequently given in a parametric form.

a. Torus
b. Prolate
c. Paraboloid
d. Parametric surface

78. Jean Baptiste _____ (March 21, 1768 - May 16, 1830) was a French mathematician and physicist best known for initiating the investigation of Fourier series and their application to problems of heat flow. The Fourier transform is also named in his honour. Fourier is also generally credited with the discovery of the greenhouse effect.

a. Joseph Fourier
b. BIBO stability
c. BDDC
d. 15 theorem

79. In mathematics and physics, a _____ associates a scalar value, which can be either mathematical in definition to every point in space. Scalar fields are often used in physics, for instance to indicate the temperature distribution throughout space or more specifically, differential geometry, the set of functions defined on a manifold define the commutative ring of functions.
   a. Symmetry of second derivatives
   b. Scalar field
   c. Level curve
   d. Vector Laplacian

80. In mathematics, the _____ is a representation of a function as an infinite sum of terms calculated from the values of its derivatives at a single point. It may be regarded as the limit of the Taylor polynomials. If the series is centered at zero, the series is also called a Maclaurin series.
   a. Taylor series
   b. 15 theorem
   c. BIBO stability
   d. BDDC

81. Continuous functions are of utmost importance in mathematics and applications. However, not all functions are continuous. If a function is not continuous at a point in its domain, one says that it has a _____ there. The set of all points of _____ of a function may be a discrete set, a dense set, or even the entire domain of the function.
   a. BDDC
   b. 15 theorem
   c. Vector
   d. Discontinuity

82. In elementary algebra, a _____ is a polynomial with two terms--the sum of two monomials--often bound by parenthesis or brackets when operated upon. It is the simplest kind of polynomial other than monomials.

   - The _____ $a^2 - b^2$ can be factored as the product of two other binomials:

     $a^2 - b^2 = (a + b)(a - b.)$

     This is a special case of the more general formula: $a^{n+1} - b^{n+1} = (a - b) \sum_{k=0}^{n} a^k b^{n-k}$.

   - The product of a pair of linear binomials (ax + b) and (cx + d) is:

     $(ax + b)(cx + d) = acx^2 + axd + bcx + bd.$

   - A _____ raised to the nth power, represented as

     $(a + b)^n$
     can be expanded by means of the _____ theorem or, equivalently, using Pascal's triangle. Taking a simple example, the perfect square _____ $(p + q)^2$ can be found by squaring the :first digit, adding twice the product of the first and second digit and finally adding the square of the second digit, to give $p^2 + 2pq + q^2$.

   a. Completing the square
   b. Partial fractions
   c. Multinomial theorem
   d. Binomial

83. In mathematics, an _____ is a function built from a finite number of exponentials, logarithms, constants, one variable, and nth roots through composition and combinations using the four elementary operations (+ - × ÷.) The trigonometric functions and their inverses are assumed to be included in the elementary functions by using complex variables and the relations between the trigonometric functions and the exponential and logarithm functions.

Elementary functions are considered a subset of special functions.

a. ALGOR
b. ACTRAN
c. AUSM
d. Elementary function

84. In vector calculus, the _____ of a scalar field is a vector field which points in the direction of the greatest rate of increase of the scalar field, and whose magnitude is the greatest rate of change.

A generalization of the _____ for functions on a Euclidean space which have values in another Euclidean space is the Jacobian. A further generalization for a function from one Banach space to another is the Fréchet derivative.

a. Lin-Tsien equation
b. Gradient
c. Symmetric derivative
d. Smooth function

Chapter 9. Conics, Parametric Equations, and Polar Coordinates

1. In geometry, the _____, pronounced , are a pair of special points used in describing conic sections. The four types of conic sections are the circle, parabola, ellipse, and hyperbola.

The focus has two equivalent defining properties; and they always fall on the major axis of symmetry of the conic.

a. BDDC
b. Foci
c. Latus rectum
d. 15 theorem

2. The _____ is the chord parallel to the directrix and passing through the focus (or one of the two foci.)

The semi-_____ (l) is half the _____.

The focal parameter (p) is the distance from the focus (or one of the two foci) to the directrix.

a. Foci
b. Latus rectum
c. 15 theorem
d. BDDC

3. A surface normal to a flat surface is a vector which is perpendicular to that surface. A normal to a non-flat surface at a point P on the surface is a vector perpendicular to the tangent plane to that surface at P. The word 'normal' is also used as an adjective: a line normal to a plane, the normal component of a force, the _____, etc. The concept of normality generalizes to orthogonality.

a. Hyperbolic paraboloid
b. Paraboloid
c. Normal vector
d. Normal line

4. In mathematics, the _____ is a conic section, the intersection of a right circular conical surface and a plane parallel to a generating straight line of that surface. Given a point (the focus) and a line (the directrix) that lie in a plane, the locus of points in that plane that are equidistant to them is a _____.

A particular case arises when the plane is tangent to the conical surface of a circle.

a. 15 theorem
b. BDDC
c. BIBO stability
d. Parabola

5. _____ generally conveys two primary meanings. The first is an imprecise sense of harmonious or aesthetically-pleasing proportionality and balance; such that it reflects beauty or perfection. The second meaning is a precise and well-defined concept of balance or 'patterned self-similarity' that can be demonstrated or proved according to the rules of a formal system: by geometry, through physics or otherwise.

a. BDDC
b. BIBO stability
c. 15 theorem
d. Symmetry

6. In physics, and more specifically kinematics, _____ is the change in velocity over time. Because velocity is a vector, it can change in two ways: a change in magnitude and/or a change in direction. In one dimension, _____ is the rate at which something speeds up or slows down.

a. ACTRAN
b. Acceleration
c. AUSM
d. ALGOR

Chapter 9. Conics, Parametric Equations, and Polar Coordinates 141

7. In mathematics and its applications, a _____ system is a system for assigning an n-tuple of numbers or scalars to each point in an n-dimensional space. This concept is part of the theory of manifolds. 'Scalars' in many cases means real numbers, but, depending on context, can mean complex numbers or elements of some other commutative ring.
   a. Cylindrical coordinate system
   b. Spherical coordinate system
   c. 15 theorem
   d. Coordinate

8. Continuous functions are of utmost importance in mathematics and applications. However, not all functions are continuous. If a function is not continuous at a point in its domain, one says that it has a _____ there. The set of all points of _____ of a function may be a discrete set, a dense set, or even the entire domain of the function.
   a. 15 theorem
   b. BDDC
   c. Vector
   d. Discontinuity

9. In mathematics, an _____, is the apparent shape of a circle viewed obliquely from outside it, as distinct from a hyperbola which is the shape seen from inside. It is the finite or bounded case of a conic section as a shape cut in a cone by a plane, the unbounded cases being the parabola, which like the _____ remains connected, and the hyperbola, which separates into two connected components or branches.

   Equivalently an _____ can be defined as the locus of points, or path traced out, in a plane such that the sum of the distances from the moving point to two fixed points remains constant.

   a. ALGOR
   b. AUSM
   c. ACTRAN
   d. Ellipse

10. In computer science and information science, _____ could also be a method or an algorithm. Again, an example will illustrate: There are systems of counting, as with Roman numerals, and various systems for filing papers, or catalogues, and various library systems, of which the Dewey Decimal _____ is an example. This still fits with the definition of components which are connected together (in this case in order to facilitate the flow of information.)
    a. BDDC
    b. 15 theorem
    c. BIBO stability
    d. System

11. In elementary mathematics, physics, and engineering, a _____ is a geometric object that has both a magnitude (or length), direction and sense, (i.e., orientation along the given direction.) A _____ is frequently represented by a line segment with a definite direction, or graphically as an arrow, connecting an initial point A with a terminal point B, and denoted by

    The magnitude of the _____ is the length of the segment and the direction characterizes the displacement of B relative to A: how much one should move the point A to 'carry' it to the point B.

    Many algebraic operations on real numbers have close analogues for vectors.

    a. BDDC
    b. Linear partial differential operator
    c. 15 theorem
    d. Vector

12. The _____ of a material is defined as its mass per unit volume. The symbol of _____ is ρ '>rho.)

Mathematically:

$$d = \frac{m}{V}$$

where:

        d is the _____,
        m is the mass,
        V is the volume.

a. BDDC
b. BIBO stability
c. 15 theorem
d. Density

13. In mathematics, a probability _____ is a function that represents a probability distribution in terms of integrals.

Formally, a probability distribution has density f, if f is a non-negative Lebesgue-integrable function $\mathbb{R} \rightarrow \mathbb{R}$ such that the probability of the interval [a, b] is given by

$$\int_a^b f(x)\,dx$$

for any two numbers a and b. This implies that the total integral of f must be 1.

a. 15 theorem
b. Factorial moment generating function
c. BDDC
d. Density function

14. _____ is a way of expressing knowledge or belief that an event will occur or has occurred. In mathematics the concept has been given an exact meaning in _____ theory, that is used extensively in such areas of study as mathematics, statistics, finance, gambling, science, and philosophy to draw conclusions about the likelihood of potential events and the underlying mechanics of complex systems.

The word _____ does not have a consistent direct definition.

a. Normal distribution
b. Probability
c. Linear regression
d. Discrete probability distributions

15. In mathematics, a _____ (pdf) is a function that represents a probability distribution in terms of integrals.

Formally, a probability distribution has density f, if f is a non-negative Lebesgue-integrable function $\mathbb{R} \to \mathbb{R}$ such that the probability of the interval [a, b] is given by

$$\int_a^b f(x)\,dx$$

for any two numbers a and b. This implies that the total integral of f must be 1.

a. BDDC
b. 15 theorem
c. Factorial moment generating function
d. Probability density function

16. _____ is any physical or virtual entity that is owned by an individual or jointly by a group of individuals. An owner of _____ has the right to consume, sell, rent, mortgage, transfer and exchange his or her _____. Important widely-recognized types of _____ include real _____, personal _____ (other physical possessions), and intellectual _____ (rights over artistic creations, inventions, etc.), although the latter is not always as widely recognized or enforced.

a. Property
b. 15 theorem
c. BDDC
d. BIBO stability

17. In geometry, _____ of a curve is found at a point that is at a distance equal to the radius of curvature lying on the normal vector. It is the point at infinity if the curvature is zero. The osculating circle to the curve is centered at the _____.

a. Kampyle of Eudoxus
b. Dolbeault operator
c. Strophoid
d. Center of curvature

18. A quantity is said to be subject to _____ if it decreases at a rate proportional to its value. Symbolically, this can be expressed as the following differential equation, where N is the quantity and λ is a positive number called the decay constant.

$$\frac{dN}{dt} = -\lambda N.$$

The solution to this equation is:

$$N(t) = N_0 e^{-\lambda t}.$$

Here N(t) is the quantity at time t, and N_0 = N(0) is the initial quantity, i.e. the quantity at time t = 0.

a. Exponential sum
b. ALGOR
c. ACTRAN
d. Exponential decay

19. The _____ is a function in mathematics. The application of this function to a value x is written as exp(x). Equivalently, this can be written in the form e^x, where e is a mathematical constant, the base of the natural logarithm, which equals approximately 2.718281828, and is also known as Euler's number.

a. ACTRAN
b. Exponential function
c. Integral part
d. Area hyperbolic functions

20. In geometry, the _____ (also semimajor axis) is used to describe the dimensions of ellipses and hyperbolae.

The major axis of an ellipse is its longest diameter, a line that runs through the centre and both foci, its ends being at the widest points of the shape. The _____ is one half of the major axis, and thus runs from the centre, through a focus, and to the edge of the ellipse.

a. BIBO stability
b. 15 theorem
c. Semi-major axis
d. BDDC

21. Let f be a differentiable function, and let f'(x) be its derivative. The derivative of f'(x) (if it has one) is written f''(x) and is called the second derivative of f. Similarly, the derivative of a second derivative, if it exists, is written f'''(x) and is called the _____ of f.

a. Mountain pass theorem
b. Differential coefficient
c. Derivative
d. Third derivative

22. In mathematics, _____ refers to any of a number of loosely related concepts in different areas of geometry. Intuitively, _____ is the amount by which a geometric object deviates from being flat, or straight in the case of a line, but this is defined in different ways depending on the context. There is a key distinction between extrinsic _____, which is defined for objects embedded in another space (usually a Euclidean space) in a way that relates to the radius of _____ of circles that touch the object, and intrinsic _____, which is defined at each point in a differential manifold.

a. Sphere
b. Lie derivative
c. Minimal surface
d. Curvature

23. In calculus, a branch of mathematics, the _____ is a measurement of how a function changes when its input changes. Loosely speaking, a _____ can be thought of as how much a quantity is changing at some given point. For example, the _____ of the position (or distance) of a vehicle with respect to time is the instantaneous velocity (respectively, instantaneous speed) at which the vehicle is traveling.

The process of finding a _____ is called differentiation. The fundamental theorem of calculus states that differentiation is the reverse process to integration.

a. Bounded function
b. Derivative
c. Semi-differentiability
d. Stationary phase approximation

24. _____ was a German mathematician, astronomer and astrologer, and key figure in the 17th century scientific revolution. He is best known for his eponymous laws of planetary motion, codified by later astronomers based on his works Astronomia nova, Harmonices Mundi, and Epitome of Copernican Astrononomy. They also provided one of the foundations for Isaac Newton's theory of universal gravitation.

a. Robin K. Bullough
b. Johannes Kepler
c. Niels Henrik David Bohr
d. MÄ dhava of Sangamagrama

25. An _____ of a real-valued function y = f(x) is a curve which describes the behavior of f as either x or y tends to infinity.

Chapter 9. Conics, Parametric Equations, and Polar Coordinates 145

In other words, as one moves along the graph of f(x) in some direction, the distance between it and the _____ eventually becomes smaller than any distance that one may specify.

a. ALGOR
b. AUSM
c. ACTRAN
d. Asymptote

26. In geometry, the _____ (or simply the tangent) to a curve at a given point is the straight line that 'just touches' the curve at that point (in the sense explained more precisely below.) As it passes through the point of tangency, the _____ is 'going in the same direction' as the curve, and in this sense it is the best straight-line approximation to the curve at that point. The same definition applies to space curves and curves in n-dimensional Euclidean space.

a. North pole
b. Lie derivative
c. Minimal surface
d. Tangent line

27. The largest and the smallest element of a set are called extreme values, absolute extrema, or extreme records.

For a differentiable function f, if $f(x_0)$ is an _____ for the set of all values f(x), and if x_0 is in the interior of the domain of f, then x_0 is a critical point, by Fermat's theorem.

In the case of a general partial order one should not confuse a least element (smaller than all other) and a minimal element (nothing is smaller.)

a. Extreme Value Theorem
b. Extreme Value
c. Integration by substitution
d. Infinitesimal

28. In calculus, the _____ states that if a real-valued function f is continuous in the closed and bounded interval [a,b], then f must attain its maximum and minimum value, each at least once. That is, there exist numbers c and d in [a,b] such that:

$$f(c) \geq f(x) \geq f(d) \quad \text{for all } x \in [a, b].$$

A related theorem is the boundedness theorem which states that a continuous function f in the closed interval [a,b] is bounded on that interval. That is, there exist real numbers m and M such that:

$$m \leq f(x) \leq M \quad \text{for all } x \in [a, b].$$

The _____ enriches the boundedness theorem by saying that not only is the function bounded, but it also attains its least upper bound as its maximum and its greatest lower bound as its minimum.

a. Integral of secant cubed
b. Infinitesimal
c. Uniform convergence
d. Extreme Value Theorem

29. In mathematics, _____ are a method of defining a curve. A simple kinematical example is when one uses a time parameter to determine the position, velocity, and other information about a body in motion.

Abstractly, a relation is given in the form of an equation, and it is shown also to be the image of functions from items such as R^n.

- a. Partial derivative
- b. Critical point
- c. Parametric equations
- d. Shift theorem

30. In mathematics, a _____ is a curve in a Euclidian plane (cf. space curve.) The most frequently studied cases are smooth plane curves (including piecewise smooth plane curves), and algebraic plane curves.
    - a. Vector area
    - b. Gyroid
    - c. Lipschitz domain
    - d. Plane curve

31. In mathematics, a (topological) _____ is defined as follows: let I be an interval of real numbers (i.e. a non-empty connected subset of $\mathbb{R}$); then a _____ γ is a continuous mapping $\gamma : I \to X$, where X is a topological space. The _____ γ is said to be simple if it is injective, i.e. if for all x, y in I, we have $\gamma(x) = \gamma(y) \implies x = y$. If I is a closed bounded interval $[a, b]$, we also allow the possibility $\gamma(a) = \gamma(b)$ (this convention makes it possible to talk about closed simple _____.)
    - a. Prolate cycloid
    - b. Tractrix
    - c. Closed curve
    - d. Curve

32. In mathematics, an _____ on a real vector space is a choice of which ordered bases are 'positively' oriented and which are 'negatively' oriented. In the three-dimensional Euclidean space, the two possible basis orientations are called right-handed and left-handed (or right-chiral and left-chiral), respectively. However, the choice of _____ is independent of the handedness or chirality of the bases (although right-handed bases are typically declared to be positively oriented, they may also be assigned a negative _____.)
    - a. ACTRAN
    - b. Unit vector
    - c. ALGOR
    - d. Orientation

33. In mathematics, a _____ is an ordered list of objects (or events). Like a set, it contains members (also called elements or terms), and the number of terms (possibly infinite) is called the length of the _____. Unlike a set, order matters, and the exact same elements can appear multiple times at different positions in the _____.
    - a. Slope
    - b. Y-intercept
    - c. 15 theorem
    - d. Sequence

34. _____ is a type of motion in which the velocity of an object changes equal amounts in equal time periods. An example of an object having _____ would be a ball rolling down a ramp. The object picks up velocity as it goes down the ramp with equal changes in time.
    - a. Uniform Acceleration
    - b. AUSM
    - c. ACTRAN
    - d. ALGOR

35. In calculus, the indefinite integral of a given function (i.e. the set of all antiderivatives of the function) is always written with a constant, the _____. This constant expresses an ambiguity inherent in the construction of antiderivatives. If a function f(x) is defined on an interval and F(x) is an antiderivative of f(x), then the set of all antiderivatives of f(x) is given by the functions F(x) + C, where C is an arbitrary constant.

Chapter 9. Conics, Parametric Equations, and Polar Coordinates 147

a. Nonelementary integral
c. Disk integration
b. Sum rule in integration
d. Constant of integration

36. A _____ is the curve defined by the path of a point on the edge of circular wheel as the wheel rolls along a straight line. It is an example of a roulette, a curve generated by a curve rolling on another curve.

The _____ is the solution to the brachistochrone problem (i.e. it is the curve of fastest descent under gravity) and the related tautochrone problem (i.e. the period of a ball rolling back and forth inside it does not depend on the ball's starting position.)

a. Tractrix
c. Cycloid
b. Prolate cycloid
d. Curtate cycloid

37. In mathematics, a _____ is a function whose definition is dependent on the value of the independent variable. Mathematically, a real-valued function f of a real variable x is a relationship whose definition is given differently on disjoint subsets of its domain

The word piecewise is also used to describe any property of a _____ that holds for each piece but may not hold for the whole domain of the function.

a. Piecewise-defined function
c. Surjective
b. Constant function
d. Range

38. A _____ is a type of manifold that is locally similar enough to Euclidean space to allow one to do calculus Any manifold can be described by a collection of charts, also known as an atlas.
a. Sphere
c. Tangent line
b. Minimal surface
d. Differentiable manifold

39. A _____ is the curve between two points that is covered in the least time by a body that starts at the first point with zero speed and is constrained to move along the curve to the second point, under the action of constant gravity and assuming no friction.

Given two points A and B, with A not lower than B, there is just one upside down cycloid that passes through A with infinite slope, passes also through B and does not have maximum points between A and B. This particular inverted cycloid is a _____. The curve does not depend on the body's mass or on the strength of the gravitational constant.

a. Space curve
c. Closed curve
b. Prolate cycloid
d. Brachistochrone curve

40. A tautochrone or isochrone curve is the curve for which the time taken by an object sliding without friction in uniform gravity to its lowest point is independent of its starting point. The curve is a cycloid, and the time is equal to >π times the square root of the radius over the acceleration of gravity.

The _____, the attempt to identify this curve, was solved by Christiaan Huygens in 1659. He proved geometrically in his Horologium oscillatorium (The Pendulum Clock, 1673) that the curve was a cycloid. This solution was later used to attack the problem of the brachistochrone curve. Jakob Bernoulli solved the problem using calculus in a paper (Acta Eruditorum, 1690) that saw the first published use of the term integral.

a. Folium of Descartes
b. Hypocycloid
c. Space curve
d. Tautochrone problem

41. Several curves are related to the cycloid. When we relax the requirement that the fixed point be on the edge of the circle, we get the _____ and the prolate cycloid. In the former case, the point tracing out the curve is inside the circle, and, in the latter case, it is outside.

a. Curtate cycloid
b. Prolate cycloid
c. Kappa curve
d. Space curve

42. In geometry, an _____ is a plane curve produced by tracing the path of a chosen point of a circle -- called epicycle -- which rolls without slipping around a fixed circle. It is a particular kind of roulette.

If the smaller circle has radius r, and the larger circle has radius R = kr, then the parametric equations for the curve can be given by either:

$$x(\theta) = (R+r)\cos\theta - r\cos\left(\frac{R+r}{r}\theta\right)$$
$$y(\theta) = (R+r)\sin\theta - r\sin\left(\frac{R+r}{r}\theta\right),$$

or:

$$x(\theta) = r(k+1)\cos\theta - r\cos((k+1)\theta)$$
$$y(\theta) = r(k+1)\sin\theta - r\sin((k+1)\theta).$$

If k is an integer, then the curve is closed, and has k cusps (i.e., sharp corners, where the curve is not differentiable.)

a. Asymptotic curve
b. ALGOR
c. Epicycloid
d. ACTRAN

43. In geometry, a _____ is a special plane curve generated by the trace of a fixed point on a small circle that rolls within a larger circle. It is comparable to the cycloid but instead of the circle rolling along a line, it rolls within a circle. The red curve is a _____ traced as the smaller black circle rolls around inside the larger blue circle (parameters are R=3.0, r=1.0, and so k=3), giving a deltoid.

If the smaller circle has radius r, and the larger circle has radius R = kr, then the parametric equations for the curve can be given by either:

$$x(\theta) = (R-r)\cos\theta + r\cos\left(\frac{R-r}{r}\theta\right)$$
$$y(\theta) = (R-r)\sin\theta - r\sin\left(\frac{R-r}{r}\theta\right),$$

or:

$$x(\theta) = r(k-1)\cos\theta + r\cos((k-1)\theta)$$
$$y(\theta) = r(k-1)\sin\theta - r\sin((k-1)\theta).$$

If k is an integer, then the curve is closed, and has k cusps (i.e., sharp corners, where the curve is not differentiable.)

a. Closed curve
b. Bullet-nose curve
c. Kappa curve
d. Hypocycloid

44. Just as the definite integral of a positive function of one variable represents the area of the region between the graph of the function and the x-axis, the _____ of a positive function of two variables represents the volume of the region between the surface defined by the function (on the three dimensional Cartesian plane where z = f(x,y)) and the plane which contains its domain. (Note that the same volume can be obtained via the triple integral -- the integral of a function in three variables -- of the constant function f(x, y, z) = 1 over the above-mentioned region between the surface and the plane.) If there are more variables, a multiple integral will yield hypervolumes of multi-dimensional functions.

a. Constant of integration
b. Double integral
c. Risch algorithm
d. Trigonometric substitution

45. Integration is an important concept in mathematics, specifically in the field of calculus and, more broadly, mathematical analysis. Given a function f of a real variable x and an interval [a, b] of the real line, the _____

$$\int_a^b f(x)\,dx,$$

is defined informally to be the net signed area of the region in the xy-plane bounded by the graph of f, the x-axis, and the vertical lines x = a and x = b.

The term '_____' may also refer to the notion of antiderivative, a function F whose derivative is the given function f.

a. Integrand
b. Integral
c. Integral test for convergence
d. Indefinite integral

46. A _____ spheroid is a spheroid in which the polar diameter is greater than the equatorial diameter. A _____ spheroid

The _____ spheroid is the shape of the ball in several sports, such as Rugby Football and Australian Rules Football. American Football and Canadian Football use a pointed _____ spheroid (also resembling a rotated vesica piscis.)

a. Parametric surface
b. Hyperbolic paraboloid
c. Prolate
d. Normal vector

47. Several curves are related to the cycloid. When we relax the requirement that the fixed point be on the edge of the circle, we get the curtate cycloid and the _____. In the former case, the point tracing out the curve is inside the circle, and, in the latter case, it is outside.

a. Prolate cycloid
b. Hypocycloid
c. Cassini oval
d. Rose

48. For some curves there is a smallest number L that is an upper bound on the length of any polygonal approximation. If such a number exists, then the curve is said to be rectifiable and the curve is defined to have _____ L.

Let C be a curve in Euclidean (or, generally, a metric) space $X = R^n$, so C is the image of a continuous function f : [a, b] → X of the interval [a, b] into X.

a. Arc length
b. Integrand
c. Integration by parametric derivatives
d. Order of integration

49. In numerical analysis, _____ constitutes a broad family of algorithms for calculating the numerical value of a definite integral, and by extension, the term is also sometimes used to describe the numerical solution of differential equations The term numerical quadrature is more or less a synonym for _____, especially as applied to one-dimensional integrals.

a. Numerical integration
b. Multigrid method
c. Meshfree methods
d. Galerkin methods

50. _____ is the long dimension of any object. The _____ of a thing is the distance between its ends, its linear extent as measured from end to end. This may be distinguished from height, which is vertical extent, and width or breadth, which are the distance from side to side, measuring across the object at right angles to the _____.

a. BIBO stability
b. 15 theorem
c. BDDC
d. Length

51. A _____ is a surface created by rotating a curve lying on some plane (the generatrix) around a straight line (the axis of rotation) that lies on the same plane.

Examples of surfaces generated by a straight line are the cylindrical and conical surfaces. A circle that is rotated about a (coplanar) axis through the center generates a sphere.

Chapter 9. Conics, Parametric Equations, and Polar Coordinates

a. Riemann sum
c. Shell integration

b. Constant of integration
d. Surface of revolution

52. In mathematics, the _____ is a two-dimensional coordinate system in which each point on a plane is determined by an angle and a distance. The _____ is especially useful in situations where the relationship between two points is most easily expressed in terms of angles and distance; in the more familiar Cartesian or rectangular coordinate system, such a relationship can only be found through trigonometric formulation.

As the coordinate system is two-dimensional, each point is determined by two polar coordinates: the radial coordinate and the angular coordinate.

a. Polar coordinate system
c. BDDC

b. BIBO stability
d. 15 theorem

53. In complex analysis, a mathematical discipline, a _____ of a meromorphic function is a certain type of singularity that behaves like the singularity of $\dfrac{1}{z^n}$ at z = 0. This means that, in particular, a _____ of the function f(z) is a point z = a such that f(z) approaches infinity uniformly as z approaches a.

Formally, suppose U is an open subset of the complex plane C, a is an element of U and f : U {a} → C is a function which is holomorphic over its domain.

a. Lacunary function
c. Pole

b. Bieberbach conjecture
d. Complex logarithm

54. In calculus, the _____ allows you to take constants outside a derivative and concentrate on differentiating the function of x itself. This is a part of the linearity of differentiation.

Suppose you have a function

$$g(x) = k \cdot f(x).$$

where k is a constant.

Use the formula for differentiation from first principles to obtain:

$$g'(x) = \lim_{h \to 0} \frac{g(x+h) - g(x)}{h}$$
$$g'(x) = \lim_{h \to 0} \frac{k \cdot f(x+h) - k \cdot f(x)}{h}$$
$$g'(x) = \lim_{h \to 0} \frac{k(f(x+h) - f(x))}{h}$$
$$g'(x) = k \lim_{h \to 0} \frac{f(x+h) - f(x)}{h} \quad (*)$$
$$g'(x) = k \cdot f'(x).$$

This is the statement of the _____, in Lagrange's notation for differentiation.

a. Product rule
b. Reciprocal Rule
c. Quotient Rule
d. Constant factor rule in differentiation

55. In mathematics, a _____ is a function whose values do not vary and thus are constant. For example, if we have the function f(x) = 4, then f is constant since f maps any value to 4. More formally, a function f : A → B is a _____ if f(x) = f(y) for all x and y in A.

a. Piecewise-defined function
b. Surjective
c. Range
d. Constant function

56. A _____ is a surface in the Euclidean space R^3 which is defined by a parametric equation with two parameters. Parametric representation is the most general way to specify a surface. Surfaces that occur in two of the main theorems of vector calculus, Stokes' theorem and divergence theorem, are frequently given in a parametric form.

a. Prolate
b. Paraboloid
c. Torus
d. Parametric surface

57. In mathematics, a _____ or rhodonea curve is a sinusoid plotted in polar coordinates. Up to similarity, these curves can all be expressed by a polar equation of the form

$$r = \cos(k\theta).$$

If k is an integer, the curve will be _____ shaped with

- 2k petals if k is even, and
- k petals if k is odd.

Chapter 9. Conics, Parametric Equations, and Polar Coordinates 153

When k is even, the entire graph of the _____ will be traced out exactly once when the value of θ changes from 0 to 2π. When k is odd, this will happen on the interval between 0 and π. (More generally, this will happen on any interval of length 2π for k even, and π for k odd.)

a. Curtate cycloid
b. Space curve
c. Rose
d. Cochleoid

58. In calculus, the _____ determines whether a given critical point of a function is a maximum, a minimum, or neither.

Suppose that f is a function and we want to determine if f has a maximum or minimum at x. If f is increasing to the left of x and decreasing to the right of x, then x is a local maximum of f.

a. Test for Divergence
b. Continuous function
c. Partial sum
d. First Derivative Test

59. A _____ is closed curve with one cusp.

In geometry, the _____ is an epicycloid with one cusp.

Rolling circle around another fixed circle produces _____ (red curve) Conformal mapping from circle to _____

- epicycloid produced as the path (or locus) of a point on the circumference of a circle as that circle rolls around another fixed circle with the same radius.

- limaçon with one cusp. The cusp is formed when the ratio of a to b in the equation is equal to one.

a. BIBO stability
b. BDDC
c. 15 theorem
d. Cardioid

60. In mathematics, _____ and minima, known collectively as extrema, are the largest value (maximum) or smallest value (minimum), that a function takes in a point either within a given neighbourhood (local extremum) or on the function domain in its entirety (global extremum.)

Throughout, a point refers to an input (x), while a value refers to an output (y): one distinguishing between the maximum value and the point (or points) at which it occurs.

A real-valued function f defined on the real line is said to have a local maximum point at the point x^*, if there exists some ε > 0, such that $f(x^*) \geq f(x)$ when $|x - x^*| < ε$.

a. Leibniz formula
b. Maxima
c. Related rates
d. Racetrack principle

Chapter 9. Conics, Parametric Equations, and Polar Coordinates

61. In calculus, the _____ is a theorem regarding the limit of a function.

The _____ is a technical result which is very important in proofs in calculus and mathematical analysis. It is typically used to confirm the limit of a function via comparison with two other functions whose limits are known or easily computed.

a. Table of limits
b. Limit of a sequence
c. 15 theorem
d. Squeeze Theorem

62. In mathematics, a _____ (or just conic) is a curve obtained by intersecting a cone (more precisely, a circular conical surface) with a plane. A _____ is therefore a restriction of a quadric surface to the plane. The conic sections were named and studied as long ago as 200 BC, when Apollonius of Perga undertook a systematic study of their properties.

a. Latus rectum
b. 15 theorem
c. BDDC
d. Conic section

63. In the two-dimensional case, a _____ perpendicularly intersects the tangent line to a curve at a given point.

The _____ is often used in computer graphics to determine a surface's orientation toward a light source for flat shading, or the orientation of each of the corners (vertices) to mimic a curved surface with Phong shading.

For a polygon (such as a triangle), a surface normal can be calculated as the vector cross product of two (non-parallel) edges of the polygon.

a. PDE surfaces
b. Hyperbolic paraboloid
c. Normal line
d. Parametric surface

64. _____, S(x) and C(x), are two transcendental functions named after Augustin-Jean Fresnel that are used in optics. They arise in the description of near field Fresnel diffraction phenomena, and are defined through the following integral representations:

$$S(x) = \int_0^x \sin(t^2)\, dt, \quad C(x) = \int_0^x \cos(t^2)\, dt.$$

The simultaneous parametric plot of S(x) and C(x) is the Cornu spiral, or clothoid.

Normalised _____, S(x) and C(x).

a. Fresnel integrals
b. Differential
c. First derivative test
d. Leibniz function

65. A _____ is a cubic curve generated by increasing or diminishing the radius vector of a variable point P on a straight line by the distance PA of the point from the foot of the perpendicular drawn from the origin to the fixed line.

The polar equation is

$$r = a\ \cos 2\theta \sec \theta.$$

The Cartesian equation is

$$y^2 = x^2 /,$$

where a is the distance of the line from the origin.

a. Strophoid
c. Macbeath surface
b. Dolbeault operator
d. Kampyle of Eudoxus

1. In mathematics, a _____ (or critical number) is a point on the domain of a function where:

   - one dimension: the derivative (or slope of the line when visualized) is equal to zero or a point where the function ceases to be differentiable.
   - in general: there are two distinct concepts: either the derivative (Jacobian) vanishes, or it is not of full rank (or, in either case, the function is not differentiable); these agree in one dimension.

Note that in one dimension, a critical value or critical number x of function f is the domain element at which the derivative is zero or undefined, whereas the associated ordered pair (x, y) is the _____. In higher dimensions a critical value is in the range whereas a _____ is in the domain.

There are two situations in which a point becomes a _____ of a function of one variable. The first of which is that the value of the first derivative is equal to zero.

   a. Multivariable calculus
   b. Differentiation operator
   c. Total derivative
   d. Critical point

2. A _____ is a reference from which measurements are made. In surveying and geodesy, a datum is a set of reference points on the earth's surface against which position measurements are made, and (often) an associated model of the shape of the earth (reference ellipsoid) to define a geographic coordinate system. Horizontal datums are used for describing a point on the earth's surface, in latitude and longitude or another coordinate system.

   a. BDDC
   b. BIBO stability
   c. 15 theorem
   d. Geodetic datum

3. In mathematics, especially in order theory, an _____ of a subset S of some partially ordered set (P, >≤) is an element of P which is greater than or equal to every element of S. The term lower bound is defined dually as an element of P which is lesser than or equal to every element of S. A set with an _____ is said to be bounded from above by that bound, a set with a lower bound is said to be bounded from below by that bound.

A subset S of a partially ordered set P may fail to have any bounds or may have many different upper and lower bounds. By transitivity, any element greater than or equal to an _____ of S is again an _____ of S, and any element lesser than or equal to any lower bound of S is again a lower bound of S. This leads to the consideration of least upper bounds: (or suprema) and greatest lower bounds (or infima.)

   a. ACTRAN
   b. AUSM
   c. ALGOR
   d. Upper bound

4. In elementary mathematics, physics, and engineering, a _____ is a geometric object that has both a magnitude (or length), direction and sense, (i.e., orientation along the given direction.) A _____ is frequently represented by a line segment with a definite direction, or graphically as an arrow, connecting an initial point A with a terminal point B, and denoted by

$\boxed{x}$.

The magnitude of the _____ is the length of the segment and the direction characterizes the displacement of B relative to A: how much one should move the point A to 'carry' it to the point B.

Many algebraic operations on real numbers have close analogues for vectors.

a. Linear partial differential operator
b. Vector
c. BDDC
d. 15 theorem

5. In physics, and more specifically kinematics, _____ is the change in velocity over time. Because velocity is a vector, it can change in two ways: a change in magnitude and/or a change in direction. In one dimension, _____ is the rate at which something speeds up or slows down.
a. ACTRAN
b. Acceleration
c. ALGOR
d. AUSM

6. Integration is an important concept in mathematics, specifically in the field of calculus and, more broadly, mathematical analysis. Given a function f of a real variable x and an interval [a, b] of the real line, the _____

$$\int_a^b f(x)\,dx,$$

is defined informally to be the net signed area of the region in the xy-plane bounded by the graph of f, the x-axis, and the vertical lines x = a and x = b.

The term '_____' may also refer to the notion of antiderivative, a function F whose derivative is the given function f.

a. Integrand
b. Indefinite integral
c. Integral test for convergence
d. Integral

7. _____ is the long dimension of any object. The _____ of a thing is the distance between its ends, its linear extent as measured from end to end. This may be distinguished from height, which is vertical extent, and width or breadth, which are the distance from side to side, measuring across the object at right angles to the _____.
a. BIBO stability
b. BDDC
c. 15 theorem
d. Length

8. _____ is any physical or virtual entity that is owned by an individual or jointly by a group of individuals. An owner of _____ has the right to consume, sell, rent, mortgage, transfer and exchange his or her _____. Important widely-recognized types of _____ include real _____, personal _____ (other physical possessions), and intellectual _____ (rights over artistic creations, inventions, etc.), although the latter is not always as widely recognized or enforced.
a. 15 theorem
b. BDDC
c. BIBO stability
d. Property

9. In mathematics, a _____ is an ordered list of objects (or events). Like a set, it contains members (also called elements or terms), and the number of terms (possibly infinite) is called the length of the _____. Unlike a set, order matters, and the exact same elements can appear multiple times at different positions in the _____.

a. Slope
c. 15 theorem
b. Sequence
d. Y-intercept

10. In mathematics, a _____ is a definite integral taken over a surface (which may be a curved set in space); it can be thought of as the double integral analog of the line integral. Given a surface, one may integrate over it scalar fields (that is, functions which return numbers as values), and vector fields (that is, functions which return vectors as values.)

Surface integrals have applications in physics, particularly with the classical theory of electromagnetism.

a. Differential operator
c. Surface integral
b. Contact
d. Symmetry of second derivatives

11. In mathematics, a _____ in a normed vector space is a vector (often a spatial vector) whose length is 1 (the unit length.) A _____ is often denoted by a lowercase letter with a superscribed caret or e;hate;, like this: $\hat{\imath}$.

In Euclidean space, the dot product of two unit vectors is simply the cosine of the angle between them.

a. Unit vector
c. Overdetermined
b. ALGOR
d. ACTRAN

12. In linear algebra, the null vector or _____ is the vector (0, 0, â€¦, 0) in Euclidean space, all of whose components are zero. It is usually written $\vec{0}$ or 0 or simply 0. A _____ has no direction.
a. Homogeneous function
c. Zero vector
b. Direction vector
d. Scalar multiplication

13. In mathematics, the _____ of two monic polynomials P and Q over a field k is defined as the product

$$\operatorname{res}(P,Q) = \prod_{(x,y):\, P(x)=0,\, Q(y)=0} (x-y),$$

of the differences of their roots, where x and y take on values in the algebraic closure of k. For non-monic polynomials with leading coefficients p and q, respectively, the above product is multiplied by

$$p^{\deg Q} q^{\deg P}.$$

- The _____ is the determinant of the Sylvester matrix (and of the Bezout matrix.)

- When Q is separable, the above product can be rewritten to

$$\operatorname{res}(P, Q) = \prod_{P(x)=0} Q(x)$$

and this expression remains unchanged if Q is reduced modulo P. Note that, when non-monic, this includes the factor $q^{\deg P}$ but still needs the factor $p^{\deg Q}$.

- Let $P' = P \mod Q$. The above idea can be continued by swapping the roles of P' and Q. However, P' has a set of roots different from that of P. This can be resolved by writing $\prod_{Q(y)=0} P'(y)$ as a determinant again, where P' has leading zero coefficients. This determinant can now be simplified by iterative expansion with respect to the column, where only the leading coefficient q of Q appears.

$$\operatorname{res}(P, Q) = q^{\deg P - \deg P'} \cdot \operatorname{res}(P', Q)$$

Continuing this procedure ends up in a variant of the Euclidean algorithm. This procedure needs quadratic runtime.

a. Resultant
b. Quadratic function
c. Leading coefficient
d. Difference polynomial

14. In mathematics, _____ is one of the basic operations defining a vector space in linear algebra Note that _____ is different from scalar product which is an inner product between two vectors.

More specifically, if K is a field and V is a vector space over K, then _____ is a function from K × V to V. The result of applying this function to c in K and v in V is denoted cv.

a. Vector-valued function
b. Scalar multiplication
c. Direction cosines
d. Homogeneous function

15. In mathematics, _____ are a concept central to linear algebra and related fields of mathematics

Suppose that K is a field and V is a vector space over K. As usual, we call elements of V vectors and call elements of K scalars.

a. Linear combinations
b. 15 theorem
c. Fundamental theorem of algebra
d. Permutation

16. A _____, $F_{net} = F_1 + F_2 + â€¦$ (also known as a resultant force) is a vector produced when two or more forces { F_1, F_2, â€¦ } act upon a single object. It is calculated by vector addition of the force vectors acting upon the object. A _____ can also be defined as the overall force acting on an object, when all the individual forces acting on the object are added together.
   a. Net force
   b. 15 theorem
   c. BDDC
   d. BIBO stability

17. In mathematics and its applications, a _____ system is a system for assigning an n-tuple of numbers or scalars to each point in an n-dimensional space. This concept is part of the theory of manifolds. 'Scalars' in many cases means real numbers, but, depending on context, can mean complex numbers or elements of some other commutative ring.
   a. 15 theorem
   b. Coordinate
   c. Spherical coordinate system
   d. Cylindrical coordinate system

18. Someone who is _____ will prefer to use this hand for everyday activities, such as writing, maintaining personal hygiene, cooking and so forth. According to a variety of studies, anywhere from 70% to 90% of the world population is _____, while most of the remaining are left-handed. A small percentage of the population can use both hands equally well; a person with this ability is deemed to be ambidextrous (though such people may still have a personal preference of one hand over the other.)
   a. BDDC
   b. 15 theorem
   c. BIBO stability
   d. Right-handed

19. _____ generally conveys two primary meanings. The first is an imprecise sense of harmonious or aesthetically-pleasing proportionality and balance; such that it reflects beauty or perfection. The second meaning is a precise and well-defined concept of balance or 'patterned self-similarity' that can be demonstrated or proved according to the rules of a formal system: by geometry, through physics or otherwise.
   a. BDDC
   b. BIBO stability
   c. 15 theorem
   d. Symmetry

20. In mathematics, an _____ on a real vector space is a choice of which ordered bases are 'positively' oriented and which are 'negatively' oriented. In the three-dimensional Euclidean space, the two possible basis orientations are called right-handed and left-handed (or right-chiral and left-chiral), respectively. However, the choice of _____ is independent of the handedness or chirality of the bases (although right-handed bases are typically declared to be positively oriented, they may also be assigned a negative _____.)
   a. ALGOR
   b. Unit vector
   c. ACTRAN
   d. Orientation

21. In computer science and information science, _____ could also be a method or an algorithm. Again, an example will illustrate: There are systems of counting, as with Roman numerals, and various systems for filing papers, or catalogues, and various library systems, of which the Dewey Decimal _____ is an example. This still fits with the definition of components which are connected together (in this case in order to facilitate the flow of information.)
   a. System
   b. 15 theorem
   c. BDDC
   d. BIBO stability

22. In calculus, a branch of mathematics, the _____ is a measurement of how a function changes when its input changes. Loosely speaking, a _____ can be thought of as how much a quantity is changing at some given point. For example, the _____ of the position (or distance) of a vehicle with respect to time is the instantaneous velocity (respectively, instantaneous speed) at which the vehicle is traveling.

The process of finding a _____ is called differentiation. The fundamental theorem of calculus states that differentiation is the reverse process to integration.

- a. Bounded function
- b. Semi-differentiability
- c. Stationary phase approximation
- d. Derivative

23. A _____ is perfectly round geometrical object in three-dimensional space, such as the shape of a round ball. Like a circle in two dimensions, a perfect _____ is completely symmetrical around its center, with all points on the surface lying the same distance r from the center point. This distance r is known as the radius of the _____.

- a. Sphere
- b. Tangent line
- c. North pole
- d. Minimal surface

24. _____ is the tendency of a force to rotate an object about an axis (or fulcrum or pivot.) Just as a force is a push or a pull, a _____ can be thought of as a twist. The symbol for _____ is τ, the Greek letter tau.

- a. BDDC
- b. BIBO stability
- c. 15 theorem
- d. Torque

25. For some curves there is a smallest number L that is an upper bound on the length of any polygonal approximation. If such a number exists, then the curve is said to be rectifiable and the curve is defined to have _____ L.

Let C be a curve in Euclidean (or, generally, a metric) space $X = R^n$, so C is the image of a continuous function $f : [a, b] \to X$ of the interval [a, b] into X.

- a. Integration by parametric derivatives
- b. Arc length
- c. Integrand
- d. Order of integration

26. In mathematics, even functions and odd functions are functions which satisfy particular symmetry relations, with respect to taking additive inverses. They are important in many areas of mathematical analysis, especially the theory of power series and Fourier series. They are named for the parity of the powers of the power functions which satisfy each condition: the function $f(x) = x^n$ is an even function if n is an even integer, and it is an _____ if n is an odd integer.

- a. Integral of secant cubed
- b. Even function
- c. Integration by substitution
- d. Odd function

27. In mathematics, _____ and minima, known collectively as extrema, are the largest value (maximum) or smallest value (minimum), that a function takes in a point either within a given neighbourhood (local extremum) or on the function domain in its entirety (global extremum.)

Throughout, a point refers to an input (x), while a value refers to an output (y): one distinguishing between the maximum value and the point (or points) at which it occurs.

A real-valued function f defined on the real line is said to have a local maximum point at the point x^*, if there exists some $\varepsilon > 0$, such that $f(x^*) \geq f(x)$ when $|x - x^*| < \varepsilon$.

    a. Leibniz formula
    b. Related rates
    c. Racetrack principle
    d. Maxima

28. A _____ is a function that does not satisfy a polynomial equation whose coefficients are themselves polynomials, in contrast to an algebraic function, which does satisfy such an equation. In other words a _____ is a function which 'transcends' algebra in the sense that it cannot be expressed in terms of a finite sequence of the algebraic operations of addition, multiplication, and root extraction.

Examples of transcendental functions include the exponential function, the logarithm, and the trigonometric functions.

    a. 15 theorem
    b. BDDC
    c. BIBO stability
    d. Transcendental function

29. In mathematics, the _____, sometimes called the direct _____ is a criterion for convergence or divergence of a series whose terms are real or complex numbers. The test determines convergence by comparing the terms of the series in question with those of a series whose convergence properties are known.

The _____ states that if the series

$$\sum_{n=1}^{\infty} b_n$$

is an absolutely convergent series and

$$|a_n| \leq |b_n|$$

for sufficiently large n, then the series

$$\sum_{n=1}^{\infty} a_n$$

converges absolutely.

    a. Comparison Test
    b. Ratio test
    c. Conditionally convergent
    d. Telescoping series

30. In mathematics, the _____ is an operation which takes two vectors over the real numbers R and returns a real-valued scalar quantity. It is the standard inner product of the orthonormal Euclidean space. It contrasts with the cross product which produces a vector result.
   a. Vector-valued function
   b. Dot product
   c. Scalar multiplication
   d. Homogeneous function

31. In mathematics, an _____ space is a vector space with the additional structure of _____. This additional structure associates each pair of vectors in the space with a scalar quantity known as the _____ of the vectors. Inner products allow the rigorous introduction of intuitive geometrical notions such as the length of a vector or the angle between two vectors.
   a. ALGOR
   b. ACTRAN
   c. AUSM
   d. Inner product

32. In mathematics, two vectors are _____ if they are perpendicular, i.e., they form a right angle. For example, a subway and the street above, although they do not physically intersect, are _____ if they cross at a right angle.
   a. ACTRAN
   b. Orthogonal
   c. AUSM
   d. ALGOR

33. When a unit vector in space is expressed, with Cartesian notation, as a linear combination of i, j, k, its three scalar components can be referred to as '_____'. The value of each component is equal to the cosine of the angle formed by the unit vector with the respective basis vector. This is one of the methods used to describe the orientation (angular position) of a straight line, segment of straight line, oriented axis, or segment of oriented axis (vector.)
   a. Direction cosines
   b. Scalar multiplication
   c. Vector-valued function
   d. Dot product

34. The _____ of an angle is the ratio of the length of the adjacent side to the length of the hypotenuse. In our case

$$\cos A = \frac{\text{adjacent}}{\text{hypotenuse}} = \frac{b}{h}.$$

The tangent of an angle is the ratio of the length of the opposite side to the length of the adjacent side. In our case

$$\tan A = \frac{\text{opposite}}{\text{adjacent}} = \frac{a}{b}.$$

The remaining three functions are best defined using the above three functions.

   a. Sine integral
   b. Trigonometric functions
   c. Trigonometric
   d. Cosine

35. In mathematics, an _____ is an infinite series of the form

$$\sum_{n=0}^{\infty}(-1)^n a_n,$$

with $a_n \geq 0$ (or $a_n \leq 0$) for all n. A finite sum of this kind is an alternating sum. An _____ converges if the terms a_n converge to 0 monotonically.

a. Uniform convergence
c. Alternating Series

b. Extreme value
d. Infinite series

36. The _____ is a method used to prove that infinite series of terms converge. It was discovered by Gottfried Leibniz and is sometimes known as Leibniz's test or the Leibniz criterion.

A series of the form

$$\sum_{n=1}^{\infty}(-1)^n a_n$$

where all the a_n are positive or 0, is called an alternating series.

a. Absolute convergence
c. Alternating Series Test

b. ACTRAN
d. Eisenstein series

37. In mathematics, the _____ is a binary operation on two vectors in a three-dimensional Euclidean space that results in another vector which is perpendicular to the plane containing the two input vectors. The algebra defined by the _____ is neither commutative nor associative. It contrasts with the dot product which produces a scalar result.

a. Cross product
c. 15 theorem

b. Fundamental theorem of algebra
d. Permutation

38. In mathematics, the _____ is a two-dimensional coordinate system in which each point on a plane is determined by an angle and a distance. The _____ is especially useful in situations where the relationship between two points is most easily expressed in terms of angles and distance; in the more familiar Cartesian or rectangular coordinate system, such a relationship can only be found through trigonometric formulation.

As the coordinate system is two-dimensional, each point is determined by two polar coordinates: the radial coordinate and the angular coordinate.

a. BDDC
c. 15 theorem

b. BIBO stability
d. Polar coordinate system

39. In mathematics, a _____ is a quadric surface of special kind. There are two kinds of paraboloids: elliptic and hyperbolic. The elliptic _____ is shaped like an oval cup and can have a maximum or minimum point.

Chapter 10. Suspension Bridges

a. PDE surfaces

c. Torus

b. Hyperbolic paraboloid

d. Paraboloid

40. In vector calculus, there are two ways of multiplying three vectors together, to make a _____ of vectors. Three vectors defining a parallelepiped

The scalar _____ is defined as the dot product of one of the vectors with the cross product of the other two.

Geometrically, the scalar _____

$$\mathbf{a} \cdot (\mathbf{b} \times \mathbf{c})$$

is the (signed) volume of the parallelepiped defined by the three vectors given.

a. Gradient theorem

c. Divergence

b. Green's theorem

d. Triple product

41. In geometry, a _____ is a three-dimensional figure formed by six parallelograms. It is to a parallelogram as a cube is to a square: Euclidean geometry supports all four notions but affine geometry admits only parallelograms and parallelepipeds. Three equivalent definitions of _____ are

- a polyhedron with six faces (hexahedron), each of which is a parallelogram,
- a hexahedron with three pairs of parallel faces, and
- a prism of which the base is a parallelogram.

The cuboid (six rectangular faces), cube (six square faces), and the rhombohedron (six rhombus faces) are all specific cases of _____.

Parallelepipeds are a subclass of the prismatoids.

a. BDDC

c. Parallelepiped

b. 15 theorem

d. BIBO stability

42. The _____ of any solid, liquid, plasma, vacuum or theoretical object is how much three-dimensional space it occupies, often quantified numerically. One-dimensional figures (such as lines) and two-dimensional shapes (such as squares) are assigned zero _____ in the three-dimensional space. _____ is commonly presented in units such as mL or cm^3 (milliliters or cubic centimeters.)

a. Volume

c. Dirac equation

b. Vector potential

d. Klein-Gordon equation

43. In mathematics, the simplest case of _____ refers to the study of problems in which one seeks to minimize or maximize a real function by systematically choosing the values of real or integer variables from within an allowed set. This (a scalar real valued objective function) is actually a small subset of this field which comprises a large area of applied mathematics and generalizes to study of means to obtain 'best available' values of some objective function given a defined domain where the elaboration is on the types of functions and the conditions and nature of the objects in the problem domain.

The first _____ technique, which is known as steepest descent, goes back to Gauss.

a. AUSM
b. ACTRAN
c. ALGOR
d. Optimization

44. In mathematics, a _____ that describes a line D is any vector

$$\overrightarrow{AB}$$

where A and B are two distinct points on the line D. If v is a _____ for D, so is kv for any nonzero scalar k; and these are in fact all of the direction vectors for the line D. Under some definitions, the _____ is required to be a unit vector, in which case each line has exactly two direction vectors, which are negatives of each other (equal in magnitude, opposite in direction.)

Any line in two-dimensional Euclidean space can be described as the set of solutions to an equation of the form

ax + by + c = 0

where a, b, c are real numbers. Then one _____ of (D) is (− b,a).

a. Dot product
b. Vector-valued function
c. Direction vector
d. Direction cosines

45. The largest and the smallest element of a set are called extreme values, absolute extrema, or extreme records.

For a differentiable function f, if $f(x_0)$ is an _____ for the set of all values f(x), and if x_0 is in the interior of the domain of f, then x_0 is a critical point, by Fermat's theorem.

In the case of a general partial order one should not confuse a least element (smaller than all other) and a minimal element (nothing is smaller.)

a. Integration by substitution
b. Extreme Value Theorem
c. Infinitesimal
d. Extreme Value

46. In calculus, the _____ states that if a real-valued function f is continuous in the closed and bounded interval [a,b], then f must attain its maximum and minimum value, each at least once. That is, there exist numbers c and d in [a,b] such that:

$$f(c) \geq f(x) \geq f(d) \quad \text{for all } x \in [a, b].$$

A related theorem is the boundedness theorem which states that a continuous function f in the closed interval [a,b] is bounded on that interval. That is, there exist real numbers m and M such that:

$$m \leq f(x) \leq M \quad \text{for all } x \in [a, b].$$

The _____ enriches the boundedness theorem by saying that not only is the function bounded, but it also attains its least upper bound as its maximum and its greatest lower bound as its minimum.

a. Extreme Value Theorem
b. Infinitesimal
c. Uniform convergence
d. Integral of secant cubed

47. In calculus, _____, was originally the use of expressions such as dx and dy and to represent 'infinitely small' (or infinitesimal) increments of quantities x and y, just as >Δx and >Δy represent finite increments of x and y respectively. So for y being a function of x, or

the derivative of y with respect to x, which later came to be viewed as

was, according to Leibniz, the quotient of an infinitesimal increment of y by an infinitesimal increment of x, or

where the right hand side is Lagrange's notation for the derivative of f at x.

Similarly, although mathematicians usually now view an integral

as a limit

where >Δx is an interval containing x_i, Leibniz viewed it as the sum (the integral sign denoting summation) of infinitely many infinitesimal quantities f(x) dx.

a. Time derivative
b. Stationary point
c. Smooth function
d. Leibniz's notation

48. In mathematics, _____ are a method of defining a curve. A simple kinematical example is when one uses a time parameter to determine the position, velocity, and other information about a body in motion.

Abstractly, a relation is given in the form of an equation, and it is shown also to be the image of functions from items such as R^n.

a. Partial derivative
b. Shift theorem
c. Critical point
d. Parametric equations

49. A _____ officer is an officer of high military rank. The term or equivalent is used by nearly every country in the world. _____ can be used as a generic term for all grades of _____ officer, or it can specifically refer to a single rank that is just called _____.

a. 15 theorem
b. BDDC
c. BIBO stability
d. General

50. A _____ is a type of map characterized by large-scale detail and quantitative representation of relief, usually using contour lines in modern mapping, but historically using a variety of methods. Traditional definitions require a _____ to show both natural and man-made features.

The Canadian Centre for Topographic Information provides this definition of a _____:

Other authors define topographic maps by contrasting them with another type of map; they are distinguished from smaller-scale 'chorographic maps' that cover large regions, 'planimetric maps' that do not show elevations, and 'thematic maps' that focus on specific topics.

a. Topographic map
b. BIBO stability
c. 15 theorem
d. BDDC

51. A surface normal to a flat surface is a vector which is perpendicular to that surface. A normal to a non-flat surface at a point P on the surface is a vector perpendicular to the tangent plane to that surface at P. The word 'normal' is also used as an adjective: a line normal to a plane, the normal component of a force, the _____, etc. The concept of normality generalizes to orthogonality.

a. Normal vector
b. Normal line
c. Paraboloid
d. Hyperbolic paraboloid

52. _____ is a term in geometry and in everyday life that refers to a property in Euclidean space of two or more lines or planes, or a combination of these. The existence and properties of parallel lines are the basis of Euclid's parallel postulate. Two lines parallel would be denoted as ABC DEF.

a. 15 theorem
b. BIBO stability
c. BDDC
d. Parallelism

53. In mathematics, the _____ of a function is the set of all 'output' values produced by that function. Sometimes it is called the image, or more precisely, the image of the domain of the function. If a function is a surjection then its _____ is equal to its codomain.
   a. Constant function
   b. Piecewise-defined function
   c. Surjective
   d. Range

54. In infinitesimal calculus, a _____ is traditionally an infinitesimally small change in a variable. For example, if x is a variable, then a change in the value of x is often denoted Δx (or δx when this change is considered to be small.) The _____ dx represents such a change, but is infinitely small.
   a. Differential
   b. Dirichlet integral
   c. The Method of Mechanical Theorems
   d. Local maximum

55. The _____ of a material is defined as its mass per unit volume. The symbol of _____ is ρ '>rho.)

Mathematically:

$$d = \frac{m}{V}$$

where:

   d is the _____,
   m is the mass,
   V is the volume.

   a. 15 theorem
   b. BIBO stability
   c. BDDC
   d. Density

56. In mathematics, a probability _____ is a function that represents a probability distribution in terms of integrals.

Formally, a probability distribution has density f, if f is a non-negative Lebesgue-integrable function $\mathbb{R} \to \mathbb{R}$ such that the probability of the interval [a, b] is given by

$$\int_a^b f(x)\,dx$$

for any two numbers a and b. This implies that the total integral of f must be 1.

   a. BDDC
   b. 15 theorem
   c. Factorial moment generating function
   d. Density function

57. A _____ is one of the most curvilinear basic geometric shapes:It has two faces, zero vertices, and zero edges. The surface formed by the points at a fixed distance from a given straight line, the axis of the _____. The solid enclosed by this surface and by two planes perpendicular to the axis is also called a _____.

a. 15 theorem
b. BDDC
c. Right circular cylinder
d. Cylinder

58. A _____ is a lens which focuses light which passes through onto a line instead of onto a point, as a spherical lens would. The curved face or faces of a _____ are sections of a cylinder, and focus the image passing through it onto a line parallel to the intersection of the surface of the lens and a plane tangent to it. The lens compresses the image in the direction perpendicular to this line, and leaves it unaltered in the direction parallel to it (in the tangent plane.)

a. BDDC
b. 15 theorem
c. BIBO stability
d. Cylindrical lens

59. In mathematics, a (topological) _____ is defined as follows: let I be an interval of real numbers (i.e. a non-empty connected subset of $\mathbb{R}$); then a _____ γ is a continuous mapping $\gamma : I \to X$, where X is a topological space. The _____ γ is said to be simple if it is injective, i.e. if for all x, y in I, we have $\gamma(x) = \gamma(y) \implies x = y$. If I is a closed bounded interval $[a, b]$, we also allow the possibility $\gamma(a) = \gamma(b)$ (this convention makes it possible to talk about closed simple _____.)

a. Closed curve
b. Tractrix
c. Curve
d. Prolate cycloid

60. An _____ is a type of quadric surface that is a higher dimensional analogue of an ellipse. The equation of a standard axis-aligned _____ body in an xyz-Cartesian coordinate system is

$$\frac{x^2}{a^2} + \frac{y^2}{b^2} + \frac{z^2}{c^2} = 1$$

where a and b are the equatorial radii (along the x and y axes) and c is the polar radius (along the z-axis), all of which are fixed positive real numbers determining the shape of the _____.

More generally, a not-necessarily-axis-aligned _____ is defined by the equation

$$\mathbf{x}^T A \mathbf{x} = 1$$

where A is a symmetric positive definite matrix and x is a vector.

a. ACTRAN
b. Ellipsoid
c. AUSM
d. ALGOR

61. The _____ is a doubly ruled surface shaped like a saddle. In a suitable coordinate system, it can be represented by the equation

$$z = \frac{x^2}{a^2} - \frac{y^2}{b^2}.$$

This is a _____ that opens up along the x-axis and down along the y-axis.

Paraboloid of revolution

With a = b an elliptic paraboloid is a paraboloid of revolution: a surface obtained by revolving a parabola around its axis.

a. Paraboloid
b. Parametric surface
c. Torus
d. Hyperbolic paraboloid

62. _____ (including exponential decay) occurs when the growth rate of a mathematical function is proportional to the function's current value. In the case of a discrete domain of definition with equal intervals it is also called geometric growth or geometric decay (the function values form a geometric progression.)

_____ is said to follow an exponential law; the simple-_____ model is known as the Malthusian growth model.

a. Oscillating
b. Isomonodromic deformation
c. Inseparable differential equation
d. Exponential growth

63. A _____ is a surface created by rotating a curve lying on some plane (the generatrix) around a straight line (the axis of rotation) that lies on the same plane.

Examples of surfaces generated by a straight line are the cylindrical and conical surfaces. A circle that is rotated about a (coplanar) axis through the center generates a sphere.

a. Shell integration
b. Surface of revolution
c. Riemann sum
d. Constant of integration

64. _____ is a type of motion in which the velocity of an object changes equal amounts in equal time periods. An example of an object having _____ would be a ball rolling down a ramp. The object picks up velocity as it goes down the ramp with equal changes in time.

a. AUSM
b. Uniform Acceleration
c. ACTRAN
d. ALGOR

65. In calculus, the indefinite integral of a given function (i.e. the set of all antiderivatives of the function) is always written with a constant, the _____. This constant expresses an ambiguity inherent in the construction of antiderivatives. If a function f(x) is defined on an interval and F(x) is an antiderivative of f(x), then the set of all antiderivatives of f(x) is given by the functions F(x) + C, where C is an arbitrary constant.

a. Disk integration
b. Nonelementary integral
c. Sum rule in integration
d. Constant of integration

66. The _____ is a three-dimensional coordinate system which essentially extends circular polar coordinates by adding a third coordinate (usually denoted z) which measures the height of a point above the plane.

The notation for this coordinate system is not uniform. The Standard ISO 31-11 establishes them as (ρ, φ, z).

a. 15 theorem
c. Coordinate
b. Spherical coordinate system
d. Cylindrical coordinate system

67. In complex analysis, a mathematical discipline, a _____ of a meromorphic function is a certain type of singularity that behaves like the singularity of $\dfrac{1}{z^n}$ at z = 0. This means that, in particular, a _____ of the function f(z) is a point z = a such that f(z) approaches infinity uniformly as z approaches a.

Formally, suppose U is an open subset of the complex plane C, a is an element of U and f : U {a} → C is a function which is holomorphic over its domain.

a. Complex logarithm
c. Lacunary function
b. Pole
d. Bieberbach conjecture

68. In calculus, the _____ allows you to take constants outside a derivative and concentrate on differentiating the function of x itself. This is a part of the linearity of differentiation.

Suppose you have a function

$$g(x) = k \cdot f(x).$$

where k is a constant.

Use the formula for differentiation from first principles to obtain:

$$g'(x) = \lim_{h \to 0} \frac{g(x+h) - g(x)}{h}$$
$$g'(x) = \lim_{h \to 0} \frac{k \cdot f(x+h) - k \cdot f(x)}{h}$$
$$g'(x) = \lim_{h \to 0} \frac{k(f(x+h) - f(x))}{h}$$
$$g'(x) = k \lim_{h \to 0} \frac{f(x+h) - f(x)}{h} \quad (*)$$
$$g'(x) = k \cdot f'(x).$$

This is the statement of the _____, in Lagrange's notation for differentiation.

a. Product rule
b. Quotient Rule
c. Reciprocal Rule
d. Constant factor rule in differentiation

69. _____ is called the proportionality constant or _____.

- If an object travels at a constant speed, then the distance traveled is proportional to the time spent travelling, with the speed being the _____.

- The circumference of a circle is proportional to its diameter, with the _____ equal to π.

- On a map drawn to scale, the distance between any two points on the map is proportional to the distance between the two locations that the points represent, with the _____ being the scale of the map.

- The force acting on a certain object due to gravity is proportional to the object's mass; the _____ between the the mass and the force is known as gravitational acceleration.

Since

$$y = kx$$

is equivalent to

$$x = \left(\frac{1}{k}\right)y,$$

it follows that if y is proportional to x, with (nonzero) proportionality constant k, then x is also proportional to y with proportionality constant 1/k.

If y is proportional to x, then the graph of y as a function of x will be a straight line passing through the origin with the slope of the line equal to the _____: it corresponds to linear growth.

a. 15 theorem
b. BDDC
c. Reduction
d. Constant of proportionality

70. If a particular point on a sphere is (arbitrarily) designated as its _____, then the corresponding antipodal point is called the south pole and the equator is the great circle that is equidistant to them. Great circles through the two poles are called lines (or meridians) of longitude, and the line connecting the two poles is called the axis of rotation. Circles on the sphere that are parallel to the equator are lines of latitude.

a. Minimal surface
b. Sphere
c. Tangent line
d. North pole

71. In mathematics, the _____ is a coordinate system for representing geometric figures in three dimensions using three coordinates: the radial distance of a point from a fixed origin, the zenith angle from the positive z-axis to the point, and the azimuth angle from the positive x-axis to the orthogonal projection of the point in the x-y plane.

Several different conventions exist for representing the three coordinates. In accordance with the International Organisation for Standardisation (ISO 31-11), in physics they are typically notated as (r, θ, φ) for radial distance, zenith, and azimuth, respectively.

a. Spherical coordinate system
c. Coordinate

b. 15 theorem
d. Cylindrical coordinate system

Chapter 11. Race Car Cornering

1. A plane curve is a curve for which X is the Euclidean plane -- these are the examples first encountered -- or in some cases the projective plane. A _____ is a curve for which X is of three dimensions, usually Euclidean space; a skew curve is a _____ which lies in no plane. These definitions also apply to algebraic curves
   a. Folium of Descartes
   b. Hypocycloid
   c. Curtate cycloid
   d. Space curve

2. A _____ is a mathematical function that maps real numbers to vectors. Vector-valued functions can be defined as:

   - $\mathbf{r}(t) = f(t)\hat{\mathbf{i}} + g(t)\hat{\mathbf{j}}$ or
   - $\mathbf{r}(t) = f(t)\hat{\mathbf{i}} + g(t)\hat{\mathbf{j}} + h(t)\hat{\mathbf{k}}$

   where f(t), g(t) and h(t) are the coordinate functions of the parameter t, and $\hat{\mathbf{i}}$, $\hat{\mathbf{j}}$, and $\hat{\mathbf{k}}$ are unit vectors. r(t) is a vector which has its tail at the origin and its head at the coordinates evaluated by the function.

   The vector shown in the graph to the right is the evaluation of the function near t=19.5 (between 6π and 6.5π; i.e., somewhat more than 3 rotations.)

   a. Vector-valued function
   b. Direction vector
   c. Scalar multiplication
   d. Direction cosines

3. In mathematics, a (topological) _____ is defined as follows: let I be an interval of real numbers (i.e. a non-empty connected subset of $\mathbb{R}$); then a _____ γ is a continuous mapping $\gamma : I \to X$, where X is a topological space. The _____ γ is said to be simple if it is injective, i.e. if for all x, y in I, we have $\gamma(x) = \gamma(y) \implies x = y$. If I is a closed bounded interval $[a, b]$, we also allow the possibility $\gamma(a) = \gamma(b)$ (this convention makes it possible to talk about closed simple _____.)
   a. Tractrix
   b. Prolate cycloid
   c. Closed curve
   d. Curve

4. In calculus, a branch of mathematics, the _____ is a measurement of how a function changes when its input changes. Loosely speaking, a _____ can be thought of as how much a quantity is changing at some given point. For example, the _____ of the position (or distance) of a vehicle with respect to time is the instantaneous velocity (respectively, instantaneous speed) at which the vehicle is traveling.

   The process of finding a _____ is called differentiation. The fundamental theorem of calculus states that differentiation is the reverse process to integration.

   a. Stationary phase approximation
   b. Bounded function
   c. Semi-differentiability
   d. Derivative

5. A _____ is a special kind of space curve, i.e. a smooth curve in three-space. As a mental image of a _____ one may take the spring (although the spring is not a curve, and so is technically not a _____, it does give a convenient mental picture.) A _____ is characterised by the fact that the tangent line at any point makes a constant angle with a fixed line.

a. BIBO stability
c. 15 theorem

b. BDDC
d. Helix

6. In mathematics, the _____ (or replacement set) of a given function is the set of 'input' values for which the function is defined. For instance, the _____ of cosine would be all real numbers, while the _____ of the square root would be only numbers greater than or equal to 0 (ignoring complex numbers in both cases.) In a representation of a function in a xy Cartesian coordinate system, the _____ is represented on the x axis (or abscissa.)

a. Domain
c. BIBO stability

b. BDDC
d. 15 theorem

7. For the largest k where $a_k \neq 0$, a_k is called the _____ of P because most often, polynomials are written starting from the left with the largest power of x. So for example the _____ of the polynomial

$$4x^5 + x^3 + 2x^2$$

is 4.

The coefficients of polynomial also may be in the other order:

$$Q(x) = a_0 x^k + a_1 x^{k-1} + \cdots + a_{k-1} x^1 + a_k$$

and must be $a_0 \neq 0$ and a_0 is the _____ of Q.

a. Discriminant
c. Resultant

b. Symmetric function
d. Leading coefficient

8. In mathematics, a _____ is a constant multiplicative factor of a certain object. For example, in the expression $9x^2$, the _____ of x^2 is 9.

The object can be such things as a variable, a vector, a function, etc.

a. Coefficient
c. Degree of the polynomial

b. Resultant
d. Binomial type

9. In mathematics, the concept of a '_____' is used to describe the behavior of a function as its argument or input either 'gets close' to some point, or as the argument becomes arbitrarily large; or the behavior of a sequence's elements as their index increases indefinitely. Limits are used in calculus and other branches of mathematical analysis to define derivatives and continuity.

In formulas, _____ is usually abbreviated as lim

a. BDDC
c. BIBO stability

b. 15 theorem
d. Limit

10. In vector calculus, the _____ of a scalar field is a vector field which points in the direction of the greatest rate of increase of the scalar field, and whose magnitude is the greatest rate of change.

A generalization of the _____ for functions on a Euclidean space which have values in another Euclidean space is the Jacobian. A further generalization for a function from one Banach space to another is the Fréchet derivative.

a. Gradient
b. Symmetric derivative
c. Smooth function
d. Lin-Tsien equation

11. In metric topology and related fields of mathematics, a set U is called _____ if, intuitively speaking, starting from any point x in U one can move by a small amount in any direction and still be in the set U. In other words, the distance between any point x in U and the edge of U is always greater than zero.

As an example, consider the _____ interval (0, 1) consisting of all real numbers x with 0 < x < 1. Here, the topology is the usual topology on the real line. We can look at this in two ways.

a. Open
b. AUSM
c. ALGOR
d. ACTRAN

12. In mathematics, the _____ , is the curve defined as follows.

Starting with a fixed circle, a point O on the circle is chosen. For any other point A on the circle, the secant line OA is drawn. The point M is diametrically opposite O. The line OA intersects the tangent at M at the point N. The line parallel to OM through N, and the line perpendicular to OM through A intersect at P. As the point A is varied, the path of P is the witch.

a. Cochleoid
b. Closed curve
c. Folium of Descartes
d. Witch of Agnesi

13. In a totally ordered set all elements are mutually comparable, so such a set can have at most one minimal element and at most one maximal element. Then, due to mutual comparability, the minimal element will also be the least element and the maximal element will also be the greatest element. Thus in a totally ordered set we can simply use the terms minimum and _____ .

a. Leibniz rule
b. Nth term
c. Racetrack principle
d. Maximum

14. In calculus, the _____ is a formula for the derivative of the composite of two functions.

In intuitive terms, if a variable, y, depends on a second variable, u, which in turn depends on a third variable, x, then the rate of change of y with respect to x can be computed as the rate of change of y with respect to u multiplied by the rate of change of u with respect to x. Schematically,

$$\frac{dy}{dx} = \frac{dy}{du} \cdot \frac{du}{dx}.$$

a. Product rule
b. Reciprocal Rule
c. Chain Rule
d. Differentiation rules

15. Continuous functions are of utmost importance in mathematics and applications. However, not all functions are continuous. If a function is not continuous at a point in its domain, one says that it has a _____ there. The set of all points of _____ of a function may be a discrete set, a dense set, or even the entire domain of the function.

a. BDDC
b. Vector
c. 15 theorem
d. Discontinuity

16. _____ is a type of motion in which the velocity of an object changes equal amounts in equal time periods. An example of an object having _____ would be a ball rolling down a ramp. The object picks up velocity as it goes down the ramp with equal changes in time.

a. ACTRAN
b. AUSM
c. Uniform Acceleration
d. ALGOR

17. In calculus, the indefinite integral of a given function (i.e. the set of all antiderivatives of the function) is always written with a constant, the _____. This constant expresses an ambiguity inherent in the construction of antiderivatives. If a function f(x) is defined on an interval and F(x) is an antiderivative of f(x), then the set of all antiderivatives of f(x) is given by the functions F(x) + C, where C is an arbitrary constant.

a. Disk integration
b. Sum rule in integration
c. Nonelementary integral
d. Constant of integration

18. _____, the behaviour of a linear autonomous system around a critical point is a _____ if the following conditions are satisifed:

Each path converges to the critical as $t \to \infty$ (or as $t \to -\infty$.) Furthermore, each path approaches the point asymptotically through a line.

a. Frobenius method
b. Laser diode rate equations
c. Growth curve
d. Node

19. In mathematics, the _____ is a two-dimensional coordinate system in which each point on a plane is determined by an angle and a distance. The _____ is especially useful in situations where the relationship between two points is most easily expressed in terms of angles and distance; in the more familiar Cartesian or rectangular coordinate system, such a relationship can only be found through trigonometric formulation.

As the coordinate system is two-dimensional, each point is determined by two polar coordinates: the radial coordinate and the angular coordinate.

a. BDDC
c. 15 theorem
b. BIBO stability
d. Polar coordinate system

20. A _____ is a type of manifold that is locally similar enough to Euclidean space to allow one to do calculus Any manifold can be described by a collection of charts, also known as an atlas.
  a. Sphere
  b. Tangent line
  c. Minimal surface
  d. Differentiable manifold

21. In mathematics and its applications, a _____ system is a system for assigning an n-tuple of numbers or scalars to each point in an n-dimensional space. This concept is part of the theory of manifolds. 'Scalars' in many cases means real numbers, but, depending on context, can mean complex numbers or elements of some other commutative ring.
  a. 15 theorem
  b. Spherical coordinate system
  c. Cylindrical coordinate system
  d. Coordinate

22. In calculus, an antiderivative, primitive or _____ of a function f is a function F whose derivative is equal to f, i.e., F ′ = f. The process of solving for antiderivatives is antidifferentiation (or indefinite integration.) Antiderivatives are related to definite integrals through the fundamental theorem of calculus: the definite integral of a function over an interval is equal to the difference between the values of an antiderivative evaluated at the endpoints of the interval.
  a. Arc length
  b. Indefinite integral
  c. Integration by parts operator
  d. Integral test for convergence

23. In mathematics, in the field of differential equations, an initial value problem is an ordinary differential equation together with specified value, called the _____, of the unknown function at a given point in the domain of the solution. In physics or other sciences, modeling a system frequently amounts to solving an initial value problem; in this context, the differential equation is an evolution equation specifying how, given initial conditions, the system will evolve with time.

An initial value problem is a differential equation

$$y'(t) = f(t, y(t)) \quad \text{with} \quad f : \mathbb{R} \times \mathbb{R} \to \mathbb{R}$$

together with a point in the domain of f

$$(t_0, y_0) \in \mathbb{R} \times \mathbb{R},$$

called the _____.

  a. ALGOR
  b. Initial condition
  c. ACTRAN
  d. AUSM

24. Integration is an important concept in mathematics, specifically in the field of calculus and, more broadly, mathematical analysis. Given a function f of a real variable x and an interval [a, b] of the real line, the _____

$$\int_a^b f(x)\,dx,$$

is defined informally to be the net signed area of the region in the xy-plane bounded by the graph of f, the x-axis, and the vertical lines x = a and x = b.

The term '_____' may also refer to the notion of antiderivative, a function F whose derivative is the given function f.

a. Integrand
b. Indefinite integral
c. Integral test for convergence
d. Integral

25. In mathematics, even functions and odd functions are functions which satisfy particular symmetry relations, with respect to taking additive inverses. They are important in many areas of mathematical analysis, especially the theory of power series and Fourier series. They are named for the parity of the powers of the power functions which satisfy each condition: the function f(x) = x^n is an even function if n is an even integer, and it is an _____ if n is an odd integer.
  a. Even function
  b. Integration by substitution
  c. Odd function
  d. Integral of secant cubed

26. In geometry, the _____ (or simply the tangent) to a curve at a given point is the straight line that 'just touches' the curve at that point (in the sense explained more precisely below.) As it passes through the point of tangency, the _____ is 'going in the same direction' as the curve, and in this sense it is the best straight-line approximation to the curve at that point. The same definition applies to space curves and curves in n-dimensional Euclidean space.
  a. North pole
  b. Minimal surface
  c. Tangent line
  d. Lie derivative

27. In elementary mathematics, physics, and engineering, a _____ is a geometric object that has both a magnitude (or length), direction and sense, (i.e., orientation along the given direction.) A _____ is frequently represented by a line segment with a definite direction, or graphically as an arrow, connecting an initial point A with a terminal point B, and denoted by

The magnitude of the _____ is the length of the segment and the direction characterizes the displacement of B relative to A: how much one should move the point A to 'carry' it to the point B.

Many algebraic operations on real numbers have close analogues for vectors.

  a. 15 theorem
  b. Linear partial differential operator
  c. BDDC
  d. Vector

28. In physics, _____ is defined as the rate of change of position. it is vector physical quantity; both speed and direction are required to define it. In the SI (metric) system, it is measured in meters per second: (m/s) or ms^{-1}.

a. BIBO stability
b. Velocity
c. 15 theorem
d. BDDC

29. In physics, and more specifically kinematics, _____ is the change in velocity over time. Because velocity is a vector, it can change in two ways: a change in magnitude and/or a change in direction. In one dimension, _____ is the rate at which something speeds up or slows down.
   a. Acceleration
   b. ALGOR
   c. AUSM
   d. ACTRAN

30. In mathematics, _____ and minima, known collectively as extrema, are the largest value (maximum) or smallest value (minimum), that a function takes in a point either within a given neighbourhood (local extremum) or on the function domain in its entirety (global extremum.)

Throughout, a point refers to an input (x), while a value refers to an output (y): one distinguishing between the maximum value and the point (or points) at which it occurs.

A real-valued function f defined on the real line is said to have a local maximum point at the point x^*, if there exists some $\varepsilon > 0$, such that $f(x^*) \geq f(x)$ when $|x - x^*| < \varepsilon$.

   a. Leibniz formula
   b. Racetrack principle
   c. Related rates
   d. Maxima

31. The first Frenet vector $e_1(t)$ is the _____ in the same direction, defined at each regular point of γ:

$$\mathbf{e}_1(t) = \frac{\gamma'(t)}{\|\gamma'(t)\|}.$$

If t = s is the natural parameter then the tangent vector has unit length, so that the formula simplifies:

$$\mathbf{e}_1(s) = \gamma'(s).$$

The _____ determines the orientation of the curve, or the forward direction, corresponding to the increasing values of the parameter.

The normal vector, sometimes called the curvature vector, indicates the deviance of the curve from being a straight line.

It is defined as

$$\overline{\mathbf{e}_2}(t) = \gamma''(t) - \langle \gamma''(t), \mathbf{e}_1(t) \rangle \mathbf{e}_1(t).$$

Its normalized form, the unit normal vector, is the second Frenet vector $e_2(t)$ and defined as

$$\mathbf{e}_2(t) = \frac{\overline{\mathbf{e}_2}(t)}{\|\overline{\mathbf{e}_2}(t)\|}.$$

The tangent and the normal vector at point t define the osculating plane at point t.

a. Unit tangent vector
b. Isothermal coordinates
c. ACTRAN
d. Invariant differential operator

32. The concept of _____ in mathematics evolved from the concept of _____ in physics. The nth _____ of a real-valued function f(x) of a real variable about a value c is

$$\mu'_n = \int_{-\infty}^{\infty} (x - c)^n f(x)\, dx.$$

It is possible to define moments for random variables in a more general fashion than moments for real values. See Moments in metric spaces.

a. Geometric mean
b. Median
c. Poisson distribution
d. Moment

33. A surface normal to a flat surface is a vector which is perpendicular to that surface. A normal to a non-flat surface at a point P on the surface is a vector perpendicular to the tangent plane to that surface at P. The word 'normal' is also used as an adjective: a line normal to a plane, the normal component of a force, the _____, etc. The concept of normality generalizes to orthogonality.

a. Paraboloid
b. Normal line
c. Hyperbolic paraboloid
d. Normal vector

34. Trigonometry is a branch of mathematics that deals with triangles, particularly those plane triangles in which one angle has 90 degrees (right triangles.) Trigonometry deals with relationships between the sides and the angles of triangles and with the _____ functions, which describe those relationships.

Trigonometry has applications in both pure mathematics and in applied mathematics, where it is essential in many branches of science and technology.

a. Trigonometric functions
b. Trigonometric integrals
c. Sine
d. Trigonometric

35. In mathematics, the _____ are functions of an angle. They are important in the study of triangles and modeling periodic phenomena, among many other applications. _____ are commonly defined as ratios of two sides of a right triangle containing the angle, and can equivalently be defined as the lengths of various line segments from a unit circle.

a. Sine integral
b. Trigonometric integrals
c. Trigonometric functions
d. Trigonometric

36. In mathematics, a _____ in a normed vector space is a vector (often a spatial vector) whose length is 1 (the unit length.) A _____ is often denoted by a lowercase letter with a superscribed caret or e;hate;, like this: $\hat{\imath}$.

In Euclidean space, the dot product of two unit vectors is simply the cosine of the angle between them.

a. ACTRAN
b. ALGOR
c. Overdetermined
d. Unit vector

37. In mathematics, a _____ is a function which preserves the given order. This concept first arose in calculus, and was later generalized to the more abstract setting of order theory.

In calculus, a function f defined on a subset of the real numbers with real values is called monotonic (also monotonically increasing or non-decreasing), if for all x and y such that x >≤ y one has f(x) >≤ f(y), so f preserves the order.

a. 15 theorem
b. Pettis integral
c. Pseudo-differential operator
d. Monotonic function

38. In mathematics, an _____ is an infinite series of the form

$$\sum_{n=0}^{\infty}(-1)^n a_n,$$

with $a_n \geq 0$ (or $a_n \leq 0$) for all n. A finite sum of this kind is an alternating sum. An _____ converges if the terms a_n converge to 0 monotonically.

a. Uniform convergence
b. Alternating Series
c. Infinite series
d. Extreme value

39. The _____ is a method used to prove that infinite series of terms converge. It was discovered by Gottfried Leibniz and is sometimes known as Leibniz's test or the Leibniz criterion.

A series of the form

$$\sum_{n=1}^{\infty}(-1)^n a_n$$

where all the a_n are positive or 0, is called an alternating series.

a. Absolute convergence
c. Eisenstein series
b. ACTRAN
d. Alternating Series Test

40. In mathematics, the _____ is a binary operation on two vectors in a three-dimensional Euclidean space that results in another vector which is perpendicular to the plane containing the two input vectors. The algebra defined by the _____ is neither commutative nor associative. It contrasts with the dot product which produces a scalar result.
   a. Permutation
   b. 15 theorem
   c. Fundamental theorem of algebra
   d. Cross product

41. Cantor defined two kinds of _____ numbers, the ordinal numbers and the cardinal numbers. Ordinal numbers may be identified with well-ordered sets, or counting carried on to any stopping point, including points after an _____ number have already been counted. Generalizing finite and the ordinary _____ sequences which are maps from the positive integers leads to mappings from ordinal numbers, and transfinite sequences.
   a. AUSM
   b. ACTRAN
   c. Infinite
   d. ALGOR

42. The terms of the series are often produced according to a certain rule, such as by a formula, by an algorithm, by a sequence of measurements, or even by a random number generator. As there are an infinite number of terms, this notion is often called an _____. Unlike finite summations, series need tools from mathematical analysis to be fully understood and manipulated.
   a. Infinite series
   b. Extreme Value Theorem
   c. Integration by substitution
   d. Extreme value

43. For some curves there is a smallest number L that is an upper bound on the length of any polygonal approximation. If such a number exists, then the curve is said to be rectifiable and the curve is defined to have _____ L.

Let C be a curve in Euclidean (or, generally, a metric) space $X = R^n$, so C is the image of a continuous function f : [a, b] → X of the interval [a, b] into X.

   a. Integration by parametric derivatives
   b. Order of integration
   c. Integrand
   d. Arc length

44. _____ is the long dimension of any object. The _____ of a thing is the distance between its ends, its linear extent as measured from end to end. This may be distinguished from height, which is vertical extent, and width or breadth, which are the distance from side to side, measuring across the object at right angles to the _____.
   a. BIBO stability
   b. 15 theorem
   c. Length
   d. BDDC

45. In mathematics, _____ refers to any of a number of loosely related concepts in different areas of geometry. Intuitively, _____ is the amount by which a geometric object deviates from being flat, or straight in the case of a line, but this is defined in different ways depending on the context. There is a key distinction between extrinsic _____, which is defined for objects embedded in another space (usually a Euclidean space) in a way that relates to the radius of _____ of circles that touch the object, and intrinsic _____, which is defined at each point in a differential manifold.
   a. Lie derivative
   b. Minimal surface
   c. Sphere
   d. Curvature

46. In mathematics, a _____ (or just conic) is a curve obtained by intersecting a cone (more precisely, a circular conical surface) with a plane. A _____ is therefore a restriction of a quadric surface to the plane. The conic sections were named and studied as long ago as 200 BC, when Apollonius of Perga undertook a systematic study of their properties.
   a. Latus rectum
   b. 15 theorem
   c. BDDC
   d. Conic section

47. In mathematics, the _____ is a criterion for the convergence (a convergence test) of an infinite series

$$\sum_{n=1}^{\infty} a_n.$$

It is particularly useful in connection with power series.

The _____ was developed first by Cauchy and so is sometimes known as the Cauchy _____ or Cauchy's radical test. The _____ uses the number

$$C = \limsup_{n \to \infty} \sqrt[n]{|a_n|},$$

where 'lim sup' denotes the limit superior, possibly ∞.

   a. Racetrack principle
   b. Related rates
   c. Mean Value Theorem
   d. Root Test

48. In geometry, _____ of a curve is found at a point that is at a distance equal to the radius of curvature lying on the normal vector. It is the point at infinity if the curvature is zero. The osculating circle to the curve is centered at the _____.
   a. Kampyle of Eudoxus
   b. Strophoid
   c. Dolbeault operator
   d. Center of curvature

49. _____ is the concept of adding accumulated interest back to the principal, so that interest is earned on interest from that moment on. The act of declaring interest to be principal is called compounding (i.e., interest is compounded.) A loan, for example, may have its interest compounded every month: in this case, a loan with $100 principal and 1% interest per month would have a balance of $101 at the end of the first month.
   a. BIBO stability
   b. BDDC
   c. Compound interest
   d. 15 theorem

50. In mathematics, a _____ is a closed surface of mass M and surface density $\sigma(x,y)$ such that:

$$M = \int \int \sigma(x,y) \, dx \, dy$$, over the closed surface.

Planar laminas can be used to determine moments of inertia, or center of mass.

a. BDDC
c. 15 theorem
b. Locally integrable function
d. Planar lamina

51. A _____ is an expression which compares quantities relative to each other. The most common examples involve two quantities, but in theory any number of quantities can be compared. In mathematical terms, they are represented by separating each quantity with a colon, for example the _____ 2:3, which is read as the _____ 'two to three'.
   a. Sequence
   c. 15 theorem
   b. Y-intercept
   d. Ratio

52. In mathematics, the _____ is a test (or 'criterion') for the convergence of a series

$$\sum_{n=0}^{\infty} a_n$$

whose terms are real or complex numbers. The test was first published by Jean le Rond d'Alembert and is sometimes known as d'Alembert's _____. The test makes use of the number

$$()$$

in the cases where this limit exists.

   a. Ratio Test
   c. Converge absolutely
   b. Telescoping series
   d. Geometric series

53. _____, S(x) and C(x), are two transcendental functions named after Augustin-Jean Fresnel that are used in optics. They arise in the description of near field Fresnel diffraction phenomena, and are defined through the following integral representations:

$$S(x) = \int_0^x \sin(t^2)\, dt, \quad C(x) = \int_0^x \cos(t^2)\, dt.$$

The simultaneous parametric plot of S(x) and C(x) is the Cornu spiral, or clothoid.

Normalised _____, S(x) and C(x).
   a. Fresnel integrals
   c. Differential
   b. First derivative test
   d. Leibniz function

Chapter 12. Satellite Receiving Dish

1. The terms '_____' and 'independent variable' are used in similar but subtly different ways in mathematics and statistics as part of the standard terminology in those subjects. They are used to distinguish between two types of quantities being considered, separating them into those available at the start of a process and those being created by it, where the latter (dependent variables) are dependent on the former (independent variables.)

In traditional calculus, a function is defined as a relation between two terms called variables because their values vary.

- a. 15 theorem
- b. BIBO stability
- c. BDDC
- d. Dependent variable

2. In calculus, a branch of mathematics, the _____ is a measurement of how a function changes when its input changes. Loosely speaking, a _____ can be thought of as how much a quantity is changing at some given point. For example, the _____ of the position (or distance) of a vehicle with respect to time is the instantaneous velocity (respectively, instantaneous speed) at which the vehicle is traveling.

The process of finding a _____ is called differentiation. The fundamental theorem of calculus states that differentiation is the reverse process to integration.

- a. Semi-differentiability
- b. Bounded function
- c. Stationary phase approximation
- d. Derivative

3. The terms 'dependent variable' and '_____' are used in similar but subtly different ways in mathematics and statistics as part of the standard terminology in those subjects. They are used to distinguish between two types of quantities being considered, separating them into those available at the start of a process and those being created by it, where the latter (dependent variables) are dependent on the former (independent variables.)

In traditional calculus, a function is defined as a relation between two terms called variables because their values vary.

- a. ACTRAN
- b. ALGOR
- c. AUSM
- d. Independent variable

4. In mathematics, the _____ (or replacement set) of a given function is the set of 'input' values for which the function is defined. For instance, the _____ of cosine would be all real numbers, while the _____ of the square root would be only numbers greater than or equal to 0 (ignoring complex numbers in both cases.) In a representation of a function in a xy Cartesian coordinate system, the _____ is represented on the x axis (or abscissa.)
- a. BIBO stability
- b. 15 theorem
- c. BDDC
- d. Domain

5. A surface normal to a flat surface is a vector which is perpendicular to that surface. A normal to a non-flat surface at a point P on the surface is a vector perpendicular to the tangent plane to that surface at P. The word 'normal' is also used as an adjective: a line normal to a plane, the normal component of a force, the _____, etc. The concept of normality generalizes to orthogonality.
- a. Hyperbolic paraboloid
- b. Normal line
- c. Paraboloid
- d. Normal vector

6. In mathematics, the _____ of a function is the set of all 'output' values produced by that function. Sometimes it is called the image, or more precisely, the image of the domain of the function. If a function is a surjection then its _____ is equal to its codomain.

   a. Range
   b. Piecewise-defined function
   c. Surjective
   d. Constant function

7. In mathematics, a _____ in a normed vector space is a vector (often a spatial vector) whose length is 1 (the unit length.) A _____ is often denoted by a lowercase letter with a superscribed caret or e;hate;, like this: $\hat{\imath}$.

In Euclidean space, the dot product of two unit vectors is simply the cosine of the angle between them.

   a. ALGOR
   b. Overdetermined
   c. ACTRAN
   d. Unit vector

8. In elementary mathematics, physics, and engineering, a _____ is a geometric object that has both a magnitude (or length), direction and sense, (i.e., orientation along the given direction.) A _____ is frequently represented by a line segment with a definite direction, or graphically as an arrow, connecting an initial point A with a terminal point B, and denoted by

The magnitude of the _____ is the length of the segment and the direction characterizes the displacement of B relative to A: how much one should move the point A to 'carry' it to the point B.

Many algebraic operations on real numbers have close analogues for vectors.

   a. Vector
   b. BDDC
   c. 15 theorem
   d. Linear partial differential operator

9. In mathematics, a _____ represents the application of one function to the results of another. For instance, the functions f: X → Y and g: Y → Z can be composed by first computing f(x) and then applying a function g to the output of f(x.)

Thus one obtains a function g ∘ f: X → Z defined by (g ∘ f)(x) = g(f(x)) for all x in X. The notation g ∘ f is read as 'g circle f', or 'g composed with f', 'g after f', 'g following f', or just 'g of f'.

   a. Piecewise-defined function
   b. Constant function
   c. Surjective
   d. Composite function

10. Call S_N the _____ to N of the sequence $\{a_n\}$, or _____ of the series. A series is the sequence of partial sums, $\{S_N\}$.

When talking about series, one can refer either to the sequence {S_N} of the partial sums, or to the sum of the series,

$$\sum_{n=0}^{\infty} a_n$$

i.e., the limit of the sequence of partial sums - it is clear which one is meant from context.

a. Maxima
b. Dirichlet integral
c. The Method of Mechanical Theorems
d. Partial sum

11. In mathematics, a _____ is a function for which, intuitively, small changes in the input result in small changes in the output. Otherwise, a function is said to be discontinuous. A _____ with a continuous inverse function is called bicontinuous. An intuitive though imprecise (and inexact) idea of continuity is given by the common statement that a _____ is a function whose graph can be drawn without lifting the chalk from the blackboard.

a. Binomial series
b. Visual Calculus
c. Hyperbolic angle
d. Continuous function

12. In mathematics, a _____ is an ordered list of objects (or events). Like a set, it contains members (also called elements or terms), and the number of terms (possibly infinite) is called the length of the _____. Unlike a set, order matters, and the exact same elements can appear multiple times at different positions in the _____.

a. Slope
b. Y-intercept
c. 15 theorem
d. Sequence

13. A _____ of a function of two variables is a curve along which the function has a constant value. In cartography, a _____ (often just called a 'contour') joins points of equal elevation (height) above a given level, such as mean sea level. A contour map is a map illustrated with contour lines, for example a topographic map, which thus shows valleys and hills, and the steepness of slopes.

a. BIBO stability
b. BDDC
c. 15 theorem
d. Contour line

14. _____ or isopotential in mathematics and physics (especially electronics) refers to a region in space where every point in it is at the same potential. This usually refers to a scalar potential, although it can also be applied to vector potentials. Often, _____ surfaces are used to visualize an (n)-dimensional scalar potential function in (n-1) dimensional space.

a. Inverse function theorem
b. Upper convected time derivative
c. Implicit function theorem
d. Equipotential

15. When the number of variables is two, this is a _____, if it is three this is a level surface, and for higher values of n the level set is a level hypersurface.

More specifically, a _____ is the set of all real-valued roots of an equation in two variables x_1 and x_2. A level surface is the set of all real-valued roots of an equation in three variables x_1, x_2 and x_3.

a. Scalar field	b. Level curve
c. Partial derivative	d. Multipole moment

16. In mathematics and physics, a _____ associates a scalar value, which can be either mathematical in definition to every point in space. Scalar fields are often used in physics, for instance to indicate the temperature distribution throughout space or more specifically, differential geometry, the set of functions defined on a manifold define the commutative ring of functions.

a. Level curve	b. Scalar field
c. Vector Laplacian	d. Symmetry of second derivatives

17. A _____ is a type of map characterized by large-scale detail and quantitative representation of relief, usually using contour lines in modern mapping, but historically using a variety of methods. Traditional definitions require a _____ to show both natural and man-made features.

The Canadian Centre for Topographic Information provides this definition of a _____:

Other authors define topographic maps by contrasting them with another type of map; they are distinguished from smaller-scale 'chorographic maps' that cover large regions, 'planimetric maps' that do not show elevations, and 'thematic maps' that focus on specific topics.

a. BDDC	b. Topographic map
c. 15 theorem	d. BIBO stability

18. In mathematics, a (topological) _____ is defined as follows: let I be an interval of real numbers (i.e. a non-empty connected subset of $\mathbb{R}$); then a _____ γ is a continuous mapping $\gamma : I \to X$, where X is a topological space. The _____ γ is said to be simple if it is injective, i.e. if for all x, y in I, we have $\gamma(x) = \gamma(y) \implies x = y$. If I is a closed bounded interval $[a, b]$, we also allow the possibility $\gamma(a) = \gamma(b)$ (this convention makes it possible to talk about closed simple _____.)

a. Closed curve	b. Prolate cycloid
c. Tractrix	d. Curve

19. In economics, the _____ functional form of production functions is widely used to represent the relationship of an output to inputs. It was proposed by Knut Wicksell (1851-1926), and tested against statistical evidence by Charles Cobb and Paul Douglas in 1900-1928.

For production, the function is

$Y = AL^{\alpha}K^{\beta}$,

where:

- Y = total production (the monetary value of all goods produced in a year)
- L = labor input
- K = capital input
- A = total factor productivity
- α and β are the output elasticities of labor and capital, respectively. These values are constants determined by available technology.

Output elasticity measures the responsiveness of output to a change in levels of either labor or capital used in production, ceteris paribus. For example if α = 0.15, a 1% increase in labor would lead to approximately a 0.15% increase in output.

a. BDDC
b. BIBO stability
c. 15 theorem
d. Cobb-Douglas

20. If a particular point on a sphere is (arbitrarily) designated as its _____, then the corresponding antipodal point is called the south pole and the equator is the great circle that is equidistant to them. Great circles through the two poles are called lines (or meridians) of longitude, and the line connecting the two poles is called the axis of rotation. Circles on the sphere that are parallel to the equator are lines of latitude.

a. Sphere
b. Minimal surface
c. Tangent line
d. North pole

21. In mathematics, the _____ is a coordinate system for representing geometric figures in three dimensions using three coordinates: the radial distance of a point from a fixed origin, the zenith angle from the positive z-axis to the point, and the azimuth angle from the positive x-axis to the orthogonal projection of the point in the x-y plane.

Several different conventions exist for representing the three coordinates. In accordance with the International Organisation for Standardisation (ISO 31-11), in physics they are typically notated as (r, θ, φ) for radial distance, zenith, and azimuth, respectively.

a. 15 theorem
b. Coordinate
c. Cylindrical coordinate system
d. Spherical coordinate system

22. In mathematics and its applications, a _____ system is a system for assigning an n-tuple of numbers or scalars to each point in an n-dimensional space. This concept is part of the theory of manifolds. 'Scalars' in many cases means real numbers, but, depending on context, can mean complex numbers or elements of some other commutative ring.

a. Spherical coordinate system
b. Coordinate
c. Cylindrical coordinate system
d. 15 theorem

23. In computer science and information science, _____ could also be a method or an algorithm. Again, an example will illustrate: There are systems of counting, as with Roman numerals, and various systems for filing papers, or catalogues, and various library systems, of which the Dewey Decimal _____ is an example. This still fits with the definition of components which are connected together (in this case in order to facilitate the flow of information.)

a. System
b. BDDC
c. BIBO stability
d. 15 theorem

24. An _____ process is a change in which the temperature of the system stays constant: ΔT = 0. This typically occurs when a system is in contact with an outside thermal reservoir (heat bath), and the change occurs slowly enough to allow the system to continually adjust to the temperature of the reservoir through heat exchange. An alternative special case in which a system exchanges no heat with its surroundings (Q = 0) is called an adiabatic process.
   a. ACTRAN
   b. ALGOR
   c. AUSM
   d. Isothermal

25. In mathematics, even functions and odd functions are functions which satisfy particular symmetry relations, with respect to taking additive inverses. They are important in many areas of mathematical analysis, especially the theory of power series and Fourier series. They are named for the parity of the powers of the power functions which satisfy each condition: the function f(x) = x^n is an even function if n is an even integer, and it is an _____ if n is an odd integer.
   a. Integration by substitution
   b. Even function
   c. Integral of secant cubed
   d. Odd function

26. In topology, the boundary of a subset S of a topological space X is the set of points which can be approached both from S and from the outside of S. More formally, it is the set of points in the closure of S, not belonging to the interior of S. An element of the boundary of S is called a _____ of S. S is boundaryless when it contains no boundary, which is to say no _____ Notations used for boundary of a set S include bd(S), fr(S), and ∂S. Some authors (for example Willard, in General Topology) use the term 'frontier', instead of boundary in an attempt to avoid confusion with the concept of boundary used in algebraic topology.
   a. BDDC
   b. BIBO stability
   c. 15 theorem
   d. Boundary point

27. In geometry, a disk (also spelled disc) is the region in a plane bounded by a circle.

A disk is said to be closed or open according to whether or not it contains the circle that constitutes its boundary. In Cartesian coordinates, the open disk of center (a,b) and radius R is given by the formula

$$D = \{(x,y) \in \mathbb{R}^2 : (x-a)^2 + (y-b)^2 < R^2\}$$

while the _____ of the same center and radius is given by

$$\overline{D} = \{(x,y) \in \mathbb{R}^2 : (x-a)^2 + (y-b)^2 \leq R^2\}.$$

The area of a closed or open disk of radius R is πR^2

   a. 15 theorem
   b. BDDC
   c. BIBO stability
   d. Closed disk

28. f'(x) is twice the absolute value function, and it does not have a derivative at zero. Similar examples show that a function can have k derivatives for any non-negative integer k but no (k + 1)-order derivative. A function that has k successive derivatives is called _____.

a. Power series	b. Differential coefficient
c. Differential calculus	d. K times differentiable

29. In mathematics, the interior of a set S consists of all points of S that are intuitively 'not on the edge of S'. A point that is in the interior of S is an _____ of S.

The exterior of a set is the interior of its complement; it consists of the points that are not in the set or its boundary.

a. AUSM	b. ACTRAN
c. Interior point	d. ALGOR

30. In metric topology and related fields of mathematics, a set U is called _____ if, intuitively speaking, starting from any point x in U one can move by a small amount in any direction and still be in the set U. In other words, the distance between any point x in U and the edge of U is always greater than zero.

As an example, consider the _____ interval (0, 1) consisting of all real numbers x with 0 < x < 1. Here, the topology is the usual topology on the real line. We can look at this in two ways.

a. ALGOR	b. AUSM
c. Open	d. ACTRAN

31. In geometry, a disk (also spelled disc) is the region in a plane bounded by a circle.

A disk is said to be closed or open according to whether or not it contains the circle that constitutes its boundary. In Cartesian coordinates, the _____ of center (a,b) and radius R is given by the formula

$$D = \{(x,y) \in \mathbb{R}^2 : (x-a)^2 + (y-b)^2 < R^2\}$$

while the closed disk of the same center and radius is given by

$$\overline{D} = \{(x,y) \in \mathbb{R}^2 : (x-a)^2 + (y-b)^2 \leq R^2\}.$$

The area of a closed or _____ of radius R is πR²

a. ACTRAN	b. ALGOR
c. AUSM	d. Open disk

32. Let f be a differentiable function, and let f'(x) be its derivative. The derivative of f'(x) (if it has one) is written f''(x) and is called the _____ of f. Similarly, the derivative of a _____, if it exists, is written f'''(x) and is called the third derivative of f.

a. Second derivative	b. Slant asymptote
c. Vertical asymptote	d. Stationary phase approximation

33. In mathematics, the concept of a '_____' is used to describe the behavior of a function as its argument or input either 'gets close' to some point, or as the argument becomes arbitrarily large; or the behavior of a sequence's elements as their index increases indefinitely. Limits are used in calculus and other branches of mathematical analysis to define derivatives and continuity.

In formulas, _____ is usually abbreviated as lim

a. BDDC
b. 15 theorem
c. BIBO stability
d. Limit

34. In geometry, the _____ or Gutschoven's curve is a two-dimensional algebraic curve resembling the Greek letter κ (kappa.)

Using the Cartesian coordinate system it can be expressed as:

$$x^2(x^2 + y^2) = a^2 y^2$$

or, using parametric equations:

$$x = a\cos t \cot t$$
$$y = a\cos t$$

In polar coordinates its equation is even simpler:

r = atanθ

It has two vertical asymptotes at $x = \pm a$, shown as dashed blue lines in the figure at right.

The _____'s curvature:

$$\kappa(\theta) = \frac{8\left(3 - \sin^2\theta\right)\sin^4\theta}{a\left[\sin^2(2\theta) + 4\right]^{\frac{3}{2}}}$$

Tangential angle:

$$\phi(\theta) = -\arctan\left[\frac{1}{2}\sin(2\theta)\right]$$

The _____ was first studied by Gérard van Gutschoven around 1662.

a. Prolate cycloid
b. Kappa curve
c. Witch of Agnesi
d. Tractrix

35. In mathematics, the _____ is a two-dimensional coordinate system in which each point on a plane is determined by an angle and a distance. The _____ is especially useful in situations where the relationship between two points is most easily expressed in terms of angles and distance; in the more familiar Cartesian or rectangular coordinate system, such a relationship can only be found through trigonometric formulation.

As the coordinate system is two-dimensional, each point is determined by two polar coordinates: the radial coordinate and the angular coordinate.

a. 15 theorem
b. BDDC
c. BIBO stability
d. Polar coordinate system

36. Continuous functions are of utmost importance in mathematics and applications. However, not all functions are continuous. If a function is not continuous at a point in its domain, one says that it has a _____ there. The set of all points of _____ of a function may be a discrete set, a dense set, or even the entire domain of the function.
a. Discontinuity
b. 15 theorem
c. BDDC
d. Vector

37. A _____ is perfectly round geometrical object in three-dimensional space, such as the shape of a round ball. Like a circle in two dimensions, a perfect _____ is completely symmetrical around its center, with all points on the surface lying the same distance r from the center point. This distance r is known as the radius of the _____.
a. Tangent line
b. Sphere
c. Minimal surface
d. North pole

38. _____ is a quantity used to predict an object's ability to resist torsion, in objects (or segments of objects) with an invariant circular cross-section and no significant warping or out-of-plane deformation. It is used to calculate the angular displacement of an object subjected to a torque. It is analogous to the area moment of inertia, which characterizes an object's ability to resist bending and is required to calculate displacement.
a. Spring equation
b. Spring constant
c. Navier-Stokes equations
d. Polar moment of inertia

39. The concept of _____ in mathematics evolved from the concept of _____ in physics. The nth _____ of a real-valued function f(x) of a real variable about a value c is

$$\mu'_n = \int_{-\infty}^{\infty} (x-c)^n f(x)\, dx.$$

It is possible to define moments for random variables in a more general fashion than moments for real values. See Moments in metric spaces.

a. Median
b. Geometric mean
c. Moment
d. Poisson distribution

40. _____, also called mass _____ or the angular mass, (SI units kg m^2) is a measure of an object's resistance to changes in its rotation rate. It is the rotational analog of mass. That is, it is the inertia of a rigid rotating body with respect to its rotation.
- a. Wave equation
- b. Moment of inertia
- c. Klein-Gordon equation
- d. Dirac equation

41. In mathematics, a _____ of a function of several variables is its derivative with respect to one of those variables with the others held constant (as opposed to the total derivative, in which all variables are allowed to vary.) Partial derivatives are useful in vector calculus and differential geometry.

The _____ of a function f with respect to the variable x is written as f'$_x$, ∂_xf, or ∂f/∂x.

- a. Jacobian
- b. Partial derivative
- c. Level curve
- d. Differentiation operator

42. In calculus, the _____ determines whether a given critical point of a function is a maximum, a minimum, or neither.

Suppose that f is a function and we want to determine if f has a maximum or minimum at x. If f is increasing to the left of x and decreasing to the right of x, then x is a local maximum of f.

- a. Partial sum
- b. Continuous function
- c. Test for Divergence
- d. First Derivative Test

43. In calculus, a branch of mathematics, the _____ is a criterion often useful for determining whether a given stationary point of a function is a local maximum or a local minimum.

The test states: If the function f is twice differentiable at a stationary point x, meaning that $f'(x) = 0$, then:

- If $f''(x) < 0$ then f has a local maximum at x.
- If $f''(x) > 0$ then f has a local minimum at x.
- If $f''(x) = 0$, the _____ says nothing about the point x, has a possible inflection point.

In the last case, the function may have a local maximum or minimum there, but the function is sufficiently 'flat' that this is undetected by the second derivative. In this case one has to examine the third derivative. Such an example is f(x) = x^4.

- a. Stationary point
- b. Symmetric derivative
- c. Linearity of differentiation
- d. Second Derivative Test

44. In mathematics, the _____ of a function y = f(x) is a function that, in some fashion, 'undoes' the effect of f The _____ of f is denoted f^{-1}. The statements y=f(x) and x=f^{-1}(y) are equivalent.

a. ALGOR
b. AUSM
c. ACTRAN
d. Inverse

45. In mathematics, if f is a function from A to B then an _____ for f is a function in the opposite direction, from B to A, with the property that a round trip (a composition) from A to B to A (or from B to A to B) returns each element of the initial set to itself. Thus, if an input x into the function f produces an output y, then inputting y into the _____ f^{-1} (read f inverse, not to be confused with exponentiation) produces the output x. Not every function has an inverse; those that do are called invertible.

a. Aristotle
b. Augustin Louis Cauchy
c. Augustin-Jean Fresnel
d. Inverse function

46. The _____ of a material is defined as its mass per unit volume. The symbol of _____ is ρ '>rho.)

Mathematically:

$$d = \frac{m}{V}$$

where:

    d is the _____,
    m is the mass,
    V is the volume.

a. BDDC
b. BIBO stability
c. Density
d. 15 theorem

47. In mathematics, a probability _____ is a function that represents a probability distribution in terms of integrals.

Formally, a probability distribution has density f, if f is a non-negative Lebesgue-integrable function $\mathbb{R} \to \mathbb{R}$ such that the probability of the interval [a, b] is given by

$$\int_a^b f(x)\,dx$$

for any two numbers a and b. This implies that the total integral of f must be 1.

a. BDDC
b. Factorial moment generating function
c. Density function
d. 15 theorem

48. _____ is a way of expressing knowledge or belief that an event will occur or has occurred. In mathematics the concept has been given an exact meaning in _____ theory, that is used extensively in such areas of study as mathematics, statistics, finance, gambling, science, and philosophy to draw conclusions about the likelihood of potential events and the underlying mechanics of complex systems.

The word _____ does not have a consistent direct definition.

a. Discrete probability distributions
c. Normal distribution
b. Linear regression
d. Probability

49. In mathematics, a _____ (pdf) is a function that represents a probability distribution in terms of integrals.

Formally, a probability distribution has density f, if f is a non-negative Lebesgue-integrable function $\mathbb{R} \to \mathbb{R}$ such that the probability of the interval [a, b] is given by

$$\int_a^b f(x)\,dx$$

for any two numbers a and b. This implies that the total integral of f must be 1.

a. Factorial moment generating function
c. BDDC
b. 15 theorem
d. Probability density function

50. In infinitesimal calculus, a _____ is traditionally an infinitesimally small change in a variable. For example, if x is a variable, then a change in the value of x is often denoted Δx (or δx when this change is considered to be small.) The _____ dx represents such a change, but is infinitely small.

a. Local maximum
c. Dirichlet integral
b. The Method of Mechanical Theorems
d. Differential

51. Integration is an important concept in mathematics, specifically in the field of calculus and, more broadly, mathematical analysis. Given a function f of a real variable x and an interval [a, b] of the real line, the _____

$$\int_a^b f(x)\,dx,$$

is defined informally to be the net signed area of the region in the xy-plane bounded by the graph of f, the x-axis, and the vertical lines x = a and x = b.

The term '_____' may also refer to the notion of antiderivative, a function F whose derivative is the given function f.

a. Indefinite integral
c. Integrand
b. Integral
d. Integral test for convergence

52. In mathematics, the _____ for convergence is a method used to test infinite series of non-negative terms for convergence. An early form of the test of convergence was developed in India by Madhava in the 14th century, and by his followers at the Kerala School. In Europe, it was later developed by Maclaurin and Cauchy and is sometimes known as the Maclaurin-Cauchy test.

a. ALGOR
c. AUSM
b. ACTRAN
d. Integral Test

53. For some curves there is a smallest number L that is an upper bound on the length of any polygonal approximation. If such a number exists, then the curve is said to be rectifiable and the curve is defined to have _____ L.

Let C be a curve in Euclidean (or, generally, a metric) space X = R^n, so C is the image of a continuous function f : [a, b] → X of the interval [a, b] into X.

a. Integration by parametric derivatives
b. Order of integration
c. Integrand
d. Arc length

54. _____ is the long dimension of any object. The _____ of a thing is the distance between its ends, its linear extent as measured from end to end. This may be distinguished from height, which is vertical extent, and width or breadth, which are the distance from side to side, measuring across the object at right angles to the _____.

a. Length
b. BIBO stability
c. 15 theorem
d. BDDC

55. In mathematics, a _____ is an approximation of a general function using a linear function (more precisely, an affine function.)

Given a differentiable function f of one real variable, Taylor's theorem for n=1 states that

$$f(x) = f(a) + f'(a)(x - a) + R_2$$

where R_2 is the remainder term. The _____ is obtained by dropping the remainder:

$$f(x) \approx f(a) + f'(a)(x - a)$$

which is true for x close to a.

a. Lin-Tsien equation
b. Smooth function
c. Point of inflection
d. Linear approximation

56. In a totally ordered set all elements are mutually comparable, so such a set can have at most one minimal element and at most one maximal element. Then, due to mutual comparability, the minimal element will also be the least element and the maximal element will also be the greatest element. Thus in a totally ordered set we can simply use the terms minimum and _____.

a. Maximum
b. Nth term
c. Racetrack principle
d. Leibniz rule

57. In calculus, the _____ is a formula for the derivative of the composite of two functions.

In intuitive terms, if a variable, y, depends on a second variable, u, which in turn depends on a third variable, x, then the rate of change of y with respect to x can be computed as the rate of change of y with respect to u multiplied by the rate of change of u with respect to x. Schematically,

$$\frac{dy}{dx} = \frac{dy}{du} \cdot \frac{du}{dx}.$$

a. Reciprocal Rule
b. Product rule
c. Chain Rule
d. Differentiation rules

58. In complex analysis, a mathematical discipline, a _____ of a meromorphic function is a certain type of singularity that behaves like the singularity of $\frac{1}{z^n}$ at z = 0. This means that, in particular, a _____ of the function f(z) is a point z = a such that f(z) approaches infinity uniformly as z approaches a.

Formally, suppose U is an open subset of the complex plane C, a is an element of U and f : U {a} → C is a function which is holomorphic over its domain.

a. Pole
b. Lacunary function
c. Complex logarithm
d. Bieberbach conjecture

59. In calculus, a method called _____ can be applied to implicitly defined functions. This method is an application of the chain rule allowing one to calculate the derivative of a function given implicitly.

As explained in the introduction, y can be given as a function of x implicitly rather than explicitly. When we have an equation R (x,y) = 0, we may be able to solve it for y and then differentiate. However, sometimes it is simpler to differentiate R(x,y) with respect to x and then solve for dy / dx.

a. Ordinary differential equation
b. Implicit function
c. Implicit differentiation
d. Automatic differentiation

60. A _____ is a mathematical equation for an unknown function of one or several variables that relates the values of the function itself and of its derivatives of various orders. they play a prominent role in engineering, physics, economics and other disciplines.

A simplified real world example of a _____ is modeling the acceleration of a ball falling through the air (considering only gravity and air resistance.)

a. Phase line
b. Structural stability
c. Differential equation
d. Caloric polynomial

61. In mathematics, the _____ of a multivariate differentiable function along a given vector V at a given point P intuitively represents the instantaneous rate of change of the function, moving through P, in the direction of V. It therefore generalizes the notion of a partial derivative, in which the direction is always taken parallel to one of the coordinate axes.

The _____ is a special case of the Gâteaux derivative.

The _____ of a scalar function $f(\vec{x}) = f(x_1, x_2, \ldots, x_n)$ along a vector $\vec{v} = (v_1, \ldots, v_n)$ is the function defined by the limit

$$\nabla_{\vec{v}} f(\vec{x}) = \lim_{h \to 0} \frac{f(\vec{x} + h\vec{v}) - f(\vec{x})}{h}.$$

Sometimes authors write D_v instead of ∇_v.

a. Differentiation of trigonometric functions
b. Symmetrically continuous
c. Linearity of differentiation
d. Directional derivative

62. A _____ is one of the most curvilinear basic geometric shapes: It has two faces, zero vertices, and zero edges. The surface formed by the points at a fixed distance from a given straight line, the axis of the _____. The solid enclosed by this surface and by two planes perpendicular to the axis is also called a _____.
a. 15 theorem
b. BDDC
c. Right circular cylinder
d. Cylinder

63. A _____ is a lens which focuses light which passes through onto a line instead of onto a point, as a spherical lens would. The curved face or faces of a _____ are sections of a cylinder, and focus the image passing through it onto a line parallel to the intersection of the surface of the lens and a plane tangent to it. The lens compresses the image in the direction perpendicular to this line, and leaves it unaltered in the direction parallel to it (in the tangent plane.)
a. BDDC
b. BIBO stability
c. 15 theorem
d. Cylindrical lens

64. In vector calculus, the _____ of a scalar field is a vector field which points in the direction of the greatest rate of increase of the scalar field, and whose magnitude is the greatest rate of change.

A generalization of the _____ for functions on a Euclidean space which have values in another Euclidean space is the Jacobian. A further generalization for a function from one Banach space to another is the Fréchet derivative.

a. Smooth function
b. Gradient
c. Symmetric derivative
d. Lin-Tsien equation

65. A _____ is a surface in the Euclidean space R^3 which is defined by a parametric equation with two parameters. Parametric representation is the most general way to specify a surface. Surfaces that occur in two of the main theorems of vector calculus, Stokes' theorem and divergence theorem, are frequently given in a parametric form.
a. Paraboloid
b. Parametric surface
c. Prolate
d. Torus

66. In the two-dimensional case, a _____ perpendicularly intersects the tangent line to a curve at a given point.

The _____ is often used in computer graphics to determine a surface's orientation toward a light source for flat shading, or the orientation of each of the corners (vertices) to mimic a curved surface with Phong shading.

For a polygon (such as a triangle), a surface normal can be calculated as the vector cross product of two (non-parallel) edges of the polygon.

a. Parametric surface
b. Hyperbolic paraboloid
c. PDE surfaces
d. Normal line

67. In geometry, the _____ (or simply the tangent) to a curve at a given point is the straight line that 'just touches' the curve at that point (in the sense explained more precisely below.) As it passes through the point of tangency, the _____ is 'going in the same direction' as the curve, and in this sense it is the best straight-line approximation to the curve at that point. The same definition applies to space curves and curves in n-dimensional Euclidean space.

a. Lie derivative
b. North pole
c. Minimal surface
d. Tangent line

68. The largest and the smallest element of a set are called extreme values, absolute extrema, or extreme records.

For a differentiable function f, if $f(x_0)$ is an _____ for the set of all values f(x), and if x_0 is in the interior of the domain of f, then x_0 is a critical point, by Fermat's theorem.

In the case of a general partial order one should not confuse a least element (smaller than all other) and a minimal element (nothing is smaller.)

a. Infinitesimal
b. Extreme Value Theorem
c. Integration by substitution
d. Extreme value

69. In mathematics, a function f defined on some set X with real or complex values is a _____ function, if the set of its values is _____. In other words, there exists a number M>0 such that

$$|f(x)| \leq M$$

for all x in X.

Sometimes, if $f(x) \leq A$ for all x in X, then the function is said to be _____ above by A.

a. Concave upwards
b. Bounded
c. Differential coefficient
d. Stationary phase approximation

70. In calculus, the _____ states that if a real-valued function f is continuous in the closed and bounded interval [a,b], then f must attain its maximum and minimum value, each at least once. That is, there exist numbers c and d in [a,b] such that:

$$f(c) \geq f(x) \geq f(d) \quad \text{for all } x \in [a, b].$$

A related theorem is the boundedness theorem which states that a continuous function f in the closed interval [a,b] is bounded on that interval. That is, there exist real numbers m and M such that:

$$m \leq f(x) \leq M \quad \text{for all } x \in [a, b].$$

The _____ enriches the boundedness theorem by saying that not only is the function bounded, but it also attains its least upper bound as its maximum and its greatest lower bound as its minimum.

a. Infinitesimal
b. Integral of secant cubed
c. Uniform convergence
d. Extreme Value Theorem

71. In a totally ordered set all elements are mutually comparable, so such a set can have at most one minimal element and at most one maximal element. Then, due to mutual comparability, the minimal element will also be the least element and the maximal element will also be the greatest element. Thus in a totally ordered set we can simply use the terms _____ and maximum.

a. Ghosts of departed quantities
b. Minimum
c. Nth term
d. Maximum

72. In mathematics, two vectors are _____ if they are perpendicular, i.e., they form a right angle. For example, a subway and the street above, although they do not physically intersect, are _____ if they cross at a right angle.

a. Orthogonal
b. AUSM
c. ACTRAN
d. ALGOR

73. _____ is used to describe the steepness, incline, gradient, or grade of a straight line. A higher _____ value indicates a steeper incline. The _____ is defined as the ratio of the 'rise' divided by the 'run' between two points on a line, or in other words, the ratio of the altitude change to the horizontal distance between any two points on the line.

a. Y-intercept
b. Slope
c. 15 theorem
d. Sequence

74. _____ is a type of motion in which the velocity of an object changes equal amounts in equal time periods. An example of an object having _____ would be a ball rolling down a ramp. The object picks up velocity as it goes down the ramp with equal changes in time.

a. ALGOR
b. AUSM
c. ACTRAN
d. Uniform Acceleration

75. The function $\log_b(x)$ depends on both b and x, but the term _____ in standard usage refers to a function of the form $\log_b(x)$ in which the base b is fixed and so the only argument is x. Thus there is one _____ for each value of the base b (which must be positive and must differ from 1.) Viewed in this way, the base-b _____ is the inverse function of the exponential function b^x.

a. BDDC
b. Logarithm function
c. 15 theorem
d. BIBO stability

76. In mathematics, a _____ (or critical number) is a point on the domain of a function where:

- one dimension: the derivative (or slope of the line when visualized) is equal to zero or a point where the function ceases to be differentiable.
- in general: there are two distinct concepts: either the derivative (Jacobian) vanishes, or it is not of full rank (or, in either case, the function is not differentiable); these agree in one dimension.

Note that in one dimension, a critical value or critical number x of function f is the domain element at which the derivative is zero or undefined, whereas the associated ordered pair (x, y) is the _____. In higher dimensions a critical value is in the range whereas a _____ is in the domain.

There are two situations in which a point becomes a _____ of a function of one variable. The first of which is that the value of the first derivative is equal to zero.

a. Differentiation operator
b. Critical point
c. Total derivative
d. Multivariable calculus

77. In physics, and more specifically kinematics, _____ is the change in velocity over time. Because velocity is a vector, it can change in two ways: a change in magnitude and/or a change in direction. In one dimension, _____ is the rate at which something speeds up or slows down.
a. ALGOR
b. ACTRAN
c. AUSM
d. Acceleration

78. Cantor defined two kinds of _____ numbers, the ordinal numbers and the cardinal numbers. Ordinal numbers may be identified with well-ordered sets, or counting carried on to any stopping point, including points after an _____ number have already been counted. Generalizing finite and the ordinary _____ sequences which are maps from the positive integers leads to mappings from ordinal numbers, and transfinite sequences.
a. AUSM
b. ALGOR
c. ACTRAN
d. Infinite

79. The terms of the series are often produced according to a certain rule, such as by a formula, by an algorithm, by a sequence of measurements, or even by a random number generator. As there are an infinite number of terms, this notion is often called an _____. Unlike finite summations, series need tools from mathematical analysis to be fully understood and manipulated.
a. Extreme value
b. Integration by substitution
c. Extreme Value Theorem
d. Infinite series

80. In mathematics, _____ and minima, known collectively as extrema, are the largest value (maximum) or smallest value (minimum), that a function takes in a point either within a given neighbourhood (local extremum) or on the function domain in its entirety (global extremum.)

Throughout, a point refers to an input (x), while a value refers to an output (y): one distinguishing between the maximum value and the point (or points) at which it occurs.

A real-valued function f defined on the real line is said to have a local maximum point at the point x*, if there exists some ε > 0, such that f(x*) ≥ f(x) when |x − x*| < ε.

a. Racetrack principle
b. Related rates
c. Maxima
d. Leibniz formula

81. In mathematics, a _____ is a point in the domain of a function of two variables which is a stationary point but not a local extremum. At such a point, in general, the surface resembles a saddle that curves up in one direction, and curves down in a different direction (like a mountain pass.) In terms of contour lines, a _____ can be recognized, in general, by a contour that appears to intersect itself.

a. Saddle point
b. BIBO stability
c. BDDC
d. 15 theorem

82. The method of _____ or ordinary _____ is used to solve overdetermined systems. _____ is often applied in statistical contexts, particularly regression analysis.

_____ can be interpreted as a method of fitting data. The best fit in the _____ sense is that instance of the model for which the sum of squared residuals has its least value, a residual being the difference between an observed value and the value given by the model.

a. 15 theorem
b. BDDC
c. BIBO stability
d. Least squares

83. The _____ of an angle is the ratio of the length of the opposite side to the length of the hypotenuse. In our case

$$\sin A = \frac{\text{opposite}}{\text{hypotenuse}} = \frac{a}{h}.$$

Note that this ratio does not depend on size of the particular right triangle chosen, as long as it contains the angle A, since all such triangles are similar.

The cosine of an angle is the ratio of the length of the adjacent side to the length of the hypotenuse.

a. Trigonometric functions
b. Sine
c. Sine integral
d. Trigonometric

84. In mathematical optimization, the method of Lagrange multipliers provides a strategy for finding the maximum/minimum of a function subject to constraints.

For example , consider the optimization problem

$$\text{maximize } f(x,y)$$
$$\text{subject to } g(x,y) = c.$$

We introduce a new variable (λ) called a _____, and study the Lagrange function defined by

$$\Lambda(x,y,\lambda) = f(x,y) - \lambda\Big(g(x,y) - c\Big).$$

If (x,y)≉ is a maximum for the original constrained problem, then there exists a λ such that (x,y,λ)≉ is a stationary point for the Lagrange function (stationary points are those points where the partial derivatives of Λ are zero.) However, not all stationary points yield a solution of the original problem.

a. BIBO stability
c. 15 theorem
b. Lagrange Multiplier
d. BDDC

85. In mathematics, the simplest case of _____ refers to the study of problems in which one seeks to minimize or maximize a real function by systematically choosing the values of real or integer variables from within an allowed set. This (a scalar real valued objective function) is actually a small subset of this field which comprises a large area of applied mathematics and generalizes to study of means to obtain 'best available' values of some objective function given a defined domain where the elaboration is on the types of functions and the conditions and nature of the objects in the problem domain.

The first _____ technique, which is known as steepest descent, goes back to Gauss.

a. Optimization
c. AUSM
b. ACTRAN
d. ALGOR

86. The _____ is an important second-order linear partial differential equation that describes the propagation of a variety of waves, such as sound waves, light waves and water waves. It arises in fields such as acoustics, electromagnetics, and fluid dynamics. Historically, the problem of a vibrating string such as that of a musical instrument was studied by Jean le Rond d'Alembert, Leonhard Euler, Daniel Bernoulli, and Joseph-Louis Lagrange.

a. Dirac equation
c. Volume
b. Lagrangian
d. Wave equation

Chapter 13. Hyperthermia Treatments for Tumors

1. In mathematics, the hyperbolic functions are analogs of the ordinary trigonometric functions. The basic hyperbolic functions are the _____ 'sinh', and the hyperbolic cosine 'cosh', from which are derived the hyperbolic tangent 'tanh', etc., in analogy to the derived trigonometric functions. The inverse hyperbolic functions are the area _____ 'arsinh' (also called 'asinh', or sometimes by the misnomer of 'arcsinh') and so on.
    a. Square root function
    b. Hyperbolic tangent
    c. Hyperbolic sine
    d. Signum function

2. In mathematics, the _____ of a function y = f(x) is a function that, in some fashion, 'undoes' the effect of f The _____ of f is denoted f⁻¹. The statements y=f(x) and x=f⁻¹(y) are equivalent.
    a. ALGOR
    b. ACTRAN
    c. AUSM
    d. Inverse

3. In mathematics, if f is a function from A to B then an _____ for f is a function in the opposite direction, from B to A, with the property that a round trip (a composition) from A to B to A (or from B to A to B) returns each element of the initial set to itself. Thus, if an input x into the function f produces an output y, then inputting y into the _____ f^{-1} (read f inverse, not to be confused with exponentiation) produces the output x. Not every function has an inverse; those that do are called invertible.
    a. Augustin-Jean Fresnel
    b. Aristotle
    c. Inverse function
    d. Augustin Louis Cauchy

4. A _____ of a curve is a line that (locally) intersects two points on the curve. The word secant comes from the Latin secare, for to cut.

It can be used to approximate the tangent to a curve, at some point P. If the secant to a curve is defined by two points, P and Q, with P fixed and Q variable, as Q approaches P along the curve, the direction of the secant approaches that of the tangent at P, assuming there is just one.

   a. Kappa curve
   b. Curve
   c. Secant line
   d. Witch of Agnesi

5. Integration is an important concept in mathematics, specifically in the field of calculus and, more broadly, mathematical analysis. Given a function f of a real variable x and an interval [a, b] of the real line, the _____

$$\int_a^b f(x)\, dx,$$

is defined informally to be the net signed area of the region in the xy-plane bounded by the graph of f, the x-axis, and the vertical lines x = a and x = b.

The term '_____' may also refer to the notion of antiderivative, a function F whose derivative is the given function f.

   a. Integral
   b. Integral test for convergence
   c. Indefinite integral
   d. Integrand

6. In mathematics, the concept of a '_____' is used to describe the behavior of a function as its argument or input either 'gets close' to some point, or as the argument becomes arbitrarily large; or the behavior of a sequence's elements as their index increases indefinitely. Limits are used in calculus and other branches of mathematical analysis to define derivatives and continuity.

In formulas, _____ is usually abbreviated as lim

a. BDDC
b. 15 theorem
c. BIBO stability
d. Limit

7. In calculus and mathematical analysis the _____ of the integral

$$\int_a^b f(x)\,dx$$

of a Riemann integrable function f defined on a closed and bounded interval [a, b] are the real numbers a and b.

_____ can also be defined for improper integrals, with the _____ of both

$$\lim_{z \to a+} \int_z^b f(x)\,dx$$

and

$$\lim_{z \to b-} \int_a^z f(x)\,dx$$

again being a and b. For an improper integral

$$\int_a^\infty f(x)\,dx$$

or

$$\int_{-\infty}^b f(x)\,dx$$

the _____ are a and ∞, or −∞ and b, respectively.

a. Differential
b. Maxima
c. Test for Divergence
d. Limits of integration

8. The _____ of an angle is the ratio of the length of the opposite side to the length of the hypotenuse. In our case

$$\sin A = \frac{\text{opposite}}{\text{hypotenuse}} = \frac{a}{h}.$$

Note that this ratio does not depend on size of the particular right triangle chosen, as long as it contains the angle A, since all such triangles are similar.

The cosine of an angle is the ratio of the length of the adjacent side to the length of the hypotenuse.

a. Trigonometric functions
b. Sine integral
c. Trigonometric
d. Sine

9. The concept of _____ in mathematics evolved from the concept of _____ in physics. The nth _____ of a real-valued function f(x) of a real variable about a value c is

$$\mu'_n = \int_{-\infty}^{\infty} (x-c)^n f(x)\, dx.$$

It is possible to define moments for random variables in a more general fashion than moments for real values. See Moments in metric spaces.

a. Poisson distribution
b. Geometric mean
c. Median
d. Moment

10. In calculus, interchange of the _____ is a methodology that transforms multiple integrations of functions into other, hopefully simpler, integrals by changing the order in which the integrations are performed.

The problem for examination is evaluation of an integral of the form:

$$\iint_D dx\, dy\; f(x,y),$$

where D is some two-dimensional area in the xy-plane. For some functions f straightforward integration is feasible, but where that is not true, the integral can sometimes be reduced to simpler form by changing the _____.

a. Arc length
b. Order of integration
c. Indefinite integral
d. Integration by parts

Chapter 13. Hyperthermia Treatments for Tumors

11. Just as the definite integral of a positive function of one variable represents the area of the region between the graph of the function and the x-axis, the _____ of a positive function of two variables represents the volume of the region between the surface defined by the function (on the three dimensional Cartesian plane where z = f(x,y)) and the plane which contains its domain. (Note that the same volume can be obtained via the triple integral -- the integral of a function in three variables -- of the constant function f(x, y, z) = 1 over the above-mentioned region between the surface and the plane.) If there are more variables, a multiple integral will yield hypervolumes of multi-dimensional functions.

   a. Constant of integration
   b. Double integral
   c. Risch algorithm
   d. Trigonometric substitution

12. A _____, in mathematics, is a polynomial function of the form $f(x) = ax^2 + bx + c$, where $a \neq 0$. The graph of a _____ is a parabola whose major axis is parallel to the y-axis.

The expression $ax^2 + bx + c$ in the definition of a _____ is a polynomial of degree 2 or a 2nd degree polynomial, because the highest exponent of x is 2.

   a. Resultant
   b. Leading coefficient
   c. Discriminant
   d. Quadratic function

13. In elementary mathematics, physics, and engineering, a _____ is a geometric object that has both a magnitude (or length), direction and sense, (i.e., orientation along the given direction.) A _____ is frequently represented by a line segment with a definite direction, or graphically as an arrow, connecting an initial point A with a terminal point B, and denoted by

The magnitude of the _____ is the length of the segment and the direction characterizes the displacement of B relative to A: how much one should move the point A to 'carry' it to the point B.

Many algebraic operations on real numbers have close analogues for vectors.

   a. Linear partial differential operator
   b. Vector
   c. BDDC
   d. 15 theorem

14. In mathematics a _____ is a construction in vector calculus which associates a vector to every point in a (locally) Euclidean space.

Vector fields are often used in physics to model, for example, the speed and direction of a moving fluid throughout space, or the strength and direction of some force, such as the magnetic or gravitational force, as it changes from point to point.

In the rigorous mathematical treatment, (tangent) vector fields are defined on manifolds as sections of a manifold's tangent bundle.

a. 15 theorem
b. BDDC
c. BIBO stability
d. Vector field

15. In calculus, a branch of mathematics, the _____ is a measurement of how a function changes when its input changes. Loosely speaking, a _____ can be thought of as how much a quantity is changing at some given point. For example, the _____ of the position (or distance) of a vehicle with respect to time is the instantaneous velocity (respectively, instantaneous speed) at which the vehicle is traveling.

The process of finding a _____ is called differentiation. The fundamental theorem of calculus states that differentiation is the reverse process to integration.

a. Bounded function
b. Stationary phase approximation
c. Semi-differentiability
d. Derivative

16. In mathematics, an _____ is a function whose integral exists. Unless specifically stated, the integral in question is usually the Lebesgue integral. Otherwise, one can say that the function is 'Riemann-integrable' (i.e., its Riemann integral exists), 'Henstock-Kurzweil-integrable,' etc.

a. ACTRAN
b. AUSM
c. Integrable function
d. ALGOR

17. A _____ is a surface in the Euclidean space R^3 which is defined by a parametric equation with two parameters. Parametric representation is the most general way to specify a surface. Surfaces that occur in two of the main theorems of vector calculus, Stokes' theorem and divergence theorem, are frequently given in a parametric form.

a. Prolate
b. Torus
c. Paraboloid
d. Parametric surface

18. _____ is a type of motion in which the velocity of an object changes equal amounts in equal time periods. An example of an object having _____ would be a ball rolling down a ramp. The object picks up velocity as it goes down the ramp with equal changes in time.

a. ALGOR
b. ACTRAN
c. AUSM
d. Uniform Acceleration

19. In mathematics and its applications, a _____ system is a system for assigning an n-tuple of numbers or scalars to each point in an n-dimensional space. This concept is part of the theory of manifolds. 'Scalars' in many cases means real numbers, but, depending on context, can mean complex numbers or elements of some other commutative ring.

a. 15 theorem
b. Cylindrical coordinate system
c. Coordinate
d. Spherical coordinate system

20. In mathematics, the _____ is a two-dimensional coordinate system in which each point on a plane is determined by an angle and a distance. The _____ is especially useful in situations where the relationship between two points is most easily expressed in terms of angles and distance; in the more familiar Cartesian or rectangular coordinate system, such a relationship can only be found through trigonometric formulation.

As the coordinate system is two-dimensional, each point is determined by two polar coordinates: the radial coordinate and the angular coordinate.

a. Polar coordinate system
c. 15 theorem
b. BIBO stability
d. BDDC

21. In geometry, a _____ is a special plane curve generated by the trace of a fixed point on a small circle that rolls within a larger circle. It is comparable to the cycloid but instead of the circle rolling along a line, it rolls within a circle. The red curve is a _____ traced as the smaller black circle rolls around inside the larger blue circle (parameters are R=3.0, r=1.0, and so k=3), giving a deltoid.

If the smaller circle has radius r, and the larger circle has radius R = kr, then the parametric equations for the curve can be given by either:

$$x(\theta) = (R - r)\cos\theta + r\cos\left(\frac{R-r}{r}\theta\right)$$
$$y(\theta) = (R - r)\sin\theta - r\sin\left(\frac{R-r}{r}\theta\right),$$

or:

$$x(\theta) = r(k-1)\cos\theta + r\cos((k-1)\theta)$$
$$y(\theta) = r(k-1)\sin\theta - r\sin((k-1)\theta).$$

If k is an integer, then the curve is closed, and has k cusps (i.e., sharp corners, where the curve is not differentiable.)

a. Bullet-nose curve
c. Closed curve
b. Kappa curve
d. Hypocycloid

22. In mathematics, a _____ is a basic technique used to simplify problems in which the original variables are replaced with new ones; the new and old variables being related in some specified way. The intent is that the problem expressed in new variables may be simpler, or else equivalent to a better understood problem.

A very simple example of a useful variable change can be seen in the problem of finding the roots of the eighth order polynomial:

$$x^8 + 3x^4 + 2 = 0$$

Eighth order polynomial equations are generally impossible to solve in terms of elementary functions.

a. Linear equation
c. Change of variables
b. Cubic function
d. Quadratic formula

23. The _____ of a material is defined as its mass per unit volume. The symbol of _____ is ρ '>rho.)

Mathematically:

$$d = \frac{m}{V}$$

where:

d is the _____,
m is the mass,
V is the volume.

a. 15 theorem
c. BIBO stability
b. BDDC
d. Density

24. In mathematics, a probability _____ is a function that represents a probability distribution in terms of integrals.

Formally, a probability distribution has density f, if f is a non-negative Lebesgue-integrable function $\mathbb{R} \rightarrow \mathbb{R}$ such that the probability of the interval [a, b] is given by

$$\int_a^b f(x)\,dx$$

for any two numbers a and b. This implies that the total integral of f must be 1.

a. 15 theorem
c. BDDC
b. Density function
d. Factorial moment generating function

25. In mathematics, an _____ on a real vector space is a choice of which ordered bases are 'positively' oriented and which are 'negatively' oriented. In the three-dimensional Euclidean space, the two possible basis orientations are called right-handed and left-handed (or right-chiral and left-chiral), respectively. However, the choice of _____ is independent of the handedness or chirality of the bases (although right-handed bases are typically declared to be positively oriented, they may also be assigned a negative _____.)

a. ACTRAN
c. ALGOR
b. Unit vector
d. Orientation

26. In mathematics, a (topological) _____ is defined as follows: let I be an interval of real numbers (i.e. a non-empty connected subset of $\mathbb{R}$); then a _____ γ is a continuous mapping $\gamma : I \rightarrow X$, where X is a topological space. The _____ γ is said to be simple if it is injective, i.e. if for all x, y in I, we have $\gamma(x) = \gamma(y) \implies x = y$. If I is a closed bounded interval $[a, b]$, we also allow the possibility $\gamma(a) = \gamma(b)$ (this convention makes it possible to talk about closed simple _____.)

a. Prolate cycloid
c. Closed curve
b. Tractrix
d. Curve

27. In mathematics, a _____ is a closed surface of mass M and surface density $\sigma(x,y)$ such that:

$$M = \int \int \sigma(x,y)\, dx\, dy$$

, over the closed surface.

Planar laminas can be used to determine moments of inertia, or center of mass.

- a. BDDC
- b. 15 theorem
- c. Locally integrable function
- d. Planar lamina

28. In geometry, _____ of a curve is found at a point that is at a distance equal to the radius of curvature lying on the normal vector. It is the point at infinity if the curvature is zero. The osculating circle to the curve is centered at the _____.
- a. Strophoid
- b. Center of curvature
- c. Kampyle of Eudoxus
- d. Dolbeault operator

29. In geometry, the _____, geometric center, or barycenter of a plane figure X is the intersection of all straight lines that divide X into two parts of equal moment about the line. Informally, it is the 'average' of all points of X. The definition extends to any object X in n-dimensional space: its _____ is the intersection of all hyperplanes that divide X into two parts of equal moment.
- a. BDDC
- b. Centroid
- c. 15 theorem
- d. BIBO stability

30. In mathematics, _____ are a method of defining a curve. A simple kinematical example is when one uses a time parameter to determine the position, velocity, and other information about a body in motion.

Abstractly, a relation is given in the form of an equation, and it is shown also to be the image of functions from items such as R^n.

- a. Parametric equations
- b. Partial derivative
- c. Shift theorem
- d. Critical point

31. In mathematics, _____ refers to any of a number of loosely related concepts in different areas of geometry. Intuitively, _____ is the amount by which a geometric object deviates from being flat, or straight in the case of a line, but this is defined in different ways depending on the context. There is a key distinction between extrinsic _____, which is defined for objects embedded in another space (usually a Euclidean space) in a way that relates to the radius of _____ of circles that touch the object, and intrinsic _____, which is defined at each point in a differential manifold.
- a. Curvature
- b. Sphere
- c. Minimal surface
- d. Lie derivative

32. In infinitesimal calculus, a _____ is traditionally an infinitesimally small change in a variable. For example, if x is a variable, then a change in the value of x is often denoted Δx (or δx when this change is considered to be small.) The _____ dx represents such a change, but is infinitely small.

a. The Method of Mechanical Theorems
b. Local maximum
c. Dirichlet integral
d. Differential

33. A _____ is a mathematical equation for an unknown function of one or several variables that relates the values of the function itself and of its derivatives of various orders. they play a prominent role in engineering, physics, economics and other disciplines.

A simplified real world example of a _____ is modeling the acceleration of a ball falling through the air (considering only gravity and air resistance.)

a. Differential equation
b. Caloric polynomial
c. Phase line
d. Structural stability

34. _____ is a term in geometry and in everyday life that refers to a property in Euclidean space of two or more lines or planes, or a combination of these. The existence and properties of parallel lines are the basis of Euclid's parallel postulate. Two lines parallel would be denoted as ABC DEF.

a. 15 theorem
b. BDDC
c. BIBO stability
d. Parallelism

35. _____ is a quantity used to predict an object's ability to resist torsion, in objects (or segments of objects) with an invariant circular cross-section and no significant warping or out-of-plane deformation. It is used to calculate the angular displacement of an object subjected to a torque. It is analogous to the area moment of inertia, which characterizes an object's ability to resist bending and is required to calculate displacement.

a. Navier-Stokes equations
b. Polar moment of inertia
c. Spring equation
d. Spring constant

36. _____, also called mass _____ or the angular mass, (SI units kg m^2) is a measure of an object's resistance to changes in its rotation rate. It is the rotational analog of mass. That is, it is the inertia of a rigid rotating body with respect to its rotation.

a. Wave equation
b. Dirac equation
c. Klein-Gordon equation
d. Moment of inertia

37. In physics (specifically mechanics and electrical engineering), _____ ω (also referred to by the terms angular speed, radial frequency, circular frequency, orbital frequency, and radian frequency) is a scalar measure of rotation rate. _____ is the magnitude of the vector quantity angular velocity. The term _____ vector $\vec{\omega}$ is sometimes used as a synonym for the vector quantity angular velocity .

a. AUSM
b. ALGOR
c. ACTRAN
d. Angular frequency

38. _____ is how much exposed area an object has. It is expressed in square units. If an object has flat faces, its _____ can be calculated by adding together the areas of its faces.

a. Lipschitz domain
b. Vector area
c. Plane curve
d. Surface area

39. In mathematics, the _____ is a representation of a function as an infinite sum of terms calculated from the values of its derivatives at a single point. It may be regarded as the limit of the Taylor polynomials. If the series is centered at zero, the series is also called a Maclaurin series.

   a. BIBO stability
   b. BDDC
   c. 15 theorem
   d. Taylor series

40. A quantity is said to be subject to _____ if it decreases at a rate proportional to its value. Symbolically, this can be expressed as the following differential equation, where N is the quantity and λ is a positive number called the decay constant.

$$\frac{dN}{dt} = -\lambda N.$$

The solution to this equation is:

$$N(t) = N_0 e^{-\lambda t}.$$

Here N(t) is the quantity at time t, and N_0 = N(0) is the initial quantity, i.e. the quantity at time t = 0.

   a. Exponential sum
   b. Exponential decay
   c. ALGOR
   d. ACTRAN

41. In mathematics, a _____ that describes a line D is any vector

$$\overrightarrow{AB}$$

where A and B are two distinct points on the line D. If v is a _____ for D, so is kv for any nonzero scalar k; and these are in fact all of the direction vectors for the line D. Under some definitions, the _____ is required to be a unit vector, in which case each line has exactly two direction vectors, which are negatives of each other (equal in magnitude, opposite in direction.)

Any line in two-dimensional Euclidean space can be described as the set of solutions to an equation of the form

   ax + by + c = 0

where a, b, c are real numbers. Then one _____ of (D) is (− b,a).

   a. Dot product
   b. Direction cosines
   c. Direction vector
   d. Vector-valued function

42. In geometry, the _____ (or simply the tangent) to a curve at a given point is the straight line that 'just touches' the curve at that point (in the sense explained more precisely below.) As it passes through the point of tangency, the _____ is 'going in the same direction' as the curve, and in this sense it is the best straight-line approximation to the curve at that point. The same definition applies to space curves and curves in n-dimensional Euclidean space.

a. North pole
b. Minimal surface
c. Lie derivative
d. Tangent line

43. A _____ is one of the most curvilinear basic geometric shapes:It has two faces, zero vertices, and zero edges. The surface formed by the points at a fixed distance from a given straight line, the axis of the _____. The solid enclosed by this surface and by two planes perpendicular to the axis is also called a _____.
a. Cylinder
b. Right circular cylinder
c. BDDC
d. 15 theorem

44. In mathematics, the _____, sometimes called the direct _____ is a criterion for convergence or divergence of a series whose terms are real or complex numbers. The test determines convergence by comparing the terms of the series in question with those of a series whose convergence properties are known.

The _____ states that if the series

$$\sum_{n=1}^{\infty} b_n$$

is an absolutely convergent series and

$$|a_n| \leq |b_n|$$

for sufficiently large n , then the series

$$\sum_{n=1}^{\infty} a_n$$

converges absolutely.

a. Ratio test
b. Comparison Test
c. Telescoping series
d. Conditionally convergent

45. In physics, and more specifically kinematics, _____ is the change in velocity over time. Because velocity is a vector, it can change in two ways: a change in magnitude and/or a change in direction. In one dimension, _____ is the rate at which something speeds up or slows down.
a. ALGOR
b. AUSM
c. ACTRAN
d. Acceleration

46. If a particular point on a sphere is (arbitrarily) designated as its _____, then the corresponding antipodal point is called the south pole and the equator is the great circle that is equidistant to them. Great circles through the two poles are called lines (or meridians) of longitude, and the line connecting the two poles is called the axis of rotation. Circles on the sphere that are parallel to the equator are lines of latitude.

a. Minimal surface
b. Sphere
c. North pole
d. Tangent line

47. In vector calculus, the _____ is shorthand for either the _____ matrix or its determinant, the _____ determinant.

In algebraic geometry the _____ of a curve means the _____ variety: a group variety associated to the curve, in which the curve can be embedded.

These concepts are all named after the mathematician Carl Gustav Jacob Jacobi.

a. Saddle surface
b. Jacobian
c. Critical point
d. Vector Laplacian

Chapter 14. Vector Analysis

1. A _____, sometimes known as an energy shield, force shield typically made of energy or charged particles, that protects a person, area or object from attacks or intrusions.

A University of Washington in Seattle group has been experimenting with using a bubble of charged plasma to surround a spacecraft, contained by a fine mesh of superconducting wire. This would protect the spacecraft from interstellar radiation and some particles without needing physical shielding.

a. 15 theorem
b. BIBO stability
c. Force field
d. BDDC

2. In elementary mathematics, physics, and engineering, a _____ is a geometric object that has both a magnitude (or length), direction and sense, (i.e., orientation along the given direction.) A _____ is frequently represented by a line segment with a definite direction, or graphically as an arrow, connecting an initial point A with a terminal point B, and denoted by

The magnitude of the _____ is the length of the segment and the direction characterizes the displacement of B relative to A: how much one should move the point A to 'carry' it to the point B.

Many algebraic operations on real numbers have close analogues for vectors.

a. BDDC
b. 15 theorem
c. Linear partial differential operator
d. Vector

3. In mathematics a _____ is a construction in vector calculus which associates a vector to every point in a (locally) Euclidean space.

Vector fields are often used in physics to model, for example, the speed and direction of a moving fluid throughout space, or the strength and direction of some force, such as the magnetic or gravitational force, as it changes from point to point.

In the rigorous mathematical treatment, (tangent) vector fields are defined on manifolds as sections of a manifold's tangent bundle.

a. BDDC
b. BIBO stability
c. 15 theorem
d. Vector field

4. In physics, _____ is defined as the rate of change of position. it is vector physical quantity; both speed and direction are required to define it. In the SI (metric) system, it is measured in meters per second: (m/s) or ms^{-1}.

a. BDDC
b. BIBO stability
c. 15 theorem
d. Velocity

5. A _____ is a model used within physics to explain how gravity exists in the universe. In its original concept, gravity was a force between point masses. Following Newton, Laplace attempted to model gravity as some kind of radiation field or fluid, and since the 19th century explanations for gravity have usually been sought in terms of a field model, rather than a point attraction.
   a. BIBO stability
   b. BDDC
   c. 15 theorem
   d. Gravitational field

6. In mathematics, the _____ of a function y = f(x) is a function that, in some fashion, 'undoes' the effect of f The _____ of f is denoted f $^{-1}$. The statements y=f(x) and x=f $^{-1}$(y) are equivalent.
   a. ALGOR
   b. ACTRAN
   c. Inverse
   d. AUSM

7. In mathematics, a (topological) _____ is defined as follows: let I be an interval of real numbers (i.e. a non-empty connected subset of $\mathbb{R}$); then a _____ γ is a continuous mapping $\gamma : I \to X$, where X is a topological space. The _____ γ is said to be simple if it is injective, i.e. if for all x, y in I, we have $\gamma(x) = \gamma(y) \implies x = y$. If I is a closed bounded interval $[a, b]$, we also allow the possibility $\gamma(a) = \gamma(b)$ (this convention makes it possible to talk about closed simple _____.)
   a. Closed curve
   b. Prolate cycloid
   c. Tractrix
   d. Curve

8. In vector calculus a _____ is a vector field which is the gradient of a scalar potential. There are two closely related concepts: path independence and irrotational vector fields. Every _____ has zero curl (and is thus irrotational), and every _____ has the path independence property.
   a. Del
   b. Green's theorem
   c. Conservative vector field
   d. Divergence Theorem

9. In mathematics, even functions and odd functions are functions which satisfy particular symmetry relations, with respect to taking additive inverses. They are important in many areas of mathematical analysis, especially the theory of power series and Fourier series. They are named for the parity of the powers of the power functions which satisfy each condition: the function f(x) = x^n is an _____ if n is an even integer, and it is an odd function if n is an odd integer.
   a. Infinite series
   b. Operational calculus
   c. Integral of secant cubed
   d. Even function

10. In physics, and more specifically kinematics, _____ is the change in velocity over time. Because velocity is a vector, it can change in two ways: a change in magnitude and/or a change in direction. In one dimension, _____ is the rate at which something speeds up or slows down.
    a. ALGOR
    b. ACTRAN
    c. Acceleration
    d. AUSM

11. In mathematics, an _____ on a real vector space is a choice of which ordered bases are 'positively' oriented and which are 'negatively' oriented. In the three-dimensional Euclidean space, the two possible basis orientations are called right-handed and left-handed (or right-chiral and left-chiral), respectively. However, the choice of _____ is independent of the handedness or chirality of the bases (although right-handed bases are typically declared to be positively oriented, they may also be assigned a negative _____.)

a. ACTRAN
c. Unit vector
b. Orientation
d. ALGOR

12. In mathematics, the _____, sometimes called the direct _____ is a criterion for convergence or divergence of a series whose terms are real or complex numbers. The test determines convergence by comparing the terms of the series in question with those of a series whose convergence properties are known.

The _____ states that if the series

$$\sum_{n=1}^{\infty} b_n$$

is an absolutely convergent series and

$$|a_n| \leq |b_n|$$

for sufficiently large n , then the series

$$\sum_{n=1}^{\infty} a_n$$

converges absolutely.

a. Ratio test
c. Conditionally convergent
b. Telescoping series
d. Comparison Test

13. In vector calculus a conservative vector field is a vector field which is the gradient of a scalar potential. There are two closely related concepts: path independence and _____ vector fields. Every conservative vector field has zero curl (and is thus _____), and every conservative vector field has the path independence property.

a. ACTRAN
c. AUSM
b. ALGOR
d. Irrotational

14. _____ is the addition of a set of numbers; the result is their sum or total. An interim or present total of a _____ process is termed the running total. The 'numbers' to be summed may be natural numbers, complex numbers, matrices, or still more complicated objects.

a. BIBO stability
c. BDDC
b. 15 theorem
d. Summation

15. In vector calculus, the _____ is an operator that measures the magnitude of a vector field's source or sink at a given point; the _____ of a vector field is a (signed) scalar. For example, consider air as it is heated or cooled. The relevant vector field for this example is the velocity of the moving air at a point.

a. Green's theorem
c. Gradient theorem
b. Divergence
d. Triple product

16. Integration is an important concept in mathematics, specifically in the field of calculus and, more broadly, mathematical analysis. Given a function f of a real variable x and an interval [a, b] of the real line, the _____

$$\int_a^b f(x)\,dx,$$

is defined informally to be the net signed area of the region in the xy-plane bounded by the graph of f, the x-axis, and the vertical lines x = a and x = b.

The term '_____' may also refer to the notion of antiderivative, a function F whose derivative is the given function f.

a. Integral test for convergence
c. Indefinite integral
b. Integrand
d. Integral

17. In mathematics, the _____ for convergence is a method used to test infinite series of non-negative terms for convergence. An early form of the test of convergence was developed in India by Madhava in the 14th century, and by his followers at the Kerala School. In Europe, it was later developed by Maclaurin and Cauchy and is sometimes known as the Maclaurin-Cauchy test.

a. ALGOR
c. AUSM
b. ACTRAN
d. Integral Test

18. In mathematics, the _____ is a criterion for the convergence (a convergence test) of an infinite series

$$\sum_{n=1}^{\infty} a_n.$$

It is particularly useful in connection with power series.

The _____ was developed first by Cauchy and so is sometimes known as the Cauchy _____ or Cauchy's radical test.
The _____ uses the number

$$C = \limsup_{n \to \infty} \sqrt[n]{|a_n|},$$

where 'lim sup' denotes the limit superior, possibly ∞.

a. Mean Value Theorem
c. Related rates
b. Racetrack principle
d. Root Test

19. In vector calculus a _____ vector field (also known as an incompressible vector field) is a vector field v with divergence zero:

$$\nabla \cdot \mathbf{v} = 0.$$

The fundamental theorem of vector calculus states that any vector field can be expressed as the sum of a conservative vector field and a _____ field. The condition of zero divergence is satisfied whenever a vector field v has only a vector potential component, because the definition of the vector potential A as:

$$\mathbf{v} = \nabla \times \mathbf{A}$$

automatically results in the identity (as can be shown, for example, using Cartesian coordinates):

$$\nabla \cdot \mathbf{v} = \nabla \cdot (\nabla \times \mathbf{A}) = 0.$$

The converse also holds: for any _____ v there exists a vector potential A such that $\mathbf{V} = \nabla \times \mathbf{A}$.

The divergence theorem, gives the equivalent integral definition of a _____ field; namely that for any closed surface S, the net total flux through the surface must be zero:

$$\iint_S \mathbf{v} \cdot d\mathbf{s} = 0$$

where $d\mathbf{s}$ is the outward normal to each surface element.

a. Bloch space
c. Principal part

b. Trigonometric series
d. Solenoidal

20. In vector calculus a _____ is a vector field v with divergence zero:

$$\nabla \cdot \mathbf{v} = 0.$$

The fundamental theorem of vector calculus states that any vector field can be expressed as the sum of a conservative vector field and a solenoidal field. The condition of zero divergence is satisfied whenever a vector field v has only a vector potential component, because the definition of the vector potential A as:

$$\mathbf{v} = \nabla \times \mathbf{A}$$

automatically results in the identity (as can be shown, for example, using Cartesian coordinates):

$$\nabla \cdot \mathbf{v} = \nabla \cdot (\nabla \times \mathbf{A}) = 0.$$

The converse also holds: for any solenoidal v there exists a vector potential A such that $\mathbf{V} = \nabla \times \mathbf{A}$.

The divergence theorem, gives the equivalent integral definition of a solenoidal field; namely that for any closed surface S, the net total flux through the surface must be zero:

$$\iint_S \mathbf{v} \cdot d\mathbf{s} = 0$$

where $d\mathbf{s}$ is the outward normal to each surface element.

a. Critical value
b. Principal part
c. Solenoidal Vector field
d. Dickman-de Bruijn function

21. In differential geometry there are a number of second-order, linear, elliptic differential operators bearing the name _____

The connection _____ is a differential operator acting on the various tensor bundles of a manifold, defined in terms of a Riemmanian- or pseudo-Riemannian metric.

a. Laplacian
b. Peetre theorem
c. Dirac operator
d. Semi-elliptic operator

22. _____ is a type of motion in which the velocity of an object changes equal amounts in equal time periods. An example of an object having _____ would be a ball rolling down a ramp. The object picks up velocity as it goes down the ramp with equal changes in time.

a. ALGOR
b. ACTRAN
c. Uniform Acceleration
d. AUSM

23. In calculus, the indefinite integral of a given function (i.e. the set of all antiderivatives of the function) is always written with a constant, the _____. This constant expresses an ambiguity inherent in the construction of antiderivatives. If a function f(x) is defined on an interval and F(x) is an antiderivative of f(x), then the set of all antiderivatives of f(x) is given by the functions F(x) + C, where C is an arbitrary constant.

a. Disk integration
b. Sum rule in integration
c. Constant of integration
d. Nonelementary integral

24. In mathematics, a _____ is a function whose definition is dependent on the value of the independent variable. Mathematically, a real-valued function f of a real variable x is a relationship whose definition is given differently on disjoint subsets of its domain

The word piecewise is also used to describe any property of a _____ that holds for each piece but may not hold for the whole domain of the function.

a. Constant function
b. Surjective
c. Range
d. Piecewise-defined function

Chapter 14. Vector Analysis

25. A _____ is a type of manifold that is locally similar enough to Euclidean space to allow one to do calculus Any manifold can be described by a collection of charts, also known as an atlas.
    a. Minimal surface
    b. Sphere
    c. Differentiable manifold
    d. Tangent line

26. In mathematics, if f is a function from A to B then an _____ for f is a function in the opposite direction, from B to A, with the property that a round trip (a composition) from A to B to A (or from B to A to B) returns each element of the initial set to itself. Thus, if an input x into the function f produces an output y, then inputting y into the _____ f^{-1} (read f inverse, not to be confused with exponentiation) produces the output x. Not every function has an inverse; those that do are called invertible.
    a. Aristotle
    b. Augustin-Jean Fresnel
    c. Inverse function
    d. Augustin Louis Cauchy

27. In mathematics, a _____ is an integral where the function to be integrated is evaluated along a curve. Various different line integrals are in use. A specific case of an integration along a closed curve in two dimensions or the complex plane is the contour integral.
    a. Picard theorem
    b. Radius of convergence
    c. Mittag-Leffler star
    d. Line integral

28. In infinitesimal calculus, a _____ is traditionally an infinitesimally small change in a variable. For example, if x is a variable, then a change in the value of x is often denoted Δx (or δx when this change is considered to be small.) The _____ dx represents such a change, but is infinitely small.
    a. Local maximum
    b. The Method of Mechanical Theorems
    c. Dirichlet integral
    d. Differential

29. In the mathematical fields of differential geometry and tensor calculus, differential forms are an approach to multivariable calculus that is independent of coordinates. A _____ of degree k, or (differential) k-form, on a smooth manifold M is a smooth section of the kth exterior power of the cotangent bundle of M. The set of all k-forms on M is a vector space commonly denoted $\Omega^k(M).$

A differential 0-form is by definition a smooth function on M. A differential 1-form is an object dual to a vector field on M.

    a. Soldering
    b. Hodge dual
    c. Two-form
    d. Differential form

30. When the number of variables is two, this is a _____, if it is three this is a level surface, and for higher values of n the level set is a level hypersurface.

More specifically, a _____ is the set of all real-valued roots of an equation in two variables x_1 and x_2. A level surface is the set of all real-valued roots of an equation in three variables x_1, x_2 and x_3.

    a. Partial derivative
    b. Level curve
    c. Scalar field
    d. Multipole moment

Chapter 14. Vector Analysis

31. A _____ of a function of two variables is a curve along which the function has a constant value. In cartography, a _____ (often just called a 'contour') joins points of equal elevation (height) above a given level, such as mean sea level. A contour map is a map illustrated with contour lines, for example a topographic map, which thus shows valleys and hills, and the steepness of slopes.

   a. BDDC
   b. BIBO stability
   c. 15 theorem
   d. Contour line

32. The _____, also known as the fundamental theorem of calculus for line integrals, says that a line integral through a gradient field (any irrotational vector field can be expressed as a gradient) can be evaluated by evaluating the original scalar field at the endpoints of the curve:

$$\phi(\mathbf{q}) - \phi(\mathbf{p}) = \int_L \nabla\phi \cdot d\mathbf{r}.$$

It is a generalisation of the fundamental theorem of calculus to any curve on a line rather than just the real line.

The _____ implies that line integrals through irrotational vector fields are path independent. In physics this theorem is one of the ways of defining a 'conservative' force.

   a. Gradient theorem
   b. Del
   c. Divergence Theorem
   d. Triple product

33. A curve γ is said to be closed or a loop if $I = [a, b]$ and if $\gamma(a) = \gamma(b)$. A _____ is thus a continuous mapping of the circle S¹; a simple _____ is also called a Jordan curve or a Jordan arc. The Jordan curve theorem states that such curves divide the plane into an 'interior' and an 'exterior'.

   a. Bullet-nose curve
   b. Kappa curve
   c. Curve
   d. Closed curve

34. The _____ is the derived unit of energy in the International System of Units. It is defined as:

$$1\,\mathrm{J} = 1\,\mathrm{kg} \cdot \mathrm{m}^2 \cdot \mathrm{s}^{-2}$$

One _____ is the amount of energy required to perform the following physical actions:

- The work done by a force of one newton travelling through a distance of one metre;
- The work required to move an electric charge of one coulomb through an electrical potential difference of one volt; or one coulomb volt, with the symbol CÂ·V;
- The work done to produce the power of one watt continuously for one second; or one watt second (compare kilowatt hour), with the symbol WÂ·s. Thus a kilowatt hour is 3,600,000 joules or 3.6 megajoules;

Chapter 14. Vector Analysis

1 _____ is equal to:

- 1×10^7 ergs (exactly)
- 1.6022×10^{19} eV (electronvolts)
- 0.2390 cal (gram calories or small calories)
- 2.3901×10^{-4} kcal (kilocalories, kilogram calories, large calories or food calories)
- 9.4782×10^{-4} BTU (British thermal unit)
- 0.7376 ftÂ·lbf (foot-pound force)
- 23.7 ftÂ·pdl (foot-poundals)
- 2.7778×10^{-7} kilowatt-hour
- 2.7778×10^{-4} watt-hour
- 9.8692×10^{-3} litre-atmosphere
- 1×10^{-44} Foe (exactly)

Units defined in terms of the _____ include:

- 1 thermochemical calorie = 4.184 J
- 1 International Table calorie = 4.1868 J
- 1 watt hour = 3600 J
- 1 kilowatt hour = 3.6×10^6 J (or 3.6 MJ)
- 1 ton TNT exploding = 4.184 GJ

Useful to remember:

- 1 _____ = 1 newton × 1 meter = 1 watt × 1 second

One _____ in everyday life is approximately:

- the energy required to lift a small apple one metre straight up.
- the energy released when that same apple falls one meter to the ground.
- the energy released as heat by a quiet person, every hundredth of a second.
- the energy required to heat one gram of dry, cool air by 1 degree Celsius.
- one hundredth of the energy a person can receive by drinking a drop of beer.
- the kinetic energy of an adult human moving a distance of about a handspan every second.

- Conversion of units
- Orders of magnitude (energy)
- Fluence

a. BDDC
c. 15 theorem
b. BIBO stability
d. Joule

35. The _____ of an object is the extra energy which it possesses due to its motion. It is defined as the work needed to accelerate a body of a given mass from rest to its current velocity. Having gained this energy during its acceleration, the body maintains this _____ unless its speed changes.
   a. Law of Conservation of Energy
   c. Kinetic energy
   b. 15 theorem
   d. BDDC

36. The _____ states that the total amount of energy in an isolated system remains constant. A consequence of this law is that energy cannot be created or destroyed. The only thing that can happen with energy in an isolated system is that it can change form, that is to say for instance kinetic energy can become thermal energy.
   a. Potential energy
   c. 15 theorem
   b. BDDC
   d. Law of Conservation of Energy

37. In probability theory and statistics, the _____ (or expectation value or mean and for continuous random variables with a density function it is the probability density -weighted integral of the possible values.

The term '_____' can be misleading.

   a. ACTRAN
   c. ALGOR
   b. Expected value
   d. AUSM

38. In calculus, the _____ states, roughly, that given a section of a smooth curve, there is at least one point on that section at which the derivative (slope) of the curve is equal (parallel) to the 'average' derivative of the section. It is used to prove theorems that make global conclusions about a function on an interval starting from local hypotheses about derivatives at points of the interval.

This theorem can be understood concretely by applying it to motion: If a car travels one hundred miles in one hour, so its average speed during that time was 100 miles per hour.

   a. Mean Value Theorem
   c. Hyperbolic angle
   b. Periodic function
   d. Limits of integration

39. _____ can be thought of as energy stored within a physical system. It is called _____ because it has the potential to be converted into other forms of energy, such as kinetic energy, and to do work in the process. The standard (SI) unit of measure for _____ is the joule, the same as for work or energy in general.
   a. 15 theorem
   c. Law of Conservation of Energy
   b. BDDC
   d. Potential energy

40. In mathematics, a _____ is a function whose values do not vary and thus are constant. For example, if we have the function f(x) = 4, then f is constant since f maps any value to 4. More formally, a function f : A → B is a _____ if f(x) = f(y) for all x and y in A.
   a. Range
   c. Surjective
   b. Constant function
   d. Piecewise-defined function

41. In vector calculus, the _____ Ostrogradskye;s theorem the _____ states that the outward flux of a vector field through a surface is equal to the triple integral of the divergence on the region inside the surface. Intuitively, it states that the sum of all sources minus the sum of all sinks gives the net flow out of a region.
   a. Divergence
   b. Del
   c. Green's theorem
   d. Divergence Theorem

Chapter 15. Functions

1. In mathematics, _____ are a method of defining a curve. A simple kinematical example is when one uses a time parameter to determine the position, velocity, and other information about a body in motion.

Abstractly, a relation is given in the form of an equation, and it is shown also to be the image of functions from items such as R^n.

   a. Shift theorem
   b. Critical point
   c. Partial derivative
   d. Parametric equations

2. A _____ is a surface in the Euclidean space R^3 which is defined by a parametric equation with two parameters. Parametric representation is the most general way to specify a surface. Surfaces that occur in two of the main theorems of vector calculus, Stokes' theorem and divergence theorem, are frequently given in a parametric form.
   a. Torus
   b. Prolate
   c. Parametric surface
   d. Paraboloid

3. In mathematics, the _____ is a two-dimensional coordinate system in which each point on a plane is determined by an angle and a distance. The _____ is especially useful in situations where the relationship between two points is most easily expressed in terms of angles and distance; in the more familiar Cartesian or rectangular coordinate system, such a relationship can only be found through trigonometric formulation.

As the coordinate system is two-dimensional, each point is determined by two polar coordinates: the radial coordinate and the angular coordinate.

   a. BIBO stability
   b. BDDC
   c. 15 theorem
   d. Polar coordinate system

4. In mathematics and its applications, a _____ system is a system for assigning an n-tuple of numbers or scalars to each point in an n-dimensional space. This concept is part of the theory of manifolds. 'Scalars' in many cases means real numbers, but, depending on context, can mean complex numbers or elements of some other commutative ring.
   a. Cylindrical coordinate system
   b. Spherical coordinate system
   c. 15 theorem
   d. Coordinate

5. A surface normal to a flat surface is a vector which is perpendicular to that surface. A normal to a non-flat surface at a point P on the surface is a vector perpendicular to the tangent plane to that surface at P. The word 'normal' is also used as an adjective: a line normal to a plane, the normal component of a force, the _____, etc. The concept of normality generalizes to orthogonality.
   a. Paraboloid
   b. Hyperbolic paraboloid
   c. Normal line
   d. Normal vector

6. In mathematics, a _____ of a function of several variables is its derivative with respect to one of those variables with the others held constant (as opposed to the total derivative, in which all variables are allowed to vary.) Partial derivatives are useful in vector calculus and differential geometry.

The _____ of a function f with respect to the variable x is written as f'_x, $\partial_x f$, or $\partial f/\partial x$.

Chapter 15. Functions

a. Level curve
b. Jacobian
c. Differentiation operator
d. Partial derivative

7. In geometry, the _____ (or simply the tangent) to a curve at a given point is the straight line that 'just touches' the curve at that point (in the sense explained more precisely below.) As it passes through the point of tangency, the _____ is 'going in the same direction' as the curve, and in this sense it is the best straight-line approximation to the curve at that point. The same definition applies to space curves and curves in n-dimensional Euclidean space.

a. Lie derivative
b. North pole
c. Minimal surface
d. Tangent line

8. In calculus, a branch of mathematics, the _____ is a measurement of how a function changes when its input changes. Loosely speaking, a _____ can be thought of as how much a quantity is changing at some given point. For example, the _____ of the position (or distance) of a vehicle with respect to time is the instantaneous velocity (respectively, instantaneous speed) at which the vehicle is traveling.

The process of finding a _____ is called differentiation. The fundamental theorem of calculus states that differentiation is the reverse process to integration.

a. Semi-differentiability
b. Stationary phase approximation
c. Bounded function
d. Derivative

9. In elementary mathematics, physics, and engineering, a _____ is a geometric object that has both a magnitude (or length), direction and sense, (i.e., orientation along the given direction.) A _____ is frequently represented by a line segment with a definite direction, or graphically as an arrow, connecting an initial point A with a terminal point B, and denoted by

The magnitude of the _____ is the length of the segment and the direction characterizes the displacement of B relative to A: how much one should move the point A to 'carry' it to the point B.

Many algebraic operations on real numbers have close analogues for vectors.

a. BDDC
b. 15 theorem
c. Linear partial differential operator
d. Vector

10. _____ is how much exposed area an object has. It is expressed in square units. If an object has flat faces, its _____ can be calculated by adding together the areas of its faces.

a. Surface area
b. Lipschitz domain
c. Plane curve
d. Vector area

11. In mathematics, a _____ is a definite integral taken over a surface (which may be a curved set in space); it can be thought of as the double integral analog of the line integral. Given a surface, one may integrate over it scalar fields (that is, functions which return numbers as values), and vector fields (that is, functions which return vectors as values.)

Surface integrals have applications in physics, particularly with the classical theory of electromagnetism.

a. Contact
b. Symmetry of second derivatives
c. Differential operator
d. Surface integral

12. In mathematics, a (topological) _____ is defined as follows: let I be an interval of real numbers (i.e. a non-empty connected subset of $\mathbb{R}$); then a _____ γ is a continuous mapping $\gamma : I \to X$, where X is a topological space. The _____ γ is said to be simple if it is injective, i.e. if for all x, y in I, we have $\gamma(x) = \gamma(y) \implies x = y$. If I is a closed bounded interval $[a, b]$, we also allow the possibility $\gamma(a) = \gamma(b)$ (this convention makes it possible to talk about closed simple _____.)

a. Closed curve
b. Curve
c. Tractrix
d. Prolate cycloid

13. Integration is an important concept in mathematics, specifically in the field of calculus and, more broadly, mathematical analysis. Given a function f of a real variable x and an interval [a, b] of the real line, the _____

$$\int_a^b f(x)\,dx,$$

is defined informally to be the net signed area of the region in the xy-plane bounded by the graph of f, the x-axis, and the vertical lines x = a and x = b.

The term '_____' may also refer to the notion of antiderivative, a function F whose derivative is the given function f.

a. Integral
b. Integrand
c. Integral test for convergence
d. Indefinite integral

14. For an orientable surface, a consistent choice of 'clockwise' (as opposed to counter-clockwise) is called an orientation, and the surface is called _____. An orientable surface admits exactly 2 orientations, and the distinction between an _____ surface and an orientable surface is subtle and frequently blurred. An orientable surface is an abstract surface that admits an orientation, while an _____ surface is a surface that is abstractly orientable, and has the additional datum of a choice of one of the 2 possible orientations.

a. AUSM
b. ALGOR
c. ACTRAN
d. Oriented

15. In mathematics, an _____ on a real vector space is a choice of which ordered bases are 'positively' oriented and which are 'negatively' oriented. In the three-dimensional Euclidean space, the two possible basis orientations are called right-handed and left-handed (or right-chiral and left-chiral), respectively. However, the choice of _____ is independent of the handedness or chirality of the bases (although right-handed bases are typically declared to be positively oriented, they may also be assigned a negative _____.)

a. ACTRAN
b. Unit vector
c. ALGOR
d. Orientation

Chapter 15. Functions

16. If a particular point on a sphere is (arbitrarily) designated as its _____, then the corresponding antipodal point is called the south pole and the equator is the great circle that is equidistant to them. Great circles through the two poles are called lines (or meridians) of longitude, and the line connecting the two poles is called the axis of rotation. Circles on the sphere that are parallel to the equator are lines of latitude.

    a. Tangent line
    b. Sphere
    c. Minimal surface
    d. North pole

17. A _____ is one of the most curvilinear basic geometric shapes:It has two faces, zero vertices, and zero edges. The surface formed by the points at a fixed distance from a given straight line, the axis of the _____. The solid enclosed by this surface and by two planes perpendicular to the axis is also called a _____.

    a. BDDC
    b. 15 theorem
    c. Right circular cylinder
    d. Cylinder

18. A surface S in the Euclidean space R^3 is _____ if a two-dimensional figure (for example,) cannot be moved around the surface and back to where it started so that it looks like its own mirror image (.) Otherwise the surface is non-_____.

    More precisely, and applicable to non-embedded surfaces, a surface is non-_____ if there is a continuous map f from the product of a 2-dimensional disk D and the unit interval [0,1] to the surface, $f : D \times [0, 1] \to S$ such that f(c,t) = f(d,t) only if c = d for every t in [0,1], and there exists a reflection map r such that f(d,0) = f(r(d),1) for every d in D.

    a. ACTRAN
    b. Orientable
    c. AUSM
    d. ALGOR

19. In the various subfields of physics, there exist two common usages of the term _____, both with rigorous mathematical frameworks.

    - In the study of transport phenomena (heat transfer, mass transfer and fluid dynamics), _____ is defined as the amount that flows through a unit area per unit time. _____ in this definition is a vector.
    - In the field of electromagnetism and mathematics, _____ is usually the integral of a vector quantity over a finite surface. The result of this integration is a scalar quantity. The magnetic _____ is thus the integral of the magnetic vector field B over a surface, and the electric _____ is defined similarly. Using this definition, the _____ of the Poynting vector over a specified surface is the rate at which electromagnetic energy flows through that surface. Confusingly, the Poynting vector is sometimes called the power _____, which is an example of the first usage of _____, above. It has units of watts per square metre (WÂ·m^{-2})

    One could argue, based on the work of James Clerk Maxwell, that the transport definition precedes the more recent way the term is used in electromagnetism. The specific quote from Maxwell is 'In the case of fluxes, we have to take the integral, over a surface, of the _____ through every element of the surface. The result of this operation is called the surface integral of the _____.

    a. BIBO stability
    b. 15 theorem
    c. BDDC
    d. Flux

20. In calculus, an _____ is the limit of a definite integral as an endpoint of the interval of integration approaches either a specified real number or ∞ or −∞ or, in some cases, as both endpoints approach limits.

Specifically, an _____ is a limit of the form

$$\lim_{b \to \infty} \int_a^b f(x)\,dx, \qquad \lim_{a \to -\infty} \int_a^b f(x)\,dx,$$

or of the form

$$\lim_{c \to b^-} \int_a^c f(x)\,dx, \qquad \lim_{c \to a^+} \int_c^b f(x)\,dx,$$

in which one takes a limit in one or the other (or sometimes both) endpoints. Improper integrals may also occur at an interior point of the domain of integration, or at multiple such points.

a. ACTRAN
b. AUSM
c. ALGOR
d. Improper integral

21. In mathematics, especially in order theory, an _____ of a subset S of some partially ordered set (P, >≤) is an element of P which is greater than or equal to every element of S. The term lower bound is defined dually as an element of P which is lesser than or equal to every element of S. A set with an _____ is said to be bounded from above by that bound, a set with a lower bound is said to be bounded from below by that bound.

A subset S of a partially ordered set P may fail to have any bounds or may have many different upper and lower bounds. By transitivity, any element greater than or equal to an _____ of S is again an _____ of S, and any element lesser than or equal to any lower bound of S is again a lower bound of S. This leads to the consideration of least upper bounds: (or suprema) and greatest lower bounds (or infima.)

a. ACTRAN
b. AUSM
c. ALGOR
d. Upper bound

22. In mathematics, a _____ is an ordered list of objects (or events). Like a set, it contains members (also called elements or terms), and the number of terms (possibly infinite) is called the length of the _____. Unlike a set, order matters, and the exact same elements can appear multiple times at different positions in the _____.

a. Slope
b. 15 theorem
c. Sequence
d. Y-intercept

23. The _____ of an angle is the ratio of the length of the adjacent side to the length of the hypotenuse. In our case

$$\cos A = \frac{\text{adjacent}}{\text{hypotenuse}} = \frac{b}{h}.$$

Chapter 15. Functions

The tangent of an angle is the ratio of the length of the opposite side to the length of the adjacent side. In our case

$$\tan A = \frac{\text{opposite}}{\text{adjacent}} = \frac{a}{b}.$$

The remaining three functions are best defined using the above three functions.

a. Trigonometric functions
b. Trigonometric
c. Sine integral
d. Cosine

24. In vector calculus, the _____ is an operator that measures the magnitude of a vector field's source or sink at a given point; the _____ of a vector field is a (signed) scalar. For example, consider air as it is heated or cooled. The relevant vector field for this example is the velocity of the moving air at a point.
a. Gradient theorem
b. Triple product
c. Divergence
d. Green's theorem

25. In vector calculus, the _____ Ostrogradskye;s theorem the _____ states that the outward flux of a vector field through a surface is equal to the triple integral of the divergence on the region inside the surface. Intuitively, it states that the sum of all sources minus the sum of all sinks gives the net flow out of a region.
a. Del
b. Divergence
c. Green's theorem
d. Divergence Theorem

26. A _____ is perfectly round geometrical object in three-dimensional space, such as the shape of a round ball. Like a circle in two dimensions, a perfect _____ is completely symmetrical around its center, with all points on the surface lying the same distance r from the center point. This distance r is known as the radius of the _____.
a. Tangent line
b. North pole
c. Minimal surface
d. Sphere

27. Let f be a differentiable function, and let f'(x) be its derivative. The derivative of f'(x) (if it has one) is written f''(x) and is called the _____ of f. Similarly, the derivative of a _____, if it exists, is written f'''(x) and is called the third derivative of f.
a. Vertical asymptote
b. Slant asymptote
c. Second Derivative
d. Stationary phase approximation

28. In calculus, a branch of mathematics, the _____ is a criterion often useful for determining whether a given stationary point of a function is a local maximum or a local minimum.

The test states: If the function f is twice differentiable at a stationary point x, meaning that $f'(x) = 0$, then:

- If $f''(x) < 0$ then f has a local maximum at x.
- If $f''(x) > 0$ then f has a local minimum at x.
- If $f''(x) = 0$, the _____ says nothing about the point x, has a possible inflection point.

In the last case, the function may have a local maximum or minimum there, but the function is sufficiently 'flat' that this is undetected by the second derivative. In this case one has to examine the third derivative. Such an example is f(x) = x⁴.

a. Stationary point
c. Linearity of differentiation
b. Symmetric derivative
d. Second Derivative Test

29. In mathematics a _____ is a construction in vector calculus which associates a vector to every point in a (locally) Euclidean space.

Vector fields are often used in physics to model, for example, the speed and direction of a moving fluid throughout space, or the strength and direction of some force, such as the magnetic or gravitational force, as it changes from point to point.

In the rigorous mathematical treatment, (tangent) vector fields are defined on manifolds as sections of a manifold's tangent bundle.

a. 15 theorem
c. Vector field
b. BDDC
d. BIBO stability

30. In mathematics and physics, a _____ associates a scalar value, which can be either mathematical in definition to every point in space. Scalar fields are often used in physics, for instance to indicate the temperature distribution throughout space or more specifically, differential geometry, the set of functions defined on a manifold define the commutative ring of functions.

a. Level curve
c. Symmetry of second derivatives
b. Vector Laplacian
d. Scalar field

31. In mathematics, the hyperbolic functions are analogs of the ordinary trigonometric functions. The basic hyperbolic functions are the _____ 'sinh', and the hyperbolic cosine 'cosh', from which are derived the hyperbolic tangent 'tanh', etc., in analogy to the derived trigonometric functions. The inverse hyperbolic functions are the area _____ 'arsinh' (also called 'asinh', or sometimes by the misnomer of 'arcsinh') and so on.

a. Square root function
c. Hyperbolic tangent
b. Signum function
d. Hyperbolic sine

32. The _____ of an angle is the ratio of the length of the opposite side to the length of the hypotenuse. In our case

$$\sin A = \frac{\text{opposite}}{\text{hypotenuse}} = \frac{a}{h}.$$

Note that this ratio does not depend on size of the particular right triangle chosen, as long as it contains the angle A, since all such triangles are similar.

The cosine of an angle is the ratio of the length of the adjacent side to the length of the hypotenuse.

a. Trigonometric
c. Sine integral

b. Trigonometric functions
d. Sine

Chapter 1

1. b	2. d	3. b	4. d	5. d	6. d	7. a	8. d	9. c	10. d
11. d	12. c	13. b	14. b	15. a	16. c	17. d	18. a	19. c	20. d
21. c	22. d	23. c	24. b	25. a	26. d	27. d	28. c	29. b	30. d
31. a	32. c	33. c	34. d	35. d	36. c	37. d	38. b	39. c	40. d
41. b	42. d	43. b	44. d	45. d	46. d	47. c	48. d	49. a	50. b
51. a	52. a	53. a	54. b	55. b	56. c	57. a	58. d	59. c	60. d
61. d	62. d	63. d	64. d	65. b	66. c	67. d	68. d	69. d	70. a
71. d	72. d	73. d	74. b	75. a	76. c	77. a	78. d	79. d	80. d
81. d	82. d	83. c	84. b	85. d	86. d	87. c	88. d	89. d	90. d
91. d	92. d	93. c	94. d	95. b	96. d	97. d	98. a	99. c	100. d
101. c	102. d	103. d	104. d	105. c	106. b	107. b	108. d		

Chapter 2

1. d	2. b	3. a	4. d	5. d	6. c	7. d	8. d	9. c	10. d
11. a	12. d	13. c	14. c	15. d	16. d	17. d	18. d	19. d	20. d
21. d	22. d	23. d	24. d	25. a	26. a	27. a	28. d	29. d	30. a
31. d	32. c	33. d	34. c	35. d	36. d	37. d	38. d	39. d	40. d
41. d	42. d	43. d	44. b	45. d	46. d				

Chapter 3

1. b	2. d	3. d	4. d	5. c	6. d	7. d	8. b	9. d	10. d
11. b	12. d	13. a	14. d	15. d	16. b	17. b	18. d	19. d	20. d
21. d	22. c	23. a	24. b	25. d	26. b	27. d	28. a	29. a	30. d
31. a	32. a	33. d	34. d	35. d	36. d	37. c	38. d	39. d	40. d
41. a	42. b	43. d	44. c	45. d	46. d	47. d	48. d	49. d	50. d
51. c									

Chapter 4

1. c	2. c	3. a	4. d	5. c	6. d	7. d	8. a	9. a	10. c
11. a	12. d	13. c	14. c	15. d	16. b	17. d	18. a	19. d	20. d
21. b	22. b	23. d	24. b	25. c	26. d	27. b	28. a	29. d	30. b
31. d	32. a	33. d	34. d	35. d	36. d	37. d	38. b	39. d	40. a
41. d	42. d	43. b	44. b	45. d	46. d	47. d			

Chapter 5

1. c	2. d	3. d	4. d	5. a	6. d	7. d	8. d	9. d	10. d
11. d	12. d	13. a	14. b	15. b	16. d	17. d	18. d	19. b	20. b
21. d	22. a	23. a	24. b	25. a	26. a	27. d	28. d	29. c	30. d
31. b	32. d	33. a	34. d	35. d	36. a	37. b	38. c	39. b	40. c
41. d	42. a	43. d	44. c	45. d	46. d	47. a	48. d	49. d	50. a
51. d	52. c	53. c	54. d	55. b	56. d	57. c	58. b	59. c	60. d
61. d	62. b	63. b	64. b	65. d	66. b	67. d	68. d	69. d	70. d
71. d	72. b	73. a	74. d	75. d	76. d	77. b	78. a	79. b	80. a
81. d	82. b	83. a	84. d	85. d	86. a	87. d	88. d	89. d	90. d
91. d	92. c	93. c	94. b	95. b	96. d	97. d	98. d	99. a	

ANSWER KEY

Chapter 6

1. a	2. c	3. a	4. d	5. c	6. b	7. a	8. c	9. d	10. d
11. a	12. b	13. d	14. d	15. a	16. c	17. d	18. d	19. b	20. c
21. a	22. c	23. d	24. b	25. d	26. d	27. c	28. a	29. d	30. d
31. d	32. d	33. a	34. a	35. b	36. d	37. d	38. d	39. b	40. d

Chapter 7

1. a	2. d	3. d	4. d	5. b	6. a	7. c	8. d	9. b	10. c
11. a	12. b	13. b	14. d	15. a	16. d	17. a	18. c	19. a	20. d
21. d	22. c	23. a	24. d	25. a	26. d	27. d	28. d	29. c	30. b
31. c	32. d	33. d	34. a	35. d	36. a	37. d	38. b	39. c	40. d
41. c	42. d	43. d							

Chapter 8

1. d	2. d	3. d	4. d	5. a	6. c	7. d	8. d	9. d	10. a
11. d	12. d	13. b	14. d	15. d	16. a	17. c	18. b	19. d	20. a
21. a	22. d	23. d	24. c	25. b	26. d	27. d	28. c	29. d	30. b
31. b	32. b	33. c	34. d	35. d	36. d	37. d	38. a	39. b	40. b
41. b	42. c	43. c	44. b	45. d	46. c	47. a	48. d	49. d	50. d
51. b	52. b	53. d	54. b	55. d	56. b	57. d	58. b	59. d	60. a
61. a	62. b	63. c	64. d	65. d	66. a	67. d	68. d	69. c	70. a
71. a	72. d	73. d	74. d	75. c	76. d	77. d	78. a	79. b	80. a
81. d	82. d	83. d	84. b						

Chapter 9

1. b	2. b	3. c	4. d	5. d	6. b	7. d	8. d	9. d	10. d
11. d	12. d	13. d	14. b	15. d	16. a	17. d	18. d	19. b	20. c
21. d	22. d	23. b	24. b	25. d	26. d	27. b	28. d	29. c	30. d
31. d	32. d	33. d	34. a	35. d	36. c	37. a	38. d	39. d	40. d
41. a	42. c	43. d	44. b	45. b	46. c	47. a	48. a	49. a	50. d
51. d	52. a	53. c	54. d	55. d	56. d	57. c	58. d	59. d	60. b
61. d	62. d	63. c	64. a	65. a					

Chapter 10

1. d	2. d	3. d	4. b	5. b	6. d	7. d	8. d	9. b	10. c
11. a	12. c	13. a	14. b	15. a	16. a	17. b	18. d	19. d	20. d
21. a	22. d	23. a	24. d	25. b	26. d	27. d	28. d	29. a	30. b
31. d	32. b	33. a	34. d	35. c	36. c	37. a	38. d	39. d	40. d
41. c	42. a	43. d	44. c	45. d	46. a	47. d	48. d	49. d	50. a
51. a	52. d	53. d	54. a	55. d	56. d	57. d	58. d	59. c	60. b
61. d	62. d	63. b	64. b	65. d	66. d	67. b	68. d	69. d	70. d
71. a									

Chapter 11

1. d	2. a	3. d	4. d	5. d	6. a	7. d	8. a	9. d	10. a
11. a	12. d	13. d	14. c	15. d	16. c	17. d	18. d	19. d	20. d
21. d	22. b	23. b	24. d	25. c	26. c	27. d	28. b	29. a	30. d
31. a	32. d	33. d	34. d	35. c	36. d	37. d	38. b	39. d	40. d
41. c	42. a	43. d	44. c	45. d	46. d	47. d	48. d	49. c	50. d
51. d	52. a	53. a							

Chapter 12

1. d	2. d	3. d	4. d	5. d	6. a	7. d	8. a	9. d	10. d
11. d	12. d	13. d	14. d	15. b	16. b	17. b	18. d	19. d	20. d
21. d	22. b	23. a	24. d	25. d	26. d	27. d	28. d	29. c	30. c
31. d	32. a	33. d	34. b	35. d	36. a	37. b	38. d	39. c	40. b
41. b	42. d	43. d	44. d	45. d	46. c	47. c	48. d	49. d	50. d
51. b	52. d	53. d	54. a	55. d	56. a	57. c	58. a	59. c	60. c
61. d	62. d	63. d	64. b	65. b	66. d	67. d	68. d	69. b	70. d
71. b	72. a	73. b	74. d	75. b	76. b	77. d	78. d	79. d	80. c
81. a	82. d	83. b	84. b	85. a	86. d				

Chapter 13

1. c	2. d	3. c	4. c	5. a	6. d	7. d	8. d	9. d	10. b
11. b	12. d	13. b	14. d	15. d	16. c	17. d	18. d	19. c	20. a
21. d	22. c	23. d	24. b	25. d	26. d	27. d	28. b	29. b	30. a
31. a	32. d	33. a	34. d	35. b	36. d	37. d	38. d	39. d	40. b
41. c	42. d	43. a	44. b	45. d	46. c	47. b			

Chapter 14

1. c	2. d	3. d	4. d	5. d	6. c	7. d	8. c	9. d	10. c
11. b	12. d	13. d	14. d	15. b	16. d	17. d	18. d	19. d	20. c
21. a	22. c	23. c	24. d	25. c	26. c	27. d	28. d	29. d	30. b
31. d	32. a	33. d	34. d	35. c	36. d	37. b	38. a	39. d	40. b
41. d									

Chapter 15

1. d	2. c	3. d	4. d	5. d	6. d	7. d	8. d	9. d	10. a
11. d	12. b	13. a	14. d	15. d	16. d	17. d	18. b	19. d	20. d
21. d	22. c	23. d	24. c	25. d	26. d	27. c	28. d	29. c	30. d
31. d	32. d								